HERE ARE JUST A FEW OF THE QUESTIONS ANSWERED IN *MOMMY MADE**

When should I add texture to my baby's diet?

How much milk is enough—and how much is too much?

Will my eating habits affect the way my baby eats?

How can I encourage my child to try new foods?

How do I deal with my twins' different eating habits?

*How do I satisfy my picky daughter's tastes
and still provide nutritious, well-rounded meals?*

Plus many more!

Martha Kimmel teaches her nationally renowned Mommy Made* cooking class at the New School for Social Research in New York City. David Kimmel, who oversees his food and beverage operation in New York, graduated with honors from the Culinary Institute of America. The Kimmels and their daughters—who have personally taste-tested each recipe—live in Montebello, New York.

*and Daddy too!

Mommy Made*

*and Daddy too!

HOME COOKING
FOR A HEALTHY BABY
AND TODDLER

*Martha and David Kimmel
with Suzanne Goldenson*

BANTAM BOOKS
NEW YORK • TORONTO • LONDON • SYDNEY • AUCKLAND

ACKNOWLEDGMENTS

All accomplishments in life come with the help of others. Thank you, Dona Accillien, Teresa Campos, Dr. Max VanGilder, Gary Goldberg, Susan Gordis, Suzanne Hamlin, Mark Kimmel and PDQ Press, Fran McCullough, Denise McGraw RD, Steven Sanders, Mariann Sauvion, Jennifer Schiff, the entire Scicchitano family, and Robert Sweeney.

When we first wrote this book , we never thought we might be so fortunate to update it ten years later. As a tribute to that accomplishment we would like to thank a very special sister, sister-in-law, aunt, and co-author extraordinaire—we love you, Suzanne Goldenson.

MOMMY MADE AND DADDY TOO!
HOME COOKING FOR A HEALTHY BABY AND TODDLER
PUBLISHING HISTORY
Bantam trade paperback published June 1990
Revised Bantam trade paperback/June 2000

Library of Congress Cataloging-in-Publication Data
Kimmel, Martha.
Mommy made—and daddy too : home cooking for healthy baby and toddler /
Martha and David Kimmel, with Suzanne Goldenson.—[10th Anniversary ed.].
p.   cm.
Originally published: 1990
Includes index.
ISBN 0-553-38090-7
1. Infants—Nutrition.   2. Toddlers—Nutrition.   3. Cookery.
I. Kimmel, David.   II. Goldenson, Suzanne, 1944–   III. Title.
RJ216.K48 2000
613.2′083—dc21   99-086434

Published simultaneously in the United States and Canada

Bantam Books are published by Bantam Books, a division of Random House, Inc. Its trademark, consisting of the words "Bantam Books" and the portrayal of a rooster, is Registered in U.S. Patent and Trademark Office and in other countries. Marca Registrada. Bantam Books, 1540 Broadway, New York, New York 10036.

PRINTED IN THE UNITED STATES OF AMERICA
RRH 10 9 8 7 6 5

CONTENTS

PREFACE

We can't believe it's been ten years since *Mommy Made and Daddy too!* was first published. Our two daughters, Teddi and Renée, are now entering their teen years! As babies, they provided the inspiration—and "tasting lab"—for our Mommy Made retail line of fresh baby food and our companion Mommy Made classes. These classes on early childhood nutrition, food introduction and preparation, plus the recipes developed for our former baby food business, gave birth to this book.

This tenth-anniversary edition of *Mommy Made and Daddy too!* reflects the perspective that only time can provide. In addition to the collective wisdom of the many parents we have taught over the years and our own personal parenting experiences, this revised edition contains the latest American Pediatric Association guidelines on early childhood nutrition; expanded sections on introducing your child to solid food and food allergies; updated information on nutrients, the food pyramid, and functional foods; more of the most frequently asked classroom questions; plus delicious new recipes.

When this book was first published in 1990, the importance of good nutrition (and exercise) was just coming to the forefront. Now, as we enter the new millennium, there is widespread awareness that by eating well (and exercising) when we are young, we train our mind and body in habits that will last a lifetime. This training has set the stage for good health in our daughters. They have turned out to be healthy eaters who have not succumbed to the dieting fads that are so prevalent in young women today.

Our focus in the past ten years has shifted from hands-on retail and teaching to educating parents through this book and our Web site (www.mommymade.com). Our goal is to empower parents to raise healthy children who can make their own healthy food choices. We hope that through this book, your child will grow up with a palate educated for delicious food and good health.

Martha & David

INTRODUCTION
Only the Best Will Do

We know it's crossed your mind: family time is so precious, so why fuss at home when cunning little jars of baby food of almost every conceivable flavor and for every feeding stage are so inexpensively and widely available in the supermarket? The answer is simple. When it comes to the health and happiness of your children, only the best will do.

Why is fresh best? Most of us growing up in the fifties were raised on commercial baby food, and our hats are off to the canning and freezing industry—it liberated Mom from the stove. But is ease really what feeding our babies is all about? We don't think so.

Perhaps the most convincing argument for opting for fresh, homemade baby food is its superior flavor. Compare a fresh, juicy Bartlett pear to a jar of baby pear puree. If the pears don't convince you which tastes better, then try the carrots or even the jarred pureed meats with a shelf life of two years. No wonder we grew up hating our vegetables! Babies react happily to good smells and vibrant colors as much as they do to vibrant tastes.

Maybe you're willing to trade taste for convenience. But we know for your baby's sake you won't be happy trading ease for nutrients. Did you know that the high temperatures necessary to give canned foods their long shelf life kill many of the nutrients in the very foods they're preserving? (The percentages are alarming. For thiamine, important for steady nerves, it's 69 percent lost; for vitamin C, which builds a strong immune system, it's 64 percent lost.) Water and air are commonly whipped into commercially jarred baby foods to give them a fluffy, smooth-as-silk texture, further diluting their vitamin and mineral content. When you make it fresh, you can avoid sugar, salt, artificial colors, fillers, additives, and preservatives; all you get is the simple, pure taste of the food itself, its nutrients intact.

With your own fresh baby food, you can also be sure of the quality, source, and safety of your ingredients—a considerable concern in this age of widespread spraying of fruits and vegetables with pesticides, hormone-injected meats, and baby food tampering. And by preparing your own fresh food, you can offer your baby more variety.

Because of these concerns, as new parents armed with professional backgrounds in the food business and early childhood development, we started our first child, Teddi, on fresh, homemade baby food. It was our way of providing only the best for her. We didn't expect to change the way other babies ate—just our own.

Thirteen years ago we were hosting a Lamaze alumni party at our house. One of our guests (a real meat-and-potatoes guy) was totally floored when he saw us take a container of freshly prepared blueberry-pear puree out of our refrigerator and feed it to Teddi. With a hint of sarcasm, he asked us if we were obsessed with the idea of fresh food—of course we didn't know yet that we were. We started to explain our philosophy and then Martha had a better idea; she jumped up and grabbed some spoons, the jar of fresh puree, and a jar of the commercially prepared purees we kept on hand for emergencies. She then proceeded to put a taste of each into our guests' mouths. The taste test was a revelation—the fresh baby food was delicious—"like real food." Our guests were also amazed by the appealing look and wonderful aroma of the fresh puree compared to its dreary commercial counterpart. And later that night (as we had warm blueberry-pear sauce on our vanilla ice cream), our guests convinced Martha to sign them up as the first students for her now regularly scheduled class in which she still conducts that convincing taste test.

The course we developed teaches proper food introduction, child nutrition, allergy detection, food preparation, storage and handling techniques, as well as purchasing information, suggestions for traveling with your baby, food presentation tips, and questions and answers to food-related parenting concerns.

As we taught more and more parents about freshly prepared baby food, more and more of them, particularly the working parents, kept asking us to prepare the food for them—they didn't always have time to do it themselves but wanted the benefits for their children. After hearing this request almost daily, we decided to do some serious homework. Our research showed a tremendous need for fresh baby food but it also told us that we had a long road ahead of us. To our already growing list of specialists we added the expertise of a Harvard food chemist, the guidance of the United States Department of Agriculture, the New York City Department of Health, and the U.S. Food and Drug Administration.

We started producing on a very limited basis, using our own delivery system. For the first few months we grew by word of mouth only. Each week we would pick up a few new customers who heard about us in their mothers' group or from their pediatrician. (As part of our initial testing, we sent samples to many of the pediatricians in Manhattan.) Timing can be everything. When the movie *Baby Boom* was released we found Mommy Made and Daddy too! suddenly on the front page of the *Wall Street Journal,* in *The New York Times, The Daily News, Vogue, Health, The Baltimore Sun, The Denver Post, The Christian Science Monitor;* we appeared on FOX, NBC, CBS, Japanese TV, and on numerous radio stations across the country. We were off and running and what started as a local fresh baby food business, started to work its way toward national distribution.

We've seen firsthand the impact that food allergies and nutrition can have on learning and behavior, and once you have that experience it's difficult to continue thinking that it doesn't much matter what you feed your children.

At no other time in your child's life is nutrition more important than in the first years. In the first 12 months your baby will triple his weight and grow 10 to 12 inches. By age three he will have doubled his height. Throughout this period 20 teeth will emerge; your baby will learn to walk, talk, and feed himself; and brain growth will be unsurpassed at any other time in his life. It's the nutrients in his food that make all this possible. And in just three hours every two weeks, you can easily prepare all your baby's food from scratch.

This book has been laid out so that you can use it as a reference manual and access it by age as well as by specific issue. It follows the pattern of Martha's lectures in our cooking classes. We suggest you read and digest the whole book before you actually begin to use it. Not enough can be said about planning ahead; pregnancy is the right time to begin thinking about how to feed your baby.

Chapter One addresses the first six months of life in which breast-feeding and formula are the focus. In Chapter Two, you will learn in detail about the systematic introduction of solid foods for allergy detection, as set forth by the American Academy of Pediatrics. Chapter Three addresses the more practical side of feeding concerns, including serving that first meal, selecting the right high chair, conquering the cup, and games children play at the table. In essence these two chapters (two and three) cover your baby's feeding needs from six months through one year. Chapter Four will give you a real hands-on understanding about nutrition and appropriate serving size guidelines for your one-to-three year old. Chapter Five is a selection of the most frequently asked questions from the parents who have taken the class and from our baby food customers. The answers we supply come from our own experiences, the specialists and doctors we work with, and other parents. The last chapter provides you with a detailed inventory of the kitchen equipment you'll need in order to make home cooking for your baby a snap.

The recipes in this book have been developed to be basic enough for solid food introduction but with enough flexibility so that they can easily be upgraded for more sophisticated tastes. In addition we have included a number of easy recipes that will appeal to all ages, all with nutrition and great taste in mind.

If it's the best of everything you want for your baby and family, we promise to give it to you. The following pages contain the most up-to-the-minute information on infant and early childhood nutrition and feeding issues, as well as our most delicious Mommy Made recipes, so you too can provide your family with fresh foods from the start!

Martha Grau Kimmel obtained her master's degree in guidance and counseling with a special emphasis on early childhood development from the University of South Florida. Martha is an instructor at the New School for Social Research in New York City, where she teaches her nationally renowned Mommy Made cooking class. Martha has also developed and teaches "Yummy In My Tummy," a hands-on cooking experience exploring the world through food, and "What's Up With Food," an interactive presentation where kids compare their favorite foods through the study of their food labels. Martha also teaches her classes privately and continues her speaking engagements nationwide. In the most simple terms, Martha is the Mommy.

David Kimmel spends his time overseeing his food and beverage operations in Rockland County, New York, helping as many of the not-for-profit organizations in his community as he can, importing fresh fruit and wine from Argentina, and most important, loving his two daughters and wife each step of the way. David is an honors graduate of The Culinary Institute of America, where he has also served as an instructor and member of their Board of Trustees.

Suzanne Kimmel Goldenson is not only Teddi and Renée's aunt but a Princeton, New Jersey, based author and book publisher. Suzanne has worked as a restaurant critic, and she has written numerous books, primarily on food and wine, including: *The Open Hearth Cookbook* and *Vintage Places: A Connoisseur's Guide to North American Vineyards and Wineries*. She is also the president and founder of Golden Sun Books, which publishes guides to leisure activities. She is married to Daniel R. Goldenson, and they are the parents of two grown sons, Andy and Jeff, who were, of course, raised on fresh food from the start!

PART I

Getting Started in the Right Direction

CHAPTER ONE

The First
Six Months

Feeding our children is where our parenting begins. From infancy on, food becomes a significant form of communicating and nurturing. When your infant cries, you run to comfort her with food. In this way she gains her first sense of relief and well-being. At the same time her hunger is being satiated, she is held, cooed to, and stroked. In this way food starts to represent security and love. Later in life food plays a central part in social gatherings, is shared on special holidays, and at times of celebration and mourning, or simply accompanies the daily ritual around the kitchen table when family business is discussed.

Mealtime is one of the richest family experiences you can share with your child. It is especially important in helping her develop healthy attitudes about nutritious foods and learn proper table manners, politeness, and respect for others. These early, positive experiences will have a tremendous impact on your child's future development.

"In psychoanalytic terms, Food and Mother mean the same thing," says Dr. Charles Clegg, a nationally prominent psychiatrist with the U.S.C. School of Medicine, specializing in eating disorders in children and adults. "And eating disorders can begin very early in life and most often do."

Today's working mother is often faced with leaving her child at a very early age. Six weeks is the national average. It is very important for parents to find a nurturing replacement for mother, Dr. Clegg explains. Babies who are cared for by adults who do not hold or touch them, except while feeding them, can wrongly teach baby that eating relieves not just hunger but also anger, depression, anxiety, and loneliness, a pattern that can lead to obesity later in life. Overeating and obesity are usually psychological problems, Dr. Clegg confirms. "Most overeaters do so because their good memories about life's experiences are surrounded by food." The best way to instill in your child a healthy attitude toward food is to spend quality time with her, holding her, playing with her—in short, simply loving her. Food should be a great pleasure, but it shouldn't answer emotional needs.

For the first few days after birth your breasts will produce colostrum until your milk comes in. Colostrum, a thin yellow fluid, contains protein and concentrated antibodies that help protect your baby from infection.

If your family has a strong history of allergies, breast-feeding your infant is strongly advised.

BREAST OR BOTTLE?

While you may not get much sleep from your child's birth to age six months, you have it easy concerning food choices. The breast, the bottle, or a combination of the two are the only choices of nourishment for your baby until he begins to eat solid foods. (Solid foods are best introduced between baby's four- and six-month birthdays.)

The decision is usually made during pregnancy, which is also the right time to start thinking about your own attitude toward feeding your children. Of course, there's flexibility in these decisions—above all, it has to work for you and your family—but what's done in the beginning can be hard to undo. So now is the time to decide on your philosophy. The very first decision, breast or bottle, is the first step in establishing your own food philosophy.

BREAST MILK

According to the American Academy of Pediatrics, breast milk is the ideal food for infants because of its nutritional composition. Babies who are breast-fed are at reduced risk for ear infections and severe diarrhea. In addition, there is some evidence that for mothers, breast-feeding reduces certain types of cancer and may prevent hip fractures later in life. As a result, most pediatricians urge expectant mothers to breast-feed.

There is also strong evidence that breast milk can strengthen a baby's developing immune system. Breast milk has no curds and is therefore very digestible and never activates allergies, an important consideration if there is a strong allergy history in your family. While breast milk may not prevent your infant from having allergies, it can possibly delay their onset and minimize the severity of their symptoms.

The World Health Organization (WHO) and many experts encourage women to breast-feed as long as possible, one year or even longer, because breast milk provides optimal nutrition and protection against infections.

FOR EVERY ACTION THERE'S A REACTION

Experts agree that during the months of breast-feeding, everything you consume will come through your breast milk. Timing of what you eat is as important as what you eat. Use your head with whatever you decide to consume, keeping in mind that *your lunch will be your baby's dinner.*

Alcohol, for example, is the most rapidly metabolized drug. It will enter your bloodstream and move through your milk very quickly. A cocktail glass of wine will have very little effect, if any, on your baby if consumed *after* feeding, and the blows will be further softened if the drink is consumed with food. The same

Expressing Breast Milk

Learning to express milk is easy and well worth the trouble. Expressing breast milk and chilling or freezing it for later use ensures that breast milk will be on hand for baby when Mom is not. It is indispensable for the working mom and for that special night out or even weekend away. The La Leche League recommends Medela breast pumps. Pumps range from manual styles that are small and portable to electric pumps for long-term or more frequent use.

goes for caffeine. Spread your intake—two to three cups of coffee or tea a day—over the course of the day and consume it only *after* feeding your baby.

When breast-feeding, vitamin and mineral supplements you take may not agree with your baby. If you are supplementing your iron to combat post-partum fatigue, we suggest that instead of popping an iron-fortified vitamin capsule, you eat iron-rich foods together with foods that are high in vitamin C, which aids the body's ability to absorb iron. (See vitamin and mineral information, page 47.)

NATURE'S SUPPLY AND DEMAND

Many first-time moms who are breast-feeding ask: "Is my baby getting enough to eat? He seems to be on a feeding frenzy and can't nurse often enough." Many of these moms erroneously feel that they are not producing enough milk. On the contrary, these "feeding frenzies" often coincide with baby's many growth spurts. The first one often occurs right around baby's two-week birthday, and subsequent spurts most often occur at six weeks, three months, and six months. (Of course, your baby may not fit this schedule perfectly.) The more your baby nurses, the more milk you will produce, so you need not worry about your baby's food supply. If it's more milk that the baby wants, take advantage of the situation and express the extra milk to use later. During growth spurts, your baby may demand feedings every two hours for a few days straight. Your body will adjust by producing what your baby needs. It's nature's way of producing the supply to satisfy the demand.

THE BOTTLE AND FORMULA

If you've decided that breast-feeding simply won't work for your lifestyle, you can feel very confident in offering your baby a formula that your doctor recommends. Your baby will thrive, and his well-being will not be compromised on regular formula. Most regular formulas are based on cow's milk. But plain cow's milk should never be given to a baby under one year of age. And under no circumstances should a baby be given goat's milk (See information on milk allergies and intolerances, pages 24–25.)

Your baby can, however, be sensitive or allergic to formula. It may, for example, surprise you that corn syrup solids are commonly used in many infant formulas, considering that corn is number three on the list of common allergy-producing foods that cause sensitivity in infants (cow's milk is number one). (See Common Allergy-Producing Foods, page 24.) If you suspect your baby needs a formula change—diarrhea, irritability, crying, and rashes are some symptoms—discuss your observations with your doctor. There is no reason in the world why you can't play what one mom called "the formula-changing game" with your baby.

BREAST AND BOTTLE TOGETHER

If you decided from the start to combine breast and bottle, it is very important that you establish your own milk supply first. You do this by having the baby breast-feed exclusively in the first six to eight weeks. In this way you will be certain that there will be plenty of breast milk, even when baby goes onto a bottle or two of formula a day. It's nice for Mom to have a break now and then and to give Dad a chance at snuggling up with his son or daughter. The combination can be the best of both worlds.

SOME FACTS ABOUT BREAST MILK YOU SHOULD KNOW

- Breast milk can be kept at room temperature (66 to 72 degrees F) for up to ten hours because of its remarkable ability to retard bacteria growth. Milk can be refrigerated for eight days. For longer storage, it can be frozen. Frozen milk can be kept up to two weeks in the freezer compartment of your refrigerator, three or four months in a separate door freezer that is opened frequently, and six months or longer in a separate freezer that stays at a constant 0 degrees F.
- If you plan to freeze your milk, do so immediately after expressing it.
- Freeze milk in individual plastic or glass storage containers or plastic nurser bags (use them doubled to avoid tearing) to cut down on waste. Always label each container with the month, date, and year.
- When freezing, do not overfill your bottles or freezer bags. Leave room for the milk to expand—about half an inch.
- To defrost or heat your expressed supply, simply immerse the bottle in warm running water until it's the temperature at which your baby likes her bottle.
- Serve warmed milk immediately. Throw away any leftovers.
- Never microwave. It heats too unevenly and can overheat the milk.
- Do not refreeze defrosted breast milk. If defrosted in the refrigerator, it will stay fresh in the refrigerator for 24 hours.
- Discard any unused portion of the bottle that your baby does not finish at feeding time. Do not save it for a later meal.

WATER

Supplemental water given in a bottle is an extra in baby's diet during the first six months. At this age, babies normally get all the hydration they need from breast milk or formula. Most infants we know at this age hate water and push proffered bottles of the stuff quickly out of their mouths. If your baby is feverish, the weather hot, or if he fusses between feedings, it's a good idea to make sure there are plenty of opportunities for him to get additional water by offering bottles between feedings. If he's thirsty he'll drink it. Don't sweeten your baby's water with sugar or corn syrup to make it more palatable. You don't want him to develop a taste for sweets. And, as we discuss in the next chapter, corn and corn products commonly cause allergic reactions in young babies. Everything else you need to know about water—tap versus bottled, flouridation and your baby's teeth, etc.—appears on pages 52–53. Water concerns when traveling with baby out of the U.S. appear on page 291.

How Much Is Enough?

In the first year of life infants naturally regulate their diet and nutrition intake. An infant who is given diluted formula will simply crave more bottles to get the nutrients she needs. Breast-fed babies will regulate themselves if given unlimited access to the breast. Paying attention to your infant's early cues about being hungry or full will help your growing child pay attention to her own internal clues about hunger and fullness. At no time should a bottle-fed baby be forced to finish her bottle. Forcing every last drop on your infant can lead to overeating later in life. Obesity is seen much more frequently in bottle-fed babies.

WEANING TO THE BOTTLE

Weaning generally becomes an issue later in your baby's life, when he's comfortable with the cup and eating a variety of solid foods. (We discuss total weaning on pages 37–38.) But for the mom who is planning to return to work before her baby's six-month birthday and has opted to breast-feed, weaning in this case has an intermediate stage—from breast to bottle.

If you have nursing or feeding concerns, your doctor or her nurse are a good place to start. Other resources include your local La Leche League and nearest hospital. Most hospitals now have a lactation consultant on staff. You can also call the La Leche League at 1–800–LA LECHE. On the East Coast, try New York City's Beth Israel Hospital's "warmline"; leave a message at 1–212–420–2939, and your call will be returned.

If you know you'll be returning to work early in your baby's first year, we urge you to think this process through at the outset. You have two choices. You can partially breast-feed, nursing your baby first thing in the morning and again in the late evening, leaving your caregiver to serve up the remaining daytime meals of either expressed breast milk or formula in bottles. Or, you can totally wean your baby to bottles of formula, giving up breast-feeding altogether. Before you decide which route to go, consider the predictability of your working hours and travel needs.

Both options work well. The important thing is not to wait too long to introduce the bottle. Older babies can be very adamant about wanting their milk exclusively from Mommy's breast and will refuse a bottle with its artificial nipple, even if it is filled with Mommy's expressed breast milk. You won't want the following to happen to your caregiver.

At four months, Alice decided it would be okay to leave baby Jennifer with Grandma for an evening. She carefully filled a bottle with expressed breast milk and left Jennifer in Grandma's loving and experienced hands. Grandma was ready with the warmed milk when Jennifer awoke for her ten o'clock bottle. But Jennifer took one suck on the rubber nipple and promptly began to cry. Repeated attempts by Grandma to get her to take the bottle—rocking, walking, singing, etc.—did nothing to alleviate Jennifer's shrieking and sobbing, which continued at an earsplitting pitch until Mom came home and breast-fed her two hours later.

Some Suggestions on Weaning from Breast to Bottle:

- Take it slowly, offering supplemental bottles of formula only after your milk supply is fully established—six to eight weeks following your baby's birth.
- Gradually increase the number of bottles until you have achieved your goal—either partial or total bottle feeding.
- Leave plenty of time for your baby to get accustomed to rubber nipples (the sucking technique is different from the breast), the new taste of formula, and perhaps even a new person feeding her.
- Sometimes a baby won't accept a bottle from Mommy, only the breast. In this case, get Dad, Grandma, or the caregiver to lend a helping hand during the transition. And be sure to leave the room so baby can't see or smell you and wrongly think the breast is available but not forthcoming. This scenario will be frustrating for everyone concerned.

CHAPTER TWO

From Four to Six Months Through One Year

Getting Started on Solid Food and Allergy Detection

Systematic food introduction and allergy detection go hand in hand in the first year. It's the single most important concept you need to understand when you begin to start your baby on solid food. And in our Mommy Made classes we spend nearly half the class time discussing this subject alone.

Food intolerances are common in babies, even if they've never appeared before in the family. Many times as children mature and develop they simply grow out of these sensitivities. But it's important to remember that your baby won't get over an allergy or sensitivity by eating more of the offending food or eating it more frequently. In fact, just the opposite will happen and perhaps worse. He may develop a full-blown allergy to the food. Certainly, if allergies are common in your family, you'll want to keep a watchful eye out for any suspicious symptoms. (We go into those later in the chapter.)

The following story made us truly realize that the responsibility for finding out as much as we can about our own children's individual needs lies on our shoulders as parents. At age nine, Jason, the oldest son of a close friend, was a boy his own mother described as "off the wall." He was easily agitated and quite hyperactive. He had to be removed from his regular classroom and placed in a program for hard-to-handle children. After a battery of tests, it was discovered that Jason was allergic to a wide variety of foods, but wheat and corn in particular. When these foods were removed from his diet, Jason settled down quickly and was placed back in his regular classroom. A little extra catch-up tutoring was all that was required for his smooth transition. His mother, however, came to us in tears one night and asked, "Why didn't somebody tell me this before?"

ARE YOU READY?

Sometime near your baby's four- to six-month birthday his doctor will announce it's time to start solid food. You may have already sensed your child's readiness for this step forward. Here are some of the things you may have noticed:

- Is he demanding to be fed at two-hour intervals or consuming over 32 ounces of formula in a day?
- Is he beginning to teethe and master sitting up without your help?
- Can he turn his head away to indicate "no more" instead of simply falling back to sleep because he is so satiated? (This may very well be the most important sign to look for. If your baby can't communicate with you that he's hungry by lunging for the breast or bottle or indicate that he is full by moving away and turning his head, you could end up overfeeding

him. Overfeeding could interfere with the baby's natural mechanism for self-regulating food and lead to overeating in later life.)

- Can he take an object in his hand and bring it directly to his mouth?
- Is he showing an interest in the food that others around him are eating? We'll never forget how Renée at five months literally grabbed Teddi's spoon one evening in a bold attempt at joining the family meal.
- Has he stopped exhibiting the tongue extrusion reflex, which simply means: Has he stopped continually sticking out his tongue at every stimulus?

In addition to these outward signs, there are also changes going on inside your baby. As baby approaches six months, the enzymes in his digestive tract are becoming mature enough to break down and digest solids, making reactions to foods less likely. Collectively all of these changes are governed by the autonomic nervous system. But for Mom and Dad it means simply that baby is getting ready for a more grown-up diet.

SYSTEMATIC FOOD INTRODUCTION

As a parent you'll be eager to see your baby's response to your favorite foods, but it's especially important to take these food steps slowly and systematically, watching carefully for food allergies. Systematic food introduction is the easiest way to detect food sensitivities before they become a problem. Your child will not mind omitting foods from her diet if it makes her feel better. And in the first year or two she won't even know what she's missing. Here's how it works:

THE GOLDEN RULE: TWO NEW FOODS A WEEK

When starting your baby on solid foods, offer only a small amount (no matter how much your baby seems to love it) of one new food for three or four days straight so a problematic food can be identified easily (see symptoms list, page 24).

If your baby appears to be sensitive to a food, stop serving that food immediately! You can try again very cautiously after a month's time, but if it still causes a reaction, it's best to wait until your baby is over 12 months old to reintroduce it. Someone we know broke out in hives every time he got near a strawberry until he reached the age of 13. He is now in his late 30s and swears strawberries are his favorite food.

Once foods have been accepted into the diet, it becomes very important to rotate foods. A food that was once a favorite can turn into a problem if served too frequently. (This holds true for adults as well. Too much of a good thing—even milk and liver—can lead to nutritional deficiencies and/or vitamin overdoses.)

In some cases children can show food sensitivities or allergies to only certain foods within that food group. Take whole milk, for example. Your one-year-old child may not be able to tolerate a cup of milk, but may be quite able to consume dairy products such as yogurt without any problem. (We discuss milk intolerances in greater detail later in this chapter.)

KEEP A RECORD

In the first year of life it's a very good idea to keep a record of the foods as you introduce them to your baby. There's a cut-out chart in the back of this book just for this purpose. Attach it to your refrigerator so you'll be sure to use it. It may save you from the following:

THE $50 APPLE

One of our students told us a story that we will never forget. She called it "The $50 Apple," because this is what a typical pediatrician's visit costs where we live. Donna took our class when her son Joey was six months old. Her pediatrician had taken a casual approach when it came time to introduce foods into Joey's diet. Things went along smoothly with Joey until one afternoon he broke out in a mysterious rash on his face and neck. Donna bundled Joey off to the doctor. When they arrived, one of the very first questions her doctor asked was "What has your baby had to eat?" Donna, searching to remember, could think only of apples. The doctor said that the rash appeared to be a reaction to food and advised her to omit apples for the next month. He went on to reassure her that the rash would probably disappear in 24 hours. And it did.

A food sensitivity is often displayed by a rash, but not always. Keeping a record of the foods you serve your baby might just clear up a mystery in your mind should your baby have a reaction to a new food; it will also save you a doctor's bill and provide you with a list of safe foods for your baby-sitter.

If your baby gets a rash or displays what appears to be a reaction to a new food, eliminate that food and the reaction should disappear within 24 hours. If it doesn't, call your doctor.

WHAT FOODS TO START WITH AND HOW TO BEGIN

Here are some specific guidelines on which solid foods are appropriate to serve your 6- to 12-month-old baby. A month-by-month food chart follows to help you plan your course of introduction.

▓ ROUND AND ROUND ▓

When starting your baby on solid foods, we think the "round robin" approach most pediatricians recommend makes the best sense. Start first with baby rice cereal mixed with expressed breast milk or formula (unless of course there is a history of rice allergy in your family or if your baby has had frequent bouts of constipation. Rice is very binding. Some other options are barley and oat cereals.) Then add a pureed fruit, next a pureed vegetable, then back to a new cereal. Leave dairy products and meat until the eighth month. We don't think going through all the fruits first makes good sense, because your baby may very well expect all foods to be sweet ones and reject the vegetables. Again, the month-by-month road map to solid food that follows will help you provide a good mix.

Once a food has passed the introduction stage, it can be served with any other accepted food. As an example, start with rice cereal, serve it for three days, and then add applesauce.

Dr. William Sears, noted pediatrician, author, and child care expert shared this tip with Martha over lunch: "An avocado is a perfect, fresh, and natural baby food choice. Its flavorful soft flesh is enjoyed by most babies and is easy for babies to digest." Avocados are also high in potassium.

▓ ALWAYS COOK FIRST FOODS ▓

All new foods, aside from ripe bananas and avocados, should be cooked before being pureed and served to baby. This helps to break down the cellulose fiber and make them more digestible. It might seem to you that a ripe, juicy pear could be peeled and then pureed. But if your baby has a reaction, you won't know if it was because of the fruit itself or because your baby couldn't fully digest it. (We began offering our girls soft, fresh fruit pieces at nine months.)

▓ CEREALS AND GRAINS ▓

Leave wheat, the most allergenic grain, until last. If there is any allergic reaction to the other, less problematic cereals—rice, oats, or barley—hold off on wheat until the end of the first year.

Rice cereal is usually baby's first food. It is not homemade un-less you count the breast milk or formula you mix with the pow-dery white flakes. But this is one commercially prepared product that's hard to beat nutritionally or to prepare as well in your own kitchen.

Most doctors recommend commercially prepared iron-fortified baby rice cereal as a child's first solid food because it supplies the iron infants need and is the least allergenic of all the baby cereals. (Mommy Made's Brown Rice Cereal, page 204, is not appropriate for an infant's very first meal. It has too much texture and is not iron-fortified or vitamin-enriched. Save it for when your baby is a bit older—eight months plus—and more adept at chewing, swallowing, and eating a wider variety of foods.)

All the major brands of baby rice cereal offer nearly the per-fect food. It doesn't matter which brand you choose, provided your choice is both vitamin-enriched and iron-fortified. (Always read the labels, because baby cereals intended for bigger ba-bies—over ten months—who are eating a wide variety of foods are sometimes not enriched or fortified.) The iron is so impor-tant because of your baby's rapid growth and because the nat-ural reserve of iron stored in the baby's liver at birth will be depleted by six months of age. The iron found in baby cereal is very easy for the baby's system to absorb and is not the same as the iron added to adult cereals.

Rice cereal will be not only your baby's first solid food, but one that will stay on his menu for many months to come. It's a handy product for traveling, because of its light weight and long shelf life. (Once opened, a box of rice cereal stored in a cool, dry place retains its optimum freshness for one month. Beyond that time, its vitamin and mineral content begin to diminish.)

Rice cereal is also a comforting and healthy food that you'll return to again and again during the first two years of your baby's life, when he's teething, suffering from an upset stomach, etc. It's also useful as a thickener for other foods.

▨ FRUITS AND VEGETABLES ▨

As a general rule of thumb, introduce yellow-hued fruits and vegetables first, orange second, and green last. (Citrus fruits, melons, and corn are the exception to the yellow-orange rule. Introduce these after ten months.)

Fruits

Start with one of the following: a perfectly ripe banana with no green anywhere on the skin (but the banana should not be so ripe that it's a candidate for banana bread), Golden Delicious applesauce (see My First Applesauce, page 116–17), or Pear Puree (page 122).

In some parts of the country, carrots, a favorite first food for babies, contain large amounts of nitrates. Young babies exposed to this chemical/fertilizer in their food can develop an unusual form of anemia (low blood count). To avoid nitrates in your baby's diet buy organically grown carrots from a source that verifies they were grown in low-nitrate soil. Serve them immediately, because storing can increase the nitrate levels in food. Commercial baby food producers are aware of this problem and screen the produce they purchase. (Spinach, beets, collard greens, and turnips are also grown in nitrate-enriched soil, but you won't be serving these foods to your baby until the end of her first year, when she is big enough to tolerate this chemical.)

Vegetables

Begin with acorn squash and then move on to butternut squash, sweet potatoes, and carrots. Leave foods like green peas and green beans until later, introducing dark green and red vegetables last. Beets, turnips, spinach, mustard, and collard greens should be introduced at the end of the first year. These vegetables have a very high natural nitrate content, which is hard on a young baby's system. Because younger babies have low stomach acidity, they can't deal with the nitrates, which can cause oxygen to be displaced in their bloodstreams—a condition known as methemoglobinemia. The baby could suffer rapid breathing, lethargy, and shortness of oxygen; if the levels are very high, this condition can even be fatal.

▧ MEAT AND MEAT SUBSTITUTES ▧

Introduce meats at about eight months, starting with skinned breast of chicken or turkey. Next try lean beef, lamb, veal, pork, liver (serve liver only once a week because of its high concentration of vitamin A), tofu, and fish. Introduce egg yolks at the end of the first year. *Avoid shellfish and egg whites in the first year.*

A lot of beginning eaters don't take to pureed meats very readily. Babies can't tell us why, but take a taste. Pureeing meats does not enhance their texture, their flavor, or their appearance. Some babies will promptly spit out your carefully poached and pulverized chicken breast. What's a mom to do? First and foremost, don't fret! Throughout baby's first year her protein needs are being met through the breast or bottle. As your baby gets bigger, you can mix in pureed vegetables with the meat to make it more palatable. *But do not hide the meat behind a favorite puree so that your baby is forced to consume it.* Your baby may quickly learn to keep her mouth shut for fear of being forced to eat something she really does not like.

▧ MILK AND MILK PRODUCTS ▧

Cow's milk should not be used to replace breast milk or formula in the first year of life. Cow's milk is way too high in salt and protein for the human baby, and its large curds make it hard to digest. Milk by-products, however, such as yogurt, can be introduced by the eighth month. Yogurt is a wonderful, ready-to-serve baby food that is rich in protein and enzymes that aid in digestion. Introduce whole milk at one year. (More about milk later in this chapter and in Chapter Four.)

h Road Map to
he First Year

We developed this road map as a way for you to get started in the right direction. If you get to the seventh month, however, and there's not a fresh peach in sight, don't panic. Simply go on to the produce that is available. When making substitutions, keep in mind the rule of thumb for vegetables and fruits: yellow first, orange and pale green next, dark green and red last.

Food Road Map for the First Year

AGE	DIET
Birth to 6 months	Breast milk or formula
4 to 6 months	Cereal and Grain Group: rice, oats
	Fruit and Vegetable Group: banana (very ripe), apple juice and applesauce, pear juice and sauce; acorn squash, butternut squash, sweet potato
5 to 7 months	Cereal and Grain Group: barley, wheat
	Fruit and Vegetable Group: peaches, plums; carrots, peas, green beans
6 to 8 months	Cereal and Grain Group: kasha (buckwheat), brown rice, bread
	Fruit and Vegetable Group: apricots; zucchini, summer squash
	Meat Group: chicken, turkey
	Milk Group: plain yogurt
7 to 9 months	Cereal and Grain Group: oat cereal circles, teething biscuits
	Fruit and Vegetable Group: papaya; avocado, asparagus
	Meat Group: lean beef
	Milk Group: cream cheese, cottage cheese, ricotta cheese

AGE	DIET
8 to 10 months	Cereal and Grain Group: egg-free pasta
	Fruit and Vegetable Group: citrus fruits, nectarines, prunes; beets, broccoli
	Meat Group: lamb, liver
	Milk Group: mild cheeses, including mozzarella, Muenster, Monterey Jack, Cheddar, and Swiss
9 to 11 months	Fruit and Vegetable Group: kiwifruit; spinach, baked white potato, parsnips
	Meat Group: veal, egg yolks
	Combination Foods (pureed): chicken with vegetables, beef with noodles or rice
10 to 12 months	Fruit and Vegetable Group: cantaloupe, watermelon, blueberries; cauliflower, cucumber, artichoke (the pureed heart), eggplant
	Meat Group: soybeans (tofu), lentils, lima beans, dried peas and beans, white-fleshed fish, pork
	Others: light seasonings, but no salt or sugar

Detour at These Foods

The following foods should be avoided during baby's first year:

- *white table sugar*
- *artificial sweeteners*
- *corn syrup*
- *shellfish*
- *egg whites or uncooked yolks*
- *fried foods*
- *unripened fruit*
- *chocolate and candy*
- *honey*
- *uncooked onions*
- *junk food such as potato chips*
- *tomatoes*
- *corn*
- *processed meat: hot dogs, bologna, salami, bacon, etc.*

BACK TO SQUARE ONE

If you're concerned that your baby may have an allergy to something in his diet, go back to the beginning if your baby is under one year.

Jane, a mother who recently enrolled in our class, did just that. When her little boy, Sam, was ten months old, he had a patch of eczema on his lower leg that appeared shortly after foods were introduced into his diet. Sam's doctor gave Jane a prescription for a cream to stop the itch and assured her that Sam would outgrow it.

When Jane took our course, we explained that in the first year it's easy to go back to the beginning of food introduction to detect for allergies. She went first to rice cereal, then on to apples, squash, oat cereal, bananas, sweet potatoes, barley cereal, and pears. During this month of starting over, Sam's eczema disappeared completely. It wasn't until Jean reintroduced carrots that the problem started to arise again in the very same spot on Sam's leg. The rest is history.

If your little one is over one year, it's a little more difficult to identify a food-related sensitivity or allergy, but not impossible. Omitting the foods on the common allergy food list (page 24) is a good starting point. If you feel that your child's problems go deeper than that, a consultation with your doctor or an allergy specialist is advised.

FRUIT JUICE

Kids love juice, and *"big* apple juice" will probably become your toddler's standing drink order. You can introduce your baby to fruit juice as early as six months. Start with a single juice pressed from one of the first fruits on the food introduction chart, such as apple or pear, and serve it up in baby's cup or bottle. Leave those gourmet fruit juice combinations, such as cranberry-grape and peach-papaya, or any juices that include berries, as well as vegetable juices, such as carrot and tomato, until after one year.

At first, dilute baby's juice with water. About 2 ounces of juice to 6 ounces of water is a good ratio. Your baby will think this weak juice/water mix tastes perfectly fine, and it will not cut his appetite or give him an overdose of vitamins.

Commercial baby juices are your best bet in the beginning. They are all fortified with vitamin C, which is not always the case with regular juice. A 4-ounce serving will give your baby all of the vitamin C she needs in a day. After 12 months, when your baby moves on to table food, you can switch over to small amounts of undiluted grown-up juice.

(Taste all juice before serving them to baby. We once ran into a six-pack of pear juice that tasted more like pear vinegar.)

FOOD INTOLERANCES AND ALLERGIES

The beauty of allergy detection in the first year of life is that most often allergic reactions are food-related as opposed to environmental. Of course there is always that outside chance that your baby could be allergic to the flowers in bloom, but it's not very likely that this sensitivity would show up in the first 12 months.

It's important to identify allergies early, because allergies that go undetected can cause complications later in life, including behavioral problems, fatigue, hyperactivity, restlessness, oversensitivity, eczema, and asthma. Food allergies in extreme cases can even cause death.

SYMPTOMS TO LOOK FOR

- rashes, especially on the face and upper body
- diaper rash
- hives
- diarrhea
- gas
- irritability or any kind of temperament change
- nasal congestion
- puffy eyes

COMMON ALLERGY-PRODUCING FOODS

Ninety percent of all food-related allergies involve the following foods. The first four are foods that in time many children will outgrow their allergic reactions to. The last four are considered lifetime allergies. None of these foods should be given to children before age three or four. Be especially careful if a parent or sibling is allergic to any of these foods, since food allergies run in families.

- cow's milk
- eggs
- wheat
- soy

- peanuts
- tree nuts
- fish
- shellfish

▓ MILK SENSITIVITY AND LACTOSE INTOLERANCE ▓

It may surprise you to see such an important and frequently consumed food as milk leading the list. But milk sensitivity and related lactose intolerance are quite common in babies and children. This is an important reason for not giving your baby cow's milk before he's a year old. (Don't forget to put the hold on ice cream too.)

Milk sensitivity is an allergy to the proteins and fats in milk. In the first year mother's milk or formula offers your baby a balanced source of protein and the right amount of fats. If you find that your baby is allergic to milk either by offering him a milk-based formula or by observing his negative reaction to your breast milk because of the dairy products you've eaten, a change in diet is in order. Your doctor may advise that you switch to a low-allergy formula and that you limit or avoid dairy products while your baby is breast-feeding.

In baby's first year whole cow's milk should not replace mother's milk or formula in the diet. Cow's milk has three times as much protein as human milk, it is very high in salt, and it has a much higher concentration of saturated fat, which is very difficult for your infant to absorb. For babies under one year of age the high amount of nutrients puts undue stress on your baby's kidneys. The large curd in the milk is also very hard for your baby to digest.

If your baby is milk-sensitive, the most common symptom he might experience is diarrhea. Frequent bouts of diarrhea are considered serious in infants, and the loss of fluids can result in dehydration. Excessive dehydration can be deadly for a small child if measures are not taken to relieve it. Other symptoms include those described earlier in this section. Many children outgrow milk allergies by the time they are two years old. But the effects on those children who are sensitive can range from mild to severe.

Another milk-related problem children can experience is lactose intolerance, a deficiency in the enzyme needed to break down milk sugar, which is frequently encountered in children from one to two years of age. This condition is often, but not always, short-lived (two to three months). Symptoms are gener-

If your child is allergic to milk, avoid dairy foods including sherbet, ice cream, butter, cheese, yogurt, and buttermilk. Read food labels, because some brands of chocolate, margarine, lunch meats, and hot dogs may contain milk protein.

CHOKING FIRST AID

1. Find out if the child can breathe, cry, or speak. See if the child has a strong cough. (A strong cough means there is little or no blockage. It may also dislodge the item if there is blockage.)
2. If the child is breathing, coughing, or speaking, carefully watch him. *Do not start first aid if there is a strong cough or if there is little or no blockage.* This can turn partial blockage into complete blockage.
3. Begin the following first aid if:
   - the child cannot breathe at all.
   - the child's airway is so blocked that there's only a weak cough and loss of color.

For Infants Under One Year Old

1. Make sure you or someone else has called for emergency medical services.
2. Place the infant face- and head-down on your forearm at a 60-degree angle. Support the head and neck. Rest your forearm firmly against your body for extra support. If the infant is large, you may want to lay the child facedown over your lap. Firmly support the head, holding it lower than the trunk.
3. Give four rapid back blows with the heel of your hand, striking high between the shoulder blades.
4. If the blockage is not relieved, turn the infant over. Lay the child down, face up, on a firm surface. Give four rapid chest thrusts over the breastbone using *two fingers*.
5. If breathing does not start, open the mouth with thumb held over tongue and fingers wrapped around lower jaw. This is called the *tongue-jaw lift*. It draws the tongue away from the back of the

throat and may help clear the airway. If you can see the foreign body, it may be removed with a sideways sweep of a finger. Never poke the finger straight into the throat. *But be very careful of finger sweeps, because they may cause further blockage.*

6. If the infant does not begin to breathe right away, place your mouth over the mouth and nose of the infant. Attempt two quick, shallow breaths. Because of the infant's size, use quick and short breaths.

7. Repeat steps 1 through 6.

For Children Over One Year Old

1. Make sure you or someone you know has called for emergency medical services.
2. Place the child on his back. Kneel at his feet. Put the heel of one hand in the midline between the navel and rib cage. Place the second hand on top of the first. Then press firmly, but gently, into the abdomen with a rapid inward and upward thrust. Repeat this six to ten times. These abdominal thrusts are called the *Heimlich maneuver.*
3. If breathing does not start, open the airway using the tongue-jaw lift technique. If you can see the foreign body, you can try to remove it with a sideways sweep of the finger. *Be careful, though, because finger sweeps may push the object farther down the airway.*
4. If the child does not begin to breathe right away, attempt to restore breathing with the mouth-to-mouth technique. If this fails, repeat a series of six to ten abdominal thrusts.
5. Repeat steps 1 through 4.

Note: In a larger child, the abdominal thrusts (Heimlich maneuver) may be performed when the victim is standing, sitting, or lying down.

Gagging and Choking

Never leave your child unattended while he is eating. Any food—even purees that are too thick—can cause gagging and choking. Hot dogs are the most common cause of choking death in children, with peanuts second. Here's a list of the most common offenders.

- hot dogs (Toddler meat sticks, a commercial baby food product, should be fed only to toddlers with lots of teeth.)
- peanuts
- popcorn
- chips (potato, corn, etc.)
- seeds of any variety
- whole grapes
- whole olives
- cherries
- corn niblets
- uncooked peas
- raw carrots or other hard vegetables
- peanut butter
- baby food that is too pasty
- cookies or crackers that crumble easily
- hard candy, including its pretty cellophane or foil wrapper
- jelly beans

ally localized in the gastrointestinal tract and include gas, bloating, cramps, and diarrhea.

If your child is lactose-intolerant, you can serve a special milk that contains the enzyme lactase. A widely available lactase-enriched milk is the Lactaid brand. Packets of this enzyme can also be purchased separately and added at home to regular containers of milk.

Depending on the degree of your child's milk intolerance, you might have perfect results feeding your child milk by-products in which the milk sugar is already broken down. These include yogurt, sour cream, acidophilus milk, buttermilk, cottage cheese, and aged cheeses such as Swiss and Parmesan.

▒ WATCH OUT FOR SOY TOO ▒

A lot of babies are allergic to soybeans and soy-based products. This is true even for the baby who is allergic to the standard milk-based formula. Your doctor can recommend a low-allergy formula if your baby falls into this category.

An easy way to check out your baby's sensitivity to soy is to introduce it (at the end of the first year) in the form of tofu. Tofu is curded soy cheese that is edible just the way you buy it. Look for it in sealed shrink packs nestled among the exotic vegetables in your supermarket. The fresh product is often available in Oriental groceries. Present tofu to your baby cut into fingers or cubes. A vegetable or fruit puree dipping sauce will perk up its bland flavor.

If you find that soy disagrees with your baby, you must become very aware that soy is hidden in many fast and prepared foods. Commercially, soy is used in ways that may surprise you. It's commonly used to stretch fast-food hamburgers, and it's part of the base in fast-food "milk" shakes. Read all labels on packaged foods too. Soy oil is a common ingredient in many prepared packaged foods you might not suspect, like cookies.

READ LABELS

As your child becomes older and eats a wider variety of foods, it will become increasingly important for you to read the fine print on food labels. Corn syrup, a widely used commercial sweetener, is a frequent ingredient in infant formula and is a common allergen in children.

Often foods you are allergic to, or their derivatives, appear on labels under unfamiliar, scientific names. The following lists will help you identify and avoid them.

▒ WHEAT-CONTAINING FOODS ▒

- bran
- cake flour
- cracker meal
- durum
- farina
- graham crackers and crumbs
- graham flour
- hydrolyzed vegetable protein (hvp)*
- malt*
- malt syrup*
- monosodium glutamate*
- phosphated flour
- semolina

*Gluten and/or wheat is often present, but not always.

▒ CORN DERIVATIVES ▒

- corn syrup
- cornmeal
- corn oil
- cornstarch
- modified food starch
- dextrin
- fructose
- maltodextrins
- dextrose
- lactic acid
- sorbitol
- mannitol
- caramel color
- alcohol

▦ EGG-CONTAINING FOODS ▦

- albumin
- globulin
- ovomucin
- ovomucoid
- silico albuminate

- vitellin
- ovovitellin
- yolk
- livetin

▦ MILK-CONTAINING FOODS ▦

- lactose
- casein
- caseinate
- potassium caseinate
- sodium caseinate

- lactalbumin
- lactoglobulin
- curds
- wheys
- milk solids

▲ ● ▦ ▲ ● ▦ ▲
FOOD ADDITIVES

Remember, any food can cause your baby a problem. But with time chances are he will be able to eat anything he likes. It may take a month, a year, or even many years. So go slowly and be patient. And if you suspect your child is allergic to any food or medication, consult your doctor.

Food additives such as coloring agents, artificial flavors, and preservatives, including sulfites, nitrates, and nitrites, can also cause allergic reactions. A photographer assigned by a New York paper to cover one of our Mommy Made classes told a nightmarish story. His daughter had to be put on medication when she was three years old. He told the class that instead of getting better, his little girl got sicker each day, until she finally had to be admitted to the hospital. She turned out to be allergic to the medication, or more specifically the coloring agent that gave the medication its pretty red color. She was switched to another brand without any dyes, quickly recovered, and went on to lead a normal life. The only thing she still avoids are foods containing any red dyes.

CHAPTER THREE

Baby's First Supper, Conquering the Cup, and Other Hands-on Feeding Matters

THE DAILY ROUTINE

Before we jump right into a description of baby's first supper, we'd like to discuss the importance of the daily routine. We can't stress enough how important it is to establish a daily feeding time when you begin to introduce solid foods. It's through repetition that your child learns new skills. And eating, like learning to talk, takes time and practice. Being a patient parent will be especially important to help this new skill become a part of your child's life. Routines also give your child a sense of identity in the family and will also prepare him for school.

One mother of an eight-month-old called us in hysterics after taking our class. "I know there is something terribly wrong with my daughter," she said. "She simply does not enjoy eating solid foods. She only wants to nurse." This mom eventually admitted that her hectic work schedule kept her from feeding her daughter solid foods every day at a certain time. And even if she did find the time, she was often in a hurry to get the job done. We urged her to be patient with the process and to establish a daily routine for feeding her baby and to try not to be in such a rush. Babies need time to learn. Lo and behold, two weeks later, her daughter was eating!

Allergy or sensitivity detection is another reason to establish a routine. *New foods should always be introduced at midday.* (Breakfast is okay too, if Mom's up for it.) This way, if the new food doesn't agree with your baby, you'll be faced with a cranky child just for the afternoon, rather than an endless, sleepless night.

BABY'S FIRST SUPPER

This is a dress rehearsal of your baby's first encounter with solid food. It features rice cereal as the entree. But you may decide to start with oat or barley cereal if your baby has had frequent bouts with constipation. (Rice is very binding.) Or you may decide to begin with a vegetable such as acorn squash if your family is especially sensitive or if you have a strong family history of allergies. (Vegetables tend to be the least problematic of the food groups for babies.)

Today is a red-letter day in your baby's life! His first real meal is an event you'll probably record in his baby book and proudly report to his grandparents on the telephone. Your baby is six months old. And at his regular checkup his doctor has given you the green light to start on solid food. Typical of new moms, you rush right from the doctor's office to the nearest market and purchase a box of baby rice cereal. (Remember to purchase a vitamin-enriched and iron-fortified brand.)

Do not mix cereal with juice! Cereal with breast milk or formula creates a complete meal.
Cereal = carbohydrates, iron, and vitamins
Breast milk or formula = fats and protein

Okay. Now all you have to do is serve it up: First, mix 2 teaspoons of rice cereal in a small dish with expressed breast milk or formula until the mixture resembles a thick soup or gravy. The formula should be at the same temperature as the bottle you normally feed your baby. Breast milk, just expressed for the meal, will of course always be at the perfect 98.6 degrees.

Now sit baby on your lap, making sure he is in an upright position with his head slightly tipped back and supported in the crook of your elbow. Tuck a cloth diaper or napkin under his chin. Using a small spoon with smooth rounded edges—a demitasse spoon is perfect—place a tiny amount of the cereal in his mouth.

At first your baby may not know what to do with the new texture. He may push it off the spoon with his tongue, let it sit in his mouth, or even try to suck it off the spoon. (The sucking need is very strong in young children, as we discussed in Chapter One, and this can prevent them from satisfying their hunger from a spoon in the beginning.) Just don't get discouraged. After all, up to this point baby has only sucked liquids for sustenance. Swallowing is a new skill he will learn quickly with a little practice when his throat muscles are developed sufficiently and become accustomed to the new task.

Soon, but not perhaps at this meal, baby will get a taste of the cereal—either by licking it off his face, sucking it from the spoon, or because it inadvertently dribbled down his throat. He'll most likely love the new experience. And once he perfects swallowing, he'll be opening his mouth like an eager little bird when the cereal-laden spoon appears before him.

That's all there is to it. But keep in mind that it may take some babies longer to get the knack of eating solids. Keep trying once a day—at approximately the same time, to establish a routine. Keep the session short. Don't persist for too long, or both you and your baby will end up frustrated. Remember, he'll do it when he's ready. And don't forget to smile. Mealtime should be a happy experience.

SOME HELPFUL TIPS

To make the first solids go down easier, give baby the breast or bottle first to take the edge off, but not fill him up. Or offer first spoonfuls of rice cereal slightly before baby's normal feeding hour so that he's not frantic for food and impatient with the new taste, texture, and challenge.

Every so often a mother will call us with despair in her voice, asking what to do with a baby who simply refuses solid foods even after many attempts. We remind the mother of the importance of a daily routine as we discussed earlier and then ask, "Is your baby breast-fed?" Most often the answer is "Yes!" As with weaning a baby from breast to bottle, it may be very difficult for your baby to want anything from Mom other than the breast. At feeding time, as hard as it may be for you, you might need to be completely out of sight and in some cases out of the house. Your baby has a very keen sense of smell and can sometimes detect you even when he can't see you. Our advice in this case is to have another person like Dad or Grandma help out at feeding time.

TOWARD THREE SQUARE MEALS A DAY

As your baby grows and both her appetite and swallowing ability develop, you'll naturally increase the amount of rice cereal served and thicken its consistency. Do this gradually, based on your own observations. Does she seem to want more after the bowl is empty? Leaning forward in anticipation of the next spoonful and crying for more are sure signs. And, of course, turning her head away and pushing the food out with her tongue are clear indications that your baby's had enough.

After you've introduced other foods, protein-rich ones in

particular, such as meat and cheese, the midday meal will become baby's dinner or main meal of the day. You'll relegate cereal to other meals such as breakfast and supper. As solid food begins to play a central role in baby's diet—usually at around ten months—you'll offer the breast, bottle, or cup only after a substantial portion of the food has been consumed or at the end of the meal.

Snacks, which are so important for the growing child, are usually breast milk or formula in the first year.

CONQUERING THE CUP

Your baby can start taking his first sips of expressed breast milk, formula, or water from a cup as early as four months while he is perched comfortably on your lap. But most moms really get serious about the cup once baby is firmly sitting up in his high chair and on solid food. We recommend starting the cup early. It's good practice in the event of an unlikely emergency when breast or bottle is unavailable.

Baby's first cup should be shallow, wide-mouthed, unbreakable, and have a large handle. (A weighted bottom sometimes helps too.) Begin by giving your baby a few sips of expressed breast milk, formula, or water at the midday meal. Hold the cup for baby and tip it up to his lips. Carefully let a few drops of the liquid trickle into his mouth. He could choke a bit if the flow is too fast. At first your child will probably be content in helping you hold the cup. Later he'll want to try it completely on his own. There's no reason why he can't practice by himself. In fact it's a good idea. Just be sure the cup is unbreakable and put only the tiniest bit of liquid in it. The first solo attempts will most likely end up down his neck or on the floor. Be patient. Encourage your baby even though he's messy.

Offer the cup between meals with juice and water for extra

practice. More water is particularly important to aid digestion if your baby is on solid foods. Offer lots of water in warm weather to avoid dehydration.

You can also try one of the training cups. These are designed to cut down on spilling and come equipped with a drinking spout lid, weighted bottom, and two handles. A drawback of the spout is that it doesn't allow your baby to learn to use his lips to control the flow of the liquid. The liquid just pours down his throat. Teddi choked on her first try with one of these cups.

FEEDING MYSELF

Some Tips on Weaning

- Always keep the bottle-fed baby in your lap to encourage dependence, not independence. When it's time for your baby to explore, he'll leave the bottle with you. Eventually, exploring and playing will be more important than bottle time on Mom's lap.
- Try to offer *only* the cup at mealtimes. At the very least, reserve the bottle or breast for last, after most or all of the food is consumed.
- Take your time. Give yourself and your baby at least a month for the whole weaning process.
- Some bigger babies who eat solid food and can drink from a cup still demand the bottle or breast. What they really may want is the suckling time, not the calories. Try a pacifier.

Many first-time parents ask when they can expect their child to begin feeding himself. Start as soon as your child can sit up in a high chair by giving him a spoon to play with. Put a little pureed food on his fingertips too and put them in his mouth. When your child shows a definite interest in feeding himself, let him practice with his own bowl and spoon. You'll know when; he'll take a swipe at the spoon or refuse to let you shovel in the food. At first it's best to let him try feeding himself after you have spooned in most of the meal. (Then you won't worry whether he's had enough to eat. And he won't become frustrated by his inability to get the food to his mouth quickly and easily enough.)

You can also try the switching game at this stage. This is an especially good trick with babies who have an independent streak about feeding themselves right from the start. When baby raises his empty spoon to his open mouth, you slip in a loaded one. Thickening purees will make them cling to the spoon better and make baby more successful at these first attempts.

As you move from purees and cereals to small pieces of food, blunt baby forks may be easier for baby to manage than spoons. Once the food is speared, no matter how wiggly the route to baby's mouth, it tends to hang on.

Finger foods are another good way to get your baby to feed himself. Strew small pieces of soft food on the high-chair tray. Your baby will love plucking up bright round peas, steamed carrot circles, and banana spears with his fingers and popping them into his mouth. At the same time, he'll also be improving his eye-hand coordination and refining his motor skills.

We know this process makes a horrible mess that sometimes seems just impossible to clean up—one mom told us she regularly hosed down the high chair in the backyard—but only through practice can your baby learn this skill. And the last thing you want is a two-year-old who just sits there waiting for you to spoon the food in. You won't have the time or the patience. The best advice we have to offer is to grin and bear the mess and be proud of your baby's growing independence and accomplishment. And don't worry about manners; they'll come later. Let baby learn one skill at a time.

WEANING FROM THE BREAST AND BOTTLE

When to wean your child from the breast and bottle is a personal choice. But Mom should begin to concern herself with this issue when her child is able to sip formula from his cup and has begun feeding himself. This is usually at about eight months. Weaning naturally fits into your child's developmental pattern. As he matures, gets more teeth, and his dexterity with cups, spoons, and finger foods improves, your baby's interest in nursing from breast or bottle will naturally diminish, if you let it.

In the beginning, hold off on the breast or bottle at your baby's biggest meal—usually midday—until he has finished most of his food. You'll see that after eating pureed chicken, sweet potato, and applesauce and drinking sips of formula and mother's milk from a cup, your baby will not be very interested in nursing or a bottle afterward.

Weaning is a gradual process. After the midday breast-feeding and bottle are eliminated, try cutting it out at another meal period next. Continue the process until you have totally weaned your child. The hardest nursing time for your baby to give up will probably be his last bedtime breast-feeding or bottle, since it is comforting and soothing.

Don't delay weaning for too long. Excessive milk drinking in older babies can lead to nutritional deficiencies and for the bottle-fed baby, bottle-mouth syndrome, a serious form of tooth decay.

Keep in mind that some babies may need to go back to the bottle or breast for a day or two, especially if they are sick or teething. And older children, well beyond the breast or bottle stage, may revert to babyish behaviors and demand a bottle if a new baby sister has one. We think it's best to give in on these occasions. Older children obviously have a lot of issues to deal with when they are suddenly forced to share the limelight with a new sibling. A bottle of milk or juice can't hurt and may offer a sense of security. We promise you, your child won't take his bottle, baby blanket, or pacifier to college with him as Grandma may threaten.

GAMES CHILDREN PLAY AT THE TABLE

The concept of eating is learned gradually. And only through interaction with the strange-looking stuff called *food* can your baby *grasp* the concept. A Middle Eastern friend of ours says, "In my country you taste with your fingers." Sometimes we wonder if our sterile eating habits are depriving us of some fantastic gratification. In any event, your baby has a great need to touch, see, smell, mush, and smear food before deciding to eat it. It's wonderful to watch the look of delight when something tasty makes it to his mouth under his own steam.

At first you will see more of this messing around than eating. At this time it is important to continue to offer spoonfuls of food while your baby explores. Almost abruptly your baby will get the hang of it and will enthusiastically make the transition to self-feeding, especially if he is with other family members at the table.

At the dinner table, and in other ways throughout the day, your baby is learning about what psychologists call *object permanence and separation*. When Mommy goes away, she comes back again. Learning this truth often starts right in the high chair. (Peekaboo is another way to help baby learn about object separation and permanence.) Our adorable Teddi would throw her spoon, her toys, or even her whole bowl of food on the floor if we were not watching, and then she would look at us and then the floor to see if she would get any of this back again.

This game is one your baby won't tire of for quite some time. Take it from us, for Mom and Dad it's boring, exasperating, and messy. For your baby, however, it's very important. We know one little boy who dumped his cup of milk over the side of his high chair every day without fail for six months until he was fully convinced that what went away would indeed return.

Probably you never thought "cutting the apron strings" would start with your tiny baby right in the kitchen. But here it is. Your child's sense of self and of who he is is all wrapped up in eating and mealtime experiences. So take a deep breath, relax, and enjoy these games, because it's these early experiences that will give your baby a trusting outlook on life.

BUT HOW WILL MY BABY LEARN TABLE MANNERS?

We think the best way to teach your child to eat in a civilized fashion is to take your meals with him as often as possible. Your baby will very much want to fit into your lifestyle and very much wants to do things to please you. By emulating your behavior he will easily learn that wiping his mouth on his napkin is far better than using his sleeve.

GEARING UP FOR MEALTIME

For such little people, babies seem to accumulate a bundle of paraphernalia. We're sure you've noticed that feeding has not escaped this proliferation of products. Airplane spoons, Splat Mats, high chairs that turn into booster seats, etc., all promise to make daily activities easier for Mom and Dad. And while some of it's hype and some of it's helpful, here's a rundown on what we consider the basics for mealtime.

BABY SPOONS AND DISHES

Every child should be born with a silver spoon in his mouth. But in reality these handsome baby gifts make better family heirlooms than they do first feeding spoons. A plastic or vinyl-coated spoon with a long handle and smooth, rounded edges is your best bet for first meals. Unlike silver, plastic does not readily absorb (and transfer to baby's mouth) heat or cold.

As your child begins feeding himself, a spoon with a short, bent handle and a deep, rounded bowl will be easiest for him to manage. And as mentioned earlier, some babies find baby forks with very safe, short, blunt tines easiest to handle.

Baby serving dishes warmed by electricity or a water bath are another popular baby gift. They are handy for keeping food warm as you dress (or undress) and position baby for dinner and while he eats. (Babies can be incredibly slow eaters.) Be wary, however, of leaving food in them for any length of time. These dishes keep food at just the perfect temperature for bacteria to grow.

When your baby begins to feed himself it's obviously time to purchase a place setting of inexpensive, shatterproof plastic that can take battering on the high-chair tray and numerous plunges to the floor.

BIBS

Bibs quickly become a necessity for baby at mealtimes. For very young babies being fed their first spoonfuls on your lap, simply tucking the cloth diaper used for burping under the chin is sufficient. But you will quickly graduate to official bibs as your baby gets bigger. In general bibs should be generous in size, easily sponged off, machine washable, and easy to fasten. Most babies have short, fat necks and are quite impatient at mealtime for you to bring on the food. They have little interest in such niceties as dressing for the occasion. Most moms find Velcro or snap fasteners quicker and easier than ties. Both, though, have a tendency to get tangled in tendrils of fine baby hair. If your child is blessed with a mop of curls, try putting the bib on backward—fastening it loosely under his chin and then twisting it around to the proper position. For more grown-up babies who are sitting up and feeding themselves, and for toddlers, molded plastic bibs with a curved lip at the bottom like a kangaroo pouch are excellent, virtually indestructible shields and catchers for dropped food and dripped liquids, although they can be rough around the neck. And in warm weather, some moms simply feed their babies dressed in diapers only. Skin is eminently washable!

We don't recommend those long-sleeved tie-on plastic shirt bibs. While they offer a lot of coverage, all the babies we know hate them; they're probably too hot and confining.

Finally, don't make yourself and your child miserable by feeding him in his best party attire! Food and formula stains are tough—sometimes impossible—to get out.

BE SEATED

Baby's first chair for eating solid food will be your lap. But you can quickly progress to a high chair. Feeding baby in a high chair will give you two free hands—one to spoon the food in with and the other to shake rattles, catch his hands as he attempts to intercept the spoon, adjust the bib, and wipe up drips. (A lot of mothers give their children toys and spoons to hold as a distraction while they are feeding them. Sometimes this works.) The youngest diners (six to eight months) will probably need a pad to cushion the seat and a pillow or two to hold them upright. Once your baby can fully sit up on his own you can do away with these props.

If you don't have the space for a full-fledged high chair, a booster seat that sits on a kitchen chair is fine. Another abbreviated baby chair is supported by its arms from the tabletop. Both of these alternatives have the advantage of being portable and easily transported for dining out. They are also much less costly than high chairs.

Be practical. Antique baby chairs and newer wicker models are charming, but babies today are bigger than their counterparts of 100 years ago, and designers have come a long way in adding safety and convenience features to the current high chairs. When selecting a high chair, look for the following:

- Sturdiness and stability (splayed legs)
- Removable and adjustable tray with a raised lip
- Safety strap that threads between baby's legs and fastens around his waist. And don't forget to use it! Many a mom has turned her back on baby for a few moments only to find on her next glance that her child is slipping under the tray to the floor, hanging only by his chin. Older children who are not buckled up will try to climb out of the chair and can be found proudly standing on the seat, displaying their achievement.
- Foot rest, so baby's legs don't dangle

• Nontoxic finish and easily washable surface. The first is a must for the teething stage, when babies are known to gnaw on anything handy.

If you're purchasing a high chair, spending a little extra for these features will be well worth the investment, especially if you're planning on future siblings. Secondhand baby furniture retains its resale value.

We don't recommend that you feed your baby in his infant seat. His head will be tilted too far back, and he might gag.

GEARING UP FOR THE SECOND CHILD

When you gear up for a second baby, you may want to rethink the obviously practical notion of using the firstborn's plates, cups, and spoons for the second—especially if your children are close in age. Our girls are only 19 months apart, and we'll never forget when Teddi looked over at her little sister Renée's place setting with a horrified expression and declared, "That's *my* dinosaur plate!" We began to realize that Teddi was having to share so much in her life—her mommy and daddy, her room, some of her clothes—that she simply wanted to draw the line. This is perfectly okay and natural. Don't always expect your first child to give in on every issue and share. It's very frustrating for them to give up center stage, and respecting their more reasonable wishes (in this case, dishes) whenever possible can help cut down on sibling rivalry.

A Clean Finish

Putting a tablecloth on the floor (under the high chair) is probably a better use of it for first eaters than draping it on the table. Obviously you won't use your best damask linen. A plastic painter's dropcloth, yesterday's newspaper, an old bed sheet, or if you want to get fancy, a Splat Mat (which is made and sold expressly for this purpose) will also save on cleanup.

CHAPTER FOUR
From One Year On

All About Nutrition

There's no escaping it; nutrition is a very important subject moms and dads need to be well versed in if they are going to feed their kids right. This information is especially important when baby turns one. For this is the age when baby's nutritional insurance policy, as we like to call it—breast milk and formula—is about to expire, and you're on the brink of the picky, picky toddler stage. Up to about 14 months, virtually all babies eat with great relish. It's the second year when your knowledge of good nutrition is really put to the test. Now the food pyramid that follows should be your guide.

The following pages will provide you with all the information you need to know about nutrition. Good nutrition is not something your child can catch up on later. And at no other time in his life will his growth rate be surpassed or good nutrition be so important. In the first year of life your baby tripled his weight and grew 10 to 12 inches. By age three, 20 teeth will have emerged, brain growth has occurred, motor skills are refined, and his personality will develop—in total a tremendous accomplishment.

It's food, of course, that makes this growth and development possible, or more specifically the nutrients found in food. Nutrients are also necessary for energy to work and play (one and the same for baby) and to remain healthy. But not all foods are equivalent in their nutritional content—some are rich in nutrients, and others are nutrient-poor—and no single food, not even milk, contains all the nutrients needed for good health and growth. Helping Mommy and Daddy make informed food choices is what good nutrition and this chapter are all about. Research now shows that early childhood dietary habits actually shape your adult health patterns. To do it right, you need to think ahead so that you don't inadvertently fall into unhealthy habits. If you dilute your baby's juice with water right from the start, for instance, he won't crave the sweetness of full-strength juice.

THE BIG PICTURE

Nutrition is a complex, scientific subject populated with vitamins, calories, proteins, fats, carbohydrates, minerals, and more. (Detailed information on specific nutrients appears in the back of this book in the Nutrition Glossary.) It's useful to have a working knowledge of this vocabulary but it's not imperative to eating healthfully. Keep your eye on the big picture, as discussed below.

NUTRIENTS: THE TOP 10

Though you don't need to understand the specific biochemical interaction among the various nutrients and the human body, it is helpful to know which nutrients are crucial to good health. Nutrients are chemical substances that build, repair, and maintain body tissues, help regulate body processes, and furnish fuel for energy.

Scientists have determined that the human body requires

about 50 nutrients. Ten of these—protein, carbohydrate, fat, vitamin A, vitamin C, thiamine, riboflavin, niacin, calcium, and iron—are considered "leader" nutrients. Fortunately, if your diet contains the proper amounts of these top 10 nutrients, you're probably consuming the right amounts of those other 40 as well.

NOT ALL FOODS ARE CREATED EQUAL

Not all foods are nutritionally equivalent. Consider the following options: a glass of milk versus a can of soda; a gelatin dessert versus an egg custard; a snack of boxed cookies versus an apple. In these examples common sense tells you which foods are more nutrient-dense, or healthier for you. However, these comparisons present extremes. In many instances the nutritional advantage of one food over another is not as obvious, such as one loaf of packaged bread over another. How are Mom and Dad to know? They have the U.S. RDA labels on food to guide them.

U.S. RDA stands for "United States Recommended Daily Allowances." These are legal standards for labeling the nutrient content in food developed by the Food and Drug Administration. U.S. RDA labels express in percentages the 10 leader nutrients and the calories in a given food. At the manufacturer's discretion 12 additional vitamins and minerals may be included. The listing is mandatory when they do not naturally occur in a food, but are added. Get in the habit of reading these labels. On your next trip to the supermarket, compare the nutritional information on a variety of staples you regularly purchase, such as your usual oatmeal with its shelfmate. While this exercise may add considerably to your shopping time, it's a one-time task. On future trips you'll be able to identify nutrient-dense brands of choice immediately.

Read Those Labels!

Food labels offer moms and dads useful information about daily nutritional requirements. These labels are easy to read and will help you make healthful choices. Labels typically give the nutritional value per serving of vitamins and minerals expressed in the percentage of the total daily recommended requirement. Labels also give the lowdown per serving on fat, salt, protein, and carbohydrates. Information on the amount of juice in juice drinks, water in canned vegetables, and sugar in canned fruit is also included, plus a list of food additives, colors, flavor enhancers, and preservatives—man-made ingredients that are common allergens.

MANY DIFFERENT FOODS LEAD TO A BALANCED DIET

Not only is variety the spice of life, but it is all-important in your diet. Variety is what ensures that you and your baby get all of the top 10 nutrients—and the other 40 as well. And if baby doesn't like Brussels sprouts—broccoli, cantaloupe, collards, and of course oranges are even better sources of vitamin C. With the abundance of foodstuffs in the average American supermarket and the myriad cuisines of the world for inspiration, there is surely an appealing as well as healthy combination of foods to suit your family's tastes.

Again, you don't need to whip out the calculator every time you plan a day's meals to guarantee your family good nutrition. After baby's first year of life you can rely on that old, familiar standard, the Food Pyramid, outlined on the next pages, as your guide to menu planning and marketing. The is the single most important aspect of this chapter. It's a primary resource on nutrition that will ensure (for the average individual) a well-balanced, nutrient-rich diet.

Vitamin and Mineral Supplements

Most children who are good eaters and eat a wide variety of foods do not need vitamin and mineral supplements. Iron is the exception to this rule. At six months babies have used up the natural stores of iron in their liver that they were born with. A good source of iron at this age is found in what is traditionally baby's first food: commercially prepared baby rice cereal. (Check the label, however. Not all baby cereals are iron-fortified.) As your baby gets older, other solid foods such as eggs, meat, whole grains, and beans provide needed iron. But just to be sure your baby is getting enough iron during the transition from breast milk or formula to solid foods, your doctor may prescribe a supplement. Some formulas are iron-fortified, so bottle-fed babies may not need additional iron. But breast-fed babies will probably need additional iron. The need for iron can show up again at 18 months, when most children are solidly on table food and drinking cow's milk.

Vitamin and mineral deficiencies can also run in families, just like allergies. One of our class parents had a potassium deficiency that both of her twin daughters inherited. If you are concerned about these issues, be sure to discuss them with your doctor.

Food Guide Pyramid for Young Children
A Daily Guide for 2- to 6-year-olds

FATS & SWEETS
Eat LESS

MILK GROUP
2
Servings

MEAT GROUP
2
Servings

VEGETABLE GROUP
3
Servings

FRUIT GROUP
2
Servings

GRAIN GROUP
6
Servings

WHAT COUNTS AS ONE SERVING?

GRAIN GROUP

1 slice of bread

$1/2$ cup cooked rice or pasta

$1/2$ cup cooked cereal

1 ounce of ready-to-eat cereal

VEGETABLE GROUP

$1/2$ cup chopped raw or cooked vegetables

1 cup raw leafy green vegetables

FRUIT GROUP

1 piece of fruit or melon wedge

$3/4$ cup of juice

$1/2$ cup unsweetened canned fruit

$1/4$ cup of dried fruit

MILK GROUP

1 cup milk or yogurt

2 ounces of cheese

MEAT GROUP

2 to 3 ounces of cooked, lean meat, poultry, or fish

$1/2$ cup of cooked dried beans or 1 egg counts as 1 ounce of lean meat

2 tablespoons peanut butter count as 1 ounce of meat

FATS AND SWEETS

Limit calories from these

Great Finger Foods

Finger foods can be any age-appropriate, soft, unseasoned table food, cut into small pieces but big enough for your baby to pick up. Serve finger food right on the high-chair tray. (Most experienced parents dispense with plates for younger babies since they always end up on the floor.) Some possibilities:

- steamed apple and pear wedges
- steamed carrot, zucchini, or summer squash circles
- steamed asparagus spears (serve whole)
- ripe banana and avocado spears
- egg-free pasta with cottage cheese
- gelatin cubes
- cut-up chicken liver
- cheese cubes
- steamed broccoli and cauliflower flowerets, with dunking sauces (pages 273–283)
- fruit butters (pages 282–283) on whole-wheat bread
- Inside-Out Sandwiches (page 224)
- Toasted Waffles with Peanut Butter, Jelly, and Fresh Fruit (page 229)
- Tasmanian Devil Eggheads (page 223)

More on Milk

Only at three years should you begin limiting baby's fat intake and switch him over to 1 percent or skim milk from the whole cow's milk introduced at 12 months. This is the age when he becomes all too aware of junk foods that are high in fat, so low-fat milk can be a wise choice.

During the course of researching and writing this book, we found that the recommendation for daily milk intake for babies over one year varied between 16 and 24 ounces. In reality babies need only small amounts of each food. One of the biggest problems facing school-aged children in this country is iron deficiency, and children who drink too much milk can easily fall into this category.

HOW MUCH IS ENOUGH FOR CHILDREN UNDER AGE 2?

Serving sizes for babies under two years are not indicated in the above guidelines. Some babies are obviously hungrier and bigger than others. Don't get out the measuring cups and spoons. For solids, offer small portions (a tablespoon or two) of each food to start. Liquids, since they spill, just a few ounces at a time. While these servings may hardly seem large enough to sustain a bird, you're not fattening a turkey for Thanksgiving. Too much food at once can overwhelm a baby and depress his appetite. You can always serve more. And some babies will want lots more! Give it to them and don't be concerned. And remember, before he's one, baby's nutritional needs are still being largely supplied by those perfect foods: breast milk and formula.

If you're worried that your child is not eating enough nutritious foods, the following should help you put matters in perspective.

- One teaspoon of peanut butter on a slice of whole-wheat bread provides one-half the recommended daily protein for a two-year-old.
- Two ounces of fresh, or vitamin C–enriched, juice gives a child all the vitamin C he needs in a day.
- One ounce of Swiss cheese has the same amount of calcium as 8 ounces of whole milk.
- Just $1/8$ to $1/4$ cup of cooked carrots provides all the vitamin A needed in a day.

If you're still concerned that your child is not receiving enough from all the food groups, keep a written record of what he eats for a week. You may be pleasantly surprised to find that snack time is providing a good deal of the daily requirements.

Is a Vegetarian Diet Appropriate for My Baby?

Vegetarianism, a diet composed primarily of plant food, is very popular today. There's no denying that a diet rich in fruits, vegetables, and grains is good for you—and your baby. Scientists have identified certain phytochemicals—carotenoids, flavonoids, and dietary fiber, which are exclusively found in these food groups—that will help your baby grow properly as well as help her ward off diseases like cancer and heart disease in the future. Since children develop their lifelong eating habits in childhood, we believe that parents must encourage their children to eat these foods. However, to avoid health risks, making the choice to raise your child exclusively vegetarian should be considered carefully.

A vegetarian diet most often falls short of daily nutritional requirements for protein; vitamins B_{12}, B_2, and D; and calcium, iron, and zinc. When the vegetarian diet is not extreme and includes dairy products and eggs, the risk of these nutritional deficiencies, with the exception of iron, is reduced considerably. But, because of your child's rapid growth in the first few years of life, very special care must be taken to provide adequate iron. And although iron is found in plant foods, it is very poorly absorbed by the body.

The other major problem with a vegetarian diet is that it is necessarily high in bulk. And your child simply may not have the capacity to eat enough to obtain the calories he needs for the energy his rapid growth requires.

If you are serious about raising a vegetarian child, it is by no means impossible and has its physical and moral benefits. Sarah, a mother we know, had this to say about her decision to raise her family as vegetarians: "I eliminated animal flesh from my family's diet because of my concern with how animals are raised in this country. Most commercial livestock are pumped with steroids, hormones, and antibiotics, which are then passed on to the consumer in the steaks, chops, etc., we eat. I didn't think these were good for my family. It also takes five pounds of grain to yield just one pound of beef," she continued, "and I was concerned about all the hungry people of the world." (A pound of grain feeds many more than a pound of beef.)

"I am not a control freak about my children's diet," Sarah added. "We were recently visiting relatives, and they decided to barbecue hamburgers one evening. I let my son enjoy to his heart's content. But at home I plan the menu. And my family eats incredibly delicious foods filled with variety and nutrition. When my children reach the age of understanding and reason, I'll provide them with the facts and leave the decision to eat meat in their hands."

For food suggestions, see combining plant proteins on page 199 as well as the Food Pyramid on page 48.

Don't believe anyone who tells you kids don't like vegetables. Babies raised on fresh food learn from the start that vegetables are delicious. That's because fresh baby food looks better, smells better, and tastes better than any jarred commercial counterpart. And the nutrients are fresh, unlike canned baby food with its shelf life of two years or more.

And remember that a balanced diet balances out over several days. If you aren't satisfied with your own findings, be sure to discuss these concerns with your baby's doctor.

TWO OTHER NECESSITIES

WATER

Water is an important nutrient. An adult's body is two-thirds water; a baby's three-quarters water. Water is a building material, a solvent, and a regulator of body temperature. It carries nutrients to cells and carries waste products away. It aids in digestion and is necessary in all chemical reactions in metabolism. We can survive only a few days without it.

The foods and beverages that we consume contain water. But it's important to drink plenty of additional water. As mentioned in Chapter One, in the first six months of life breast milk and formula provide adequate hydration. As your baby grows older and solid food becomes the mainstay of his diet, his need for water will become greater. There's no need to force water on your baby, as breast milk contains all the water baby needs, but it's a good idea to get him accustomed to it at an early age.

At four to six months you can offer your baby water in a cup. The novelty of the cup will probably make the sips go down more readily. This also helps your baby begin to learn that he doesn't always need to quench his thirst with the breast or bottle.

"Do I need to serve my baby bottled water?" and "Should I boil it first?" are common questions about water many moms ask. No. The filtered, fluoridated city water that flows right from your kitchen tap is perfectly fine for your baby. (All municipal water must meet certain government standards.)

If you live in the country and depend on a private well for your water supply, it's a good idea to have it tested annually. Some local health departments have inspectors who provide this service. They will dispatch a sample of your water to the lab of the state department of health. Other municipalities will refer you to a certified testing laboratory. (A list of the latter appears in your Yellow Pages.) In both cases there is usually a fee of anywhere from $15 to $25 for the standard water analysis. If you rely on a private well for your water, be sure to tell your baby's doctor, who will probably want to supplement his diet with fluoride.

FIBER

Fiber, or roughage, is not a nutrient. But it keeps bowel movements regular and helps eliminate bile acids, sterols, and fat from the system. The average American diet is low in fiber. And while high-fiber diets are effective in treating constipation in children and preventing childhood obesity, it has not been proven that a high-fiber diet protects them from diseases in later life that are suspected of being linked to low-fiber diets such as adult-onset diabetes, atherosclerotic heart disease, and cancer of the colon. The Committee on Nutrition of the American Academy of Pediatrics recommends that a "substantial amount of fiber probably should be eaten to ensure normal laxation." Experts recommend that from age two on, children should consume grams of fiber totaling age plus 5 each day. So, your three-year-old needs 8 grams, whereas a ten-year-old needs 15.

Take it slowly. For babies under one no added fiber is usually needed. But as more and more solid foods are introduced, it's a good idea to instill healthy eating habits by offering fiber-rich foods. Bran and whole-grain cereals such as oatmeal are the best sources of fiber and the easiest way to increase fiber intake. If your toddler thinks these cereals are yucky, try disguising fiber. Serve our fiber-rich Banana-Bran Muffins and Oatmeal Raisin Cookies (pages 252 and 248) at breakfast and snacktime. They're sure to be a big hit. You can also hide fiber by sprinkling it on casseroles and adding it to meat loaf, meatballs, and hamburgers. Fruits and vegetables and beans are also good sources of fiber, especially prunes, apples, strawberries, raspberries, bananas, plums, peaches, pears, cantaloupe, and cherries; green beans, broccoli, carrots, and lettuce; pinto and kidney beans. And be sure to make your baby's sandwiches with whole-wheat bread; it's higher in fiber than white and even rye. When Teddi and Renée were toddlers, and sat down to watch *Sesame Street,* instead of cookies and milk, we served up garbanzo beans right out of the can. Steamed cauliflower florets with Russian dressing (page 273) were another favorite.

GOOD NUTRITION THROUGHOUT THE DAY

Once your baby is drinking whole cow's milk and eating solid foods, it's important to continue to spread his daily nutrient needs over the course of the day.

Start the day with a good breakfast! Breakfast should provide about one quarter of the day's total nutrients. It's a fact that breakfast eaters have more energy throughout the day, and getting your child into this habit will stand her in good stead when she begins school.

Lunch and dinner should each supply one third of the day's total nutrients.

Complete the rest of the day's requirements with nutritious snacks.

SNACKS

Snacks become increasingly important as your child turns into a busy, busy toddler. Because she is burning up so much energy, distracted by more interesting activities—like discovering the world—and has a limited capacity, your child simply may not be able to eat enough food at one meal to tide her over to the next. Offer her at least two snacks a day to keep her going; one at mid-morning and a second in the afternoon.

Snacks also provide Mom with a wonderful opportunity to round out baby's diet. While cookies and milk may automatically spring to mind, be nutritiously creative. Snack food can be anything from our special Peanut Butter Bananarama Shake (page 269) to a mini-meal of leftover cooked vegetables and meat or a bowl of cut-up fresh fruit topped with a dollop of yogurt.

If you feel snacks are turning into meals and your child is not hungry at the appointed mealtimes, you might consider adjusting his dining hours.

Remember, what your baby eats is more important than when he eats it. Some children, like adults, fare better with small meals throughout the day. And most children generally quit eating two to three hours before bedtime.

THE "BAD" FOODS

SALT

Every once in a while a parent will call us and ask, "Can I salt this baby food a little bit? It tastes so bland." Our response is always *no!* There's really little place for additional salt in your baby's diet. Salt (sodium) is a necessary nutrient. But in excess it can be toxic to young children. Enough salt to satisfy normal dietary requirements is generally available in foods naturally.

Occasionally in our recipes we do suggest adding a pinch of salt. But in general, do not salt food for children under one year or serve them canned foods or processed meats such as canned spaghetti and soups, bacon, hot dogs, and bologna. These foods are loaded with salt, which a young child's kidneys are not developed enough to filter sufficiently. Between the ages of one and three the amount of daily sodium that is considered safe and adequate is contained in only $1/4$ teaspoon of salt. (If you have a family history of high blood pressure or kidney disease, you may want to rethink even this small amount. Discuss this with your doctor.)

Fresh, unsalted foods will taste perfectly wonderful to your baby's developing palate. If the adults in your family must have salt, let them add it at the table. But keep in mind that your toddlers learn by your actions.

▲ ● ■ ▲
SWEETS

By his first birthday—perhaps sooner if he has older siblings— your baby will most likely be introduced to sweets. Like the rest of us, he'll probably love them. Try to reserve them for treats or special occasions, after nutritious meals and snacks are consumed. Sugary foods are usually nutrient-poor. They will satisfy your child's hunger, but will only fill him with empty calories. Sugar is also one of the culprits in obesity, a leading cause of tooth decay, and the root of some behavior problems. Sweets are also an appetite depressant and send a signal to the brain that the meal is over. In the Mommy Made recipes we use as little sugar as possible to sweeten foods and to ensure the proper chemical reaction in baking.

Above all, don't offer sweets as a reward; diet clinics are

filled with overweight adults struggling to find rewards and treats for themselves that won't end up on their hips.

Sugar comes in many forms. Don't be deceived by the healthy aura surrounding raw or unrefined sugar in gourmet and natural foods stores. It's really no better for you than the cheaper white granulated stuff packaged in your supermarket.

Molasses, on the other hand, a by-product of the sugar refining process, is the sweetener of choice. It contains valuable nutrients, iron in particular. The darkest molasses—blackstrap—is the most nutritious. It is often used as a fortifier and can have a laxative effect.

Brown sugar is processed sugar that gets its lovely, rich color from added molasses. As a result, brown sugar contains a few more vitamins and minerals than white. The darker the brown sugar, the higher the molasses content and its nutritional value.

A much more expensive and less nutritious sweetening alternative to molasses and brown sugar is *maple syrup.* A touch on your baby's French toast, pancakes, or waffles won't hurt and will be a real treat. Use only 100 percent maple syrup. It *is* more expensive. But it will taste better, and it will contain no potentially allergy-causing extenders such as corn syrup, which is the predominate ingredient in most pancake syrups.

Honey is not the health food it's cracked up to be. Although it contains about the same amount of vitamins as brown sugar, it is lower in minerals and contains more calories than white sugar. In addition, honey can be contaminated with botulism spores, which cause severe food poisoning and even death in very young children. Although scientists are not precisely sure why, this bacterium does not affect older children or adults. *Do not give honey to children under one year.* (Honey used in baking is the exception to this rule, since high heat kills the spores.)

Corn syrup—both light and dark—is another sweetener to avoid before age one. Like honey, corn syrup has been found occasionally to be contaminated with botulism. (Heating the corn syrup kills the spores.)

SWEETS AND YOUR BABY'S TEETH

Even before your baby's teeth emerge, oral care is important. Here's how to avoid baby-bottle tooth decay, which is caused by sugary liquids pooling up around the gums and on emerging teeth. Never allow your baby to fall asleep with a bottle containing breast milk, formula, milk, juice, or any sweetened beverage in her mouth. If your baby needs to be comforted between mealtimes or to fall asleep, offer water in the bottle or a pacifier.

From the very first day clean around your baby's gums. Do this with your finger wrapped in sterile gauze. This should become a daily ritual after each feeding. Continue this until you introduce the toothbrush.

Begin brushing your baby's teeth as soon as they emerge. As soon as your child has an interest in brushing her teeth, let her try, but Mommy or Daddy should finish the job. You'll know when your child is ready to be fully responsible for brushing her teeth on her own. Introduce dental floss once 20 teeth have appeared.

Ask your pediatrician if you need to add fluoride to your baby's diet. Establish a good relationship between your dentist and your child early on. Schedule a friendly visit to your dentist around your baby's first birthday.

As your baby grows and begins to eat solid food, remember that sticky foods like raisins, crackers, cookies, and even bread are more likely to lead to tooth decay than a soda or a lollipop. Be sure to brush your baby's teeth after these foods and treats—which are high in carbohydrates—are eaten, or at the very least have your child drink a lot of water to rinse his mouth out well.

Introducing the Toothbrush

When should you begin brushing your baby's teeth? As soon as they appear. In preparation for tooth brushing, we began wiping out Teddi's mouth daily with a damp, sterile gauze pad as soon as we brought her home from the hospital. Eventually as she became bigger we moved on to a clean, wet washcloth. When her first teeth emerged, she was accustomed to having someone stick something in her mouth and was comfortable with Mom and Dad wiping her teeth down. At one year, we introduced the toothbrush. It's adorable to see your one-year-old open her mouth with four teeth in place when she sees the toothbrush coming. At two, we let Teddi brush her own teeth. It became a family ritual that took place twice a day. She had a go at it first, then she sat on our lap and we finished up the job. One thing Teddi didn't master until she got a little older was spitting out the toothpaste, but the tiny bit she swallowed didn't hurt.

CAFFEINE

We remind you that caffeine is an outright "no-no" for children. It has no nutritional value and is an addictive stimulant. Caffeine is found in coffee, tea, some sodas (colas in particular), and even in chocolate in small amounts. While young children are not normally served these foods, it's best to steer clear of caffeine before it becomes a habit.

"BAD" FOODS CHILDREN NEED: FAT AND CHOLESTEROL

According to the American Academy of Pediatrics, the nutritional needs of infants, children, and even adolescents are markedly different from those of adults. *Absolutely avoid fad and special diets when feeding your baby unless specified by your doctor. The risk you run is that once your child's body is deprived of a certain nutrient during an important stage of development, often there is no going back and repairing the damage.*

Fat is crucial to your baby's diet. It provides vitamins A, D, E, and K, and it's a source of linoleic acid, without which babies would suffer growth retardation and skin problems. Fat also provides the most concentrated source of energy. And babies need lots of energy because of their rapid growth. According to the American Academy of Pediatrics Committee on Nutrition, at least 30 to 40 percent of a child's daily calories should be derived from fat. (By comparison, the American Heart Association recommends that adults restrict their dietary intake of fat to less than 30 percent.) Infants also need fats, for growth and brain development, but their dietary fat requirements are fulfilled by breast milk and formula. The time to be concerned with fat intake in your child's diet is when she discovers junk food, at around age three. But this does not mean limiting your child's caloric intake.

Cholesterol, another adult no-no, is on the good food list for kids. While the whole scoop isn't in on the role cholesterol plays in a baby's development, research indicates it is crucial to the development of the nervous system. Cholesterol is a structural part of all the body's cells, but especially brain and nerve cells. And it is necessary for normal bodily functions. Breast milk is naturally high in cholesterol, and as your child grows, his body will produce the cholesterol he needs. You'll probably want to keep the eggs to a maximum of four a week for your child age one to three. Eggs have excellent nutritional value for children.

CHAPTER FIVE

When Baby Says No!
Food and Nutrition in
the Real World

Okay. We know the road to feeding babies and toddlers is not as smooth and simple as we've laid it out. Your baby will try all kinds of funny and not-so-funny shenanigans with his dinner before he's finished with Mom and Dad. He may stop eating everything but a favorite food for days on end or seemingly eat everything in sight. He may paint his food all over the high chair, smear it into his hair, or store it in his cheeks for what seems to you like weeks.

Some of the reasons for baby's changing food tastes and un-cooperative behavior can be traced to real physical changes like teething or growth cycles. Others can be attributed to his emerging personality and taste preferences. Still others can stem from the early psychological connections he has made with food. Here are some of the most commonly asked questions from our classes, and the solutions we found.

In practice, people—especially babies—are not robots. They won't always consume the proper amount of nutritious foods in the right combinations every day. Try to take a larger view of your baby's diet—look at the variety of foods consumed on a weekly or monthly, rather than a daily, basis. No child will intentionally starve himself. And nutritionally things even out over time—provided you're serving a variety of healthy foods.

If you're still concerned about your baby's eating habits, naturally you should speak with your doctor. Having a supportive doctor can really help to relieve anxiety about your baby's growth and development. Our doctor is always ready to have his patients brought by for a weigh-in and height check. These measurements are placed on a standardized percentile chart so you can see if your baby's growth is on a healthy progression or curve. Don't worry about which percentile your baby falls into, it's the steady growth pattern that's important.

We've addressed these issues at the ages they are most likely to first appear. But, some, such as teething, temporary food fixations, and feasting or fasting can strike any time.

BIRTH TO 6 MONTHS

FEEDING ON DEMAND OR BY THE CLOCK

"I'm very nervous about nursing my baby every time he cries, although he seems hungry. My mom, a retired pediatric nurse, feels very strongly about feeding by the clock, but my instincts say just the opposite. And the crying drives me crazy."

Feeding on demand or by the clock? Try a little bit of both. Another mom who was advised to feed by the clock felt the same way. "Leaving my baby to cry seemed unrewarding to me as well as to my baby. Every time I went to my crying little boy and began to hold and feed him, I calmed down and of course so did he." We feel a flexible, semi-demand feeding schedule is the best approach. If your baby starts to cry shortly after feeding, his problem may not be hunger. He may need to burp or he may just need more suckling time. In the very first months, we noticed that our daughters often simply had a desire to suckle and would stay close to the breast for up to 25 minutes. But if a reasonable amount of time has passed, two, maybe three hours, chances are your baby would like some more breast milk or formula. In Chapter One (page 6) we discuss growth spurts. At these times, feeding on demand is clearly in your baby's best interest.

If your baby seems to be having digestive problems on a demand feeding schedule, try to feed him more by the clock. Some babies have immature digestive systems that are overwhelmed by frequent feeding.

"How do I know I am producing enough breast milk for my baby?"

"Insufficient milk is real," says Ruth Lawrence, a neonatologist and member of La Leche League International's Health Advisory Council. "Sometimes it's due to lack of support and information. Sometimes it's unavoidable." Here are some warning signs that you may not be producing enough breast milk for your baby (from "Dr. Mom's Guide to Breastfeeding," *Pediatrics in Review*): minimal or no breast changes during pregnancy; lack of engorgement after delivery; milk doesn't come in by the fifth day; no audible gulps from your baby; your newborn loses more than 10 percent of his birth weight; your baby produces fewer than six wet diapers daily; after day three, your baby produces fewer than three or four stools daily; after day four, your baby seems to be nursing continuously and is never satisfied.

Another good breastfeeding resource is *The Complete Book of Breastfeeding,* by Marvin S. Eiger, M.D., and Sally Wendkos Olds.

GOAT'S MILK VERSUS FORMULA

"My neighbor feeds her baby goat's milk instead of formula or breast milk. She says it's the latest thing. Am I missing something? Should I give it to my baby too?"

Absolutely not. Although we know this is a current fad, it's ill-advised. Goat's milk is perfect for baby goats. But it's way too high in sodium and very low in some important B vitamins and is potentially dangerous for human babies.

SKIP THE SPICE WHEN BREAST-FEEDING

"Can my baby be allergic to my breast milk? I've noticed that he cried and cried after a feeding given shortly after I devoured a spicy hoagie."

No. But your baby can be sensitive to the foods you eat that are passed on to him in your breast milk. We know the answer to this one firsthand. Shortly after Renée was born, we went out for a wonderful dinner—lasagne, garlic bread, a fresh Caesar salad, and chocolate cannoli. We toasted our second baby's arrival with glasses of the house Chianti. When we returned home, Renée eagerly nursed. However, her midnight meal turned into our early-morning nightmare. Renée's system was simply more sensitive than our first child's. As a result of our night out, she had an upset stomach for almost two days.

6 MONTHS TO 1 YEAR

ENDING BREAST-FEEDING

"When should I stop breast-feeding?"

When you should stop is a personal choice. The American Academy of Pediatrics recommends that breast-feeding be encouraged for the first year of life. I nursed Teddi for ten months and then got pregnant with Renée (You can get pregnant while nursing!), and thinking ahead to life with two babies, began to wean Teddi. Renée weaned herself after ten months. She was clearly more interested in crawling off to play with Teddi than in breast-feeding.

FEEDING TWINS

"I have twins. Do you have any special advice for starting them on solid food?"

My neighbor, Miriam, started out feeding her twins, Ari and Phoebe, the usual way for parents with twins—one bowl, one spoon for both, alternating the open mouths. As Ari and Phoebe got older, their personalities began to emerge. At eight months Ari became a slow eater, preferring to pluck up small pieces of cut-up food from his high-chair tray. Phoebe, on the other hand, wanted her mom to shovel it in. She couldn't eat fast enough.

HICCUPS

"My baby frequently gets the hiccups during feeding. What should I do?"

Most babies will get the hiccups from time to time. If they occur during mealtime try the following: change the baby's position, offer a sip of water, or wait until the hiccups are over before continuing to feed. To reduce the likeliness of hiccups happening during mealtime, try to feed your baby when he is calm and not frantically hungry.

FOOD INTRODUCTION

"Is the three-day introduction schedule really long enough to determine if a food is allergy producing? A book I just read recommends one week."

We recommend three days, because it's long enough to determine if your baby has a reaction to a food—but not so long that you run the risk of further sensitizing him to it in the process. In our research we have found that consuming too much of a new food over a longer period of time can bring on a problem that may not have occurred using the shorter, three-day trial.

CEREAL FIRST

"My doctor says at six months I can start my baby on any of the first foods on your introduction chart, including: applesauce, pears, banana, squash, and, of course, cereal. Why do you recommend baby rice cereal first?"

It's the iron in the fortified baby cereals that makes them so appropriate for baby's first food at six months. At this age your baby's natural stores of iron are almost exhausted and the form of iron in fortified baby cereal is readily absorbed by his body. Also rice is the least allergenic of all the cereal grains.

STRAIN IT?

"Do I need to strain my fresh baby food? In the supermarket, the commercially prepared baby foods are always labeled *strained.*"

Baby's first foods do not need to be strained, but they do need to be smooth so that they are easy to swallow. On pages 101–103, we give information on making your foods smooth or chunky depending on your baby's development. Your thick purees can easily be thinned with mother's milk, formula, or water.

A SMOOTH TRANSITION

"I'm about to start my baby on solid food. How do I help her make the transition from four big bottles to three meals a day?"

With food introduction we always recommend that you serve solids at the same time each day to establish a routine. Eventually, a pattern will be set and you'll be able to know when feeding time occurs. This will probably take place somewhere about the ninth or tenth month. Ideally what you're striving for is three meals and two snacks a day by baby's first birthday. This may not happen exactly on schedule, and some children may really do better with small meals throughout the day. If it's possible, have your baby join you at the table at mealtimes. Children who eat with their families establish the three-meal pattern more quickly and with greater ease.

"JUST HOW MUCH IS ENOUGH?"

This is a question we can't seem to answer enough times.

One mother shared her doctor's sensible advice with us: "I can't say how much to feed your baby, because I won't be at the table when she is eating. If she seems hungry, feed her more (new foods are obviously the exception) and if she's through, take her word for it."

TEETHING: A SORE SUBJECT

"My daughter is having a terrible time with teething. She's cranky, frequently wakes up at night crying, and worst of all won't eat a thing. What can I do to make her feel better and make sure she's getting enough nourishment?"

Teething is tough on babies and Mom and Dad too—and it goes on for almost three years. Teeth typically begin to emerge

at about six months and teething continues off and on until about age three. Put yourself in your baby's place. It's easy to understand why cutting teeth can cause tears and crankiness. Before teething, the mouth represented a source of contentment to your baby. It is how he eats and gets his milk, and it's the source of Mommy's and Daddy's kisses. Baby also learns about the world by exploring it with his mouth, chewing and tasting everything in sight at about four months. Then these horrid teeth arrive and disrupt mealtime and turn the pleasure-seeking mouth into a sore subject!

Teething creates sore, swollen gums and causes normally good eaters and sleepers temporarily to refuse all food except for breast and bottle—and sometimes these as well—and to awaken parents in the middle of the night with cries of pain. Your baby may also run a fever and suffer from diarrhea and diaper rash. Don't worry about solid foods during these periods.

Breast milk and formula, which most teething babies find comforting, provide enough nutrients during these spells. Some soothing foods can ease the pain and discomfort, as well as provide additional nourishment; look for them after the recipes in the special foods section, pages 287–291.

FAST AND FEAST

"I can't figure my son Jeffrey out. One week he eats like a truck driver and the next he seems to live on air. Is this normal?"

A baby's appetite can be as changeable as the weather. Lots of things can put her off her feed temporarily and upset Mommy or Daddy's best-laid menu plans. Teething, for example, is notorious for depressing mini-appetites. Colds are another turnoff. Appetites will also vary from day to day with the energy expended and even the outside temperature. (During a summer heat wave Teddi once ate nothing but watermelon for three days straight.) Fresh air and active play sessions in the sandbox or wading pool are likely to produce a hungrier child than an afternoon of TV. Likewise, baby will probably be more interested in food on a cold day, rather than on a hot, humid one when everything and everyone is wilted.

Children also eat more when they are growing rapidly. During the first year your child's appetite relative to his size will seem enormous. But after age one, when growth tapers off, so will the need for food—and subsequently baby's appetite. This is the time for parents to give especially careful attention to good nutrition.

HOLD THE VEGETABLES, PLEASE

"I can't understand this. My baby doesn't like vegetables. I know when kids get bigger this can be a problem. But my baby is just starting out on food. How could she be so opinionated at such a young age? What can I do to change her mind, before it's too late?"

It's understandable why first-time eaters don't always take to vegetables. After the sweetness of breast milk, formula, applesauce, and pureed pears, veggies may seem bland by comparison. Here are some ways to win your tyke over to his vegetables: (These suggestions hold for other disliked foods too.)

- Be sure all vegetables are cooked so that they retain good color and some texture. (See Chapter Six.)
- Enjoy them together. Liking and disliking are contagious. If you don't like vegetables, chances are your baby won't either.
- Offer older babies vegetables as finger food with zippy dipping sauces. Broccoli trees always fascinate even the choosiest eaters.
- Talk to your child about vegetables. When our daughters were just beginning to speak we talked to them about what we liked to eat and why. They repeated the same words and then followed our actions—and in the process tasted a great many foods. Of course, they didn't like them all. But they did try them, and at least the vegetables had a fighting chance, before being scrapped for visual or other non-taste-related reasons.
- If none of the suggestions above work, grate the vegetables and tuck them into spaghetti sauce, meat loaf, or soup. One vegetable hater we know adores homemade soup, which happens to be her only source of veggies. Or serve fruits in place of vegetables. They provide many of the same vitamins and minerals. But watch out; too many fruits may cause diarrhea.

THE YUCKY FACE

"I tried butternut squash on Teresa this week and she made a sour-looking, yucky face with every mouthful. I thought it seemed cruel to continue with the squash, because I felt her facial expressions told me she hated the stuff."

It's not always easy to read a baby's facial expressions. Baby Teresa might very well have been making the face at the new texture, underlying taste, or even the temperature of the food. As another mother quickly pointed out: "Be assured if Teresa doesn't like a particular food, she won't open her mouth for more. That's what I discovered with my baby. When I gave Sean his first bite of peas, he made certain it was his last bite. The fact that Teresa ate three bites of the squash tells you she probably thought the stuff was o.k.!" Research concurs. Your baby's facial expressions are often unrelated to actual likes and dislikes.

BRING ON THE REAL FOOD!

"When should I add texture to my baby's diet? Joshua is eight months old and seems bored with the soupy purees I'm offering him."

A lumpier texture that will encourage your baby to chew more and use his tongue can be added as early as the sixth month for some babies. For others a much later introduction will be better. One mother who enrolled in our classes offered her experience: "I found that my son enjoyed food that had more texture right from the start and loved pushing his tongue around the lumpier sauces." Another mom, however, pregnant with number two chimed in: "My first child refused anything that wasn't smooth as silk until she was well into her second year of life." Like everyone else, babies are individuals and we encourage you to respect their tastes.

STRIKE WHILE THE IRON'S HOT

"I'm very confused," said Cynthia, a first-time parent. "My aunt warned me not to offer finger foods to Nora before she was one year old. She's says she'll choke on the pieces. Nora is only eight months old and doesn't seem to want to wait."

We all know from firsthand experience that advice is every-where and even the pearls of wisdom from the most seasoned grandmothers and aunts don't always apply. Most babies we know are a lot like Nora, ready to be "hands-on with food" well before their first birthday. Another mom in the class offered this advice to Cynthia: "If you discourage your baby from learning what she seems ready to learn, you'll be fostering a don't-do-it-yourself outlook and she may be unwilling to learn these skills later when you feel the time is ripe."

I DON'T LIKE IT NOW—BUT MAYBE LATER

"Do babies have a preference for foods? My baby seems to hate what most babies love—sweet potatoes."

Everyone, including your baby, is entitled to food likes and dislikes. If your baby rejects something, take no for an answer for a month or two and then try again. If he still says no, take his word for it. One mother whose first child disliked squash intensely as a baby was amazed when at age two he devoured a bowl of pureed acorn squash intended for his baby brother—and even asked for more.

1 YEAR AND BEYOND

MILK: TOO MUCH OF A GOOD THING

"My doctor told me that when my baby reaches one year, I should be careful that he doesn't drink too much milk in place of other iron-rich foods."

Yes, overdoing milk can cause iron deficiencies in children. And iron deficiency is one of the biggest problems facing school-aged children in this country.

Milk should be considered a food, not a beverage to quench thirst. Dr. Max VanGilder of New York's Lenox Hill and St. Luke's Hospital has conducted considerable research on the subject. He offers this advice: "Children in the second year of life and the years following need a variety of foods so that their diets offer them balance from all the major food groups. It's a fact that your child's appetite will taper off in the second year. And it's a good thing! If they continued to triple their weight, you'd have a 200-pound toddler on your hands by age three. But you want to be careful not to fill them up on just one food, such as milk. Your one-year-old needs about .81 grams of protein per one pound of weight. This comes out to about 20 grams of protein for a 25-pound child. One ounce of whole cow's milk supplies one gram of protein. But you don't want to fulfill your toddler's protein needs with milk alone, primarily because it's a very poor source of iron."

The bottom line: Balance is the key you should strive for when feeding your child. Dr. VanGilder's professional recommendation is: no more than 16 ounces a day of cow's milk for baby after one year.

MONKEY SEE, MONKEY DO

"I'm always dieting and in a rush to get to work on time, so the most I ever eat for breakfast is a bite of dry toast and a cup of black coffee. I know it's important for my child to eat a good breakfast. Will my breakfast habits affect his?"

Not enough can be said about parents' setting a good example. Don't fall into the trap of admonishing your child to "do as I say, but not as I do." Children learn by mimicking their parents and peers. If you want your child to eat nutritious meals and snacks, you'd better join him at the table, beginning at breakfast. Breakfast, a meal most grown-ups skip or skimp on, is still the most important meal of the day. Protein consumed at breakfast helps you concentrate better and breakfast eaters tend to be better eaters throughout the day. (For more information on the nutritional benefits of breakfast see page 54.)

If both parents are working, this meal may also be a very meaningful one to share with your children from an emotional point of view. Talking about dreams, the day to come, and an upcoming family event can have a very positive impact on your child and help him face the day without you.

But note that some children are not ready to eat the moment they wake up. If that's the case with your child, try serving breakfast a bit later. Make breakfast one of the last things your child does in the morning after washing and dressing. Also try varying the breakfast menu. Be creative and offer a favorite food, even if it's more typically a lunch or dinner item. Soup for breakfast, pasta with cheese, peanut butter on whole wheat toast? Why not. Breakfast is about getting a nutritious start to the day, not about cereal and eggs.

TABLE TALK

"My husband and I love good food and are always eager and willing to try new tastes. How do we instill this delight in interesting food with our young daughter?"

You've asked the right people. We love and appreciate good food—in fact it's our business—and it was something we wanted to teach our children too. When our daughters were big enough to join us at the dinner table in their high chairs, we would talk to them about the foods we were eating. Sometimes we'd comment on a food's particular color or shape. Other times we would talk about how it tasted: salty, sweet, spicy, etc. Sometimes we'd also make funny faces to go along with these words. Then we'd taste the foods with our girls. They loved the close involvement and quickly began imitating us. In the process, they were willing to taste and appreciate lots of new and quite sophisticated foods at a very early age.

ALL DONE

"When I was growing up, I was expected to eat everything on my plate. I remember sitting at the table for hours after everyone had finished and gone, staring at some shriveled-up lima beans I had to swallow before I could go out and play. I don't plan to raise my baby this way, but I do want to encourage him to eat well. What's a good middle position to take without being too permissive?"

Don't enroll your child in the clean plate club! Remember when your mother coaxed, "One for Daddy," or "Here comes the airplane into the hangar" as she spooned in the food? When you were older were you required to sit at the table for hours until the last bit of food was consumed or subjected to endless lectures on starving children in the world? Try not to make the same mistakes with your children. Let your child's own natural appetite determine how much he eats. Learn to simply take the food away without a fuss when baby starts to play with it, spit it out, hold it in his cheeks, or feed it to the family pet circling under the high chair. Eating a lot of food is not necessarily a ticket to good health. And if food becomes a *cause célèbre* in your household, you can count on baby to pick up on its importance immediately and cleverly use it as a weapon to assert himself. As one friend put it, "The only real power children have is what goes in, and what comes out."

Should you ever force a child to eat, to try a strange food, for instance? Some famous gourmets say yes and credit their stern parents with their sensitive palates. But we're uncomfortable with any force-feeding—coaxing or other strategies work better, we think.

As your baby grows, don't be pressured to keep up with the Joneses. If you see that your neighbor's child eats three meals a day at seven months and your baby is still warming up to breakfast, don't worry. Your baby is an individual with his own growth and developmental timetable. Feeding, remember, is like learning to walk. It is not a task to force on your child, but rather a skill to be enjoyed.

It's just as important to avoid praising a child for eating as it is to avoid chastising her for not eating. Statements like "How wonderful that you ate your vegetables!" as well as "I'm disappointed that you didn't eat your fish" infuse food with values beyond nutrition and can set the stage for emotionally motivated eating later on. Also, never use food as a reward for good behavior or for a job well done. Try a special outing with your little one instead. Showing your appreciation this way is much more appropriate and does not send the message that food equals love.

DESSERT!

"We all eat together as a family and for my husband dinner's not complete unless there's dessert. How do I teach Rebecca about desserts and their place in her diet?"

Dessert becomes a capital issue as baby gets bigger. There's almost no way to avoid dessert unless you live on a desert island with no TV, supermarket, or other children. But the good news is, there's no need to. There's nothing wrong with a cookie or two or an occasional sweet. In fact, cookies provide needed fat in a child's diet. Children who are never given a taste of these forbidden fruits usually grow up to be inordinately fond of them. We know of one closet cookie eater whose mom swore up and down that she never allowed him to have sugar. Well, her good intentions backfired. Her clever, resourceful child was hoarding a stash of cookies at a neighbor's house and spending all of his allowance on candy bars and cakes. Here are some suggestions for keeping the balance in check that have worked in our house:

- Don't entirely delete sweets and desserts from your child's diet.
- Serve nutrient-rich desserts such as rice pudding and custard (see recipes, pages 239–246).

- Offer nutritious desserts such as fruit salad and pudding as a part of the meal, not as a reward (or withheld as a punishment) for good behavior or a clean plate. Insisting on a clean plate before dessert can lead to overeating and obesity.
- Don't say no to sweets; just teach your children a healthy approach to food and the pleasures of eating.

PROTEIN DOESN'T HAVE TO MEAN MEAT

"Now that my baby is one year old, I'm weaning her off formula. How will I be certain she gets enough protein? Up to this point, she has turned up her nose at pureed meats."

Protein can come in many tasty forms for your toddler to enjoy. Milk and dairy products are excellent sources of protein, as are tofu and eggs. Unlike adults, children can safely consume up to four eggs a week until they are three years old. Dried peas and beans can also be a good source of protein, although you need to understand how to combine them in cooking to provide complete protein. (See page 199 in the recipe section.) One of our girls' favorite sources of vegetable protein is hummus dip (page 275). We remember at a birthday party for one of Teddi's three-year-old friends we offered to bring a snack for the adults. We served our hummus dip with cut-up fresh vegetables. To everyone's surprise, the kids ate more of this nutritious treat than the adults. Michael, the birthday boy, called it "the dunking station." And after that all his friends took turns at dunking the fresh veggies.

BINGING ON MILK

"I know this is weird, but my daughter, Susan, refused everything but milk for six weeks when she turned one."

As hard as it was for Susan's parents, on their doctor's advice they just went along with her milk-only phase until she finally went back onto a varied diet again. Amazingly, Susan stayed on her growth curve through this period. If your child gives up solids and goes on a liquid diet, be sure you are offering enough water. Your child may simply be trying to tell you she's thirsty.

HEALTH FOOD THAT'S NOT HEALTHY

"My husband and I are real health food nuts. Now that our son is on table food, we would like to share our healthy concoctions with him. Are raw eggs in blended drinks safe for him? And how about carrot juice?"

It is unwise to feed raw eggs to your son—or anyone else, for that matter. Raw eggs are often contaminated with salmonella bacterium, which causes food poisoning. Cooked eggs are perfectly safe.

Go easy on the carrot juice. Carrot juice is unusually high in vitamin A. Just half a cup contains 16 times a baby's daily requirements for this vitamin—a dangerous, nearly toxic amount.

NO FOOD, MOMMY

"I'm worried to death; my 18-month-old has stopped eating entirely."

Unlike the first year, when your child's weight nearly tripled, in the second year he gains only five pounds. And as baby's growth rate drops, so does his appetite. This sounds logical in principle, but when your 14-month-old's eating comes to a screeching halt, you may still worry. We did when our girls reached this stage. It's very difficult to remain objective and not nag when it comes to your own flesh and blood.

Keep track of how much food your child *is* consuming for several days; you may be surprised to discover how much it really is. Toddlers are little people—just an ounce or two of protein or half a cup of milk is a full serving.

A good way to get them eating again is to arrange to have your child eat with a friend's child—the social aspect of eating is enormous, even at this tender age. In one study, it was only a matter of days before a toddler who refused to eat a loathed food decided, after watching his peers gobble it up, that it was, in fact, his favorite food. However, choose your child's dining companions carefully; this phenomenon can also work in reverse. A lobster lover we know turned completely off lobster after his midwestern cousins declared it to be disgusting.

A child's autonomy is very much wrapped up in food. It's important to make mealtime a happy experience. If you fight with your child over what and how much he eats, he may quickly get the upper hand and refuse another bite. To a child, trying to have the world his way defines who he is; it's an important part of becoming an individual. If there is to be a battle—and if your toddler is normal, there will be battles—it's better to take a stand on something else, like picking up his toys.

TRY IT; MAYBE YOU'LL LIKE IT

"Now that my child eats dinner with us, can I expect him to eat the same foods we enjoy, such as asparagus?"

Even though you might think that your child may not like a food because it is too sophisticated or because you don't like it, it could turn out to be one of his favorites. Our girls were always willing to try a tiny taste of everything as long as one of us was eating the food with them. Pesto sauce on corkscrew pasta and even eggplant is very popular in our household. Renée at 17 months learned to love blue cheese by swiping a piece off her daddy's plate. When your child is old enough, having him help you prepare the new food can also encourage him to taste it.

If your little one constantly refuses to eat what you have prepared, ask him what he doesn't like about the food. We know one little boy who told his mother that he hated the color brown and loved the color red. Mom quickly omitted the meat loaf and the gravy from the menu. Instead, she offered spaghetti and meatballs covered with tomato sauce and mixed in grated vegetables to round out the meal. Naturally, strawberries and watermelon became household favorites as well. And once this mom used ketchup to make funny faces on formerly yucky yellow eggs, they became a treasured food.

THE GRUB IS ALWAYS GREENER . . .

"No matter how hard I try, I just can't be that cool and collected when my child doesn't eat. I come from a long line of mothers and grandmothers whose mission in life was to feed their families well."

If you cannot be that laid-back about your child's diet, try a little loving deceit. Food is always more interesting when someone else is consuming it with gusto. Handouts of nutritious snacks such as broccoli spears and cheese cubes are much more delicious when they come from Mommy's (or Daddy's) plate or the cutting board.

This worked well for us when Teddi (about 18 months) refused to eat her vegetables. We filled a dessert bowl with them, and Martha sat down on the couch and began to eat them. As Teddi ambled by and looked into the bowl, Martha offered her a piece. Teddi said, "Ummm, good, Mommy!" as she ate one, then another. Before we knew it, she'd cleaned up the sweet potato chunks and green beans—foods that had disinterested her on her own plate.

For the older child—three, four, and five years—who is finicky about foods, getting him involved in selecting and preparing the food for a meal can help. Take him to the grocery store with you. Let him pick out the fruits, vegetables, and meat that will be served at dinnertime. If it's hamburgers, let him make the patties when you get home. With a little instruction young children can also wash lettuce and snap green beans. And with help from Mom or Dad, they can even beat the scrambled eggs and serve their little sister. Not only do we guarantee that your child will polish off every last bite of his creation with a grin, but he will gain feelings of self-confidence, importance, and new skills in the bargain.

Looking Good Enough to Eat

- Pour pancake batter initials, letters, numbers, and half moons on your griddle. (Cookie cutters make good molds.) Combine half moons with small circles on the serving plate for smiley faces.
- Write your baby's name in ketchup on his eggs.
- Layer colorful fruit puree with yogurt or cottage cheese in a clear plastic cup.
- Add pea eyes, carrot mouths, and parsley and cheese hair to stuffed baked potatoes.
- Use plenty of pasta shapes and varieties in your cooking—they are fanciful, colorful, and ready to use.

DOES IT LOOK GOOD ENOUGH TO EAT?

"Time is short in our house. But I read that kids appreciate pretty, attractively presented food. Is it worth the extra fuss?"

If the food you feed your toddler doesn't look good enough to eat, it should! Just like grown-ups, children eat with their eyes. They love beautiful colors and interesting shapes. Serve red beets with bright carrots and emerald-green broccoli. Turn a peanut butter and jelly or egg salad sandwich into a fanciful rabbit with a twist of a cookie cutter. You can also create different shapes and animals with pancake batter. When we were kids, we loved our mom's Mickey Mouse pancakes. One big pancake formed the face, two little ones the ears. Banana slices served as eyes; raisins were the nose and mouth. And sometimes, as an extra-special treat, she'd even toss in a couple of chocolate chips.

PEANUT BUTTER AND JELLY FOREVER

"My kid's had peanut butter and jelly for lunch for the last three weeks. He won't touch anything else. When will this end? And can he grow up healthy on such a limited diet?"

If your toddler makes a food choice and sticks with it for weeks or even months, you might begin to wonder if it's actually possible to live on peanut butter and jelly forever. If this were not the case, the world would be a very sick place. Temporary food fixations are very popular among the toddler set and completely normal. Don't despair. We've all been there! Usually, if not too big an issue is made of the food in question, your child will eventually get bored and move on to something else or acquire a renewed appreciation for a discarded favorite. The classic children's book on binging, *Bread and Jam for Frances* by Russell and Lillian Hoban, has convinced many a three-year-old of the joys of eating a variety of foods. Always remember too that nutrition is a continuous process that is built on over time and your child's fussiness over foods and learning to say no to virtually everything represent in part the separation process and the realization of his independent self.

EVEN EXCHANGES

"My daughter, Amanda, has reached the terrible twos and is *very* picky about what she eats. How do I satisfy her tastes, yet still provide a nutritious, well-rounded diet?"

Don't force your child to eat any food. Be flexible. If your child regularly spits out spinach and liver, respect his tastes. There are plenty of other foods that will provide the same vitamins and minerals and will go down a lot easier. At breakfast time, if the traditional staples of hot cereal and eggs won't fly— or if they literally do, try leftovers from last night's dinner or grilled cheese on whole wheat. Teddi and Renée still love Lo Mein with Sesame and Peanuts, page 197, for breakfast, lunch, and dinner.

SUPERMARKET SURVIVAL

"Lately my child has been having tantrums in the supermarket if I refuse to purchase candy or some other treat. I try to avoid the aisles with the worst stuff but there's even Life Savers and chewing gum racks at the checkout. Any suggestions?"

Fair Trades

If you're tired of nagging "Drink your milk!" or "Eat your meat!" try these even exchanges.

The calcium supplied by $1/3$ cup of fresh whole milk can also be found in:

- $1/3$ cup of whole milk yogurt
- $1/2$ ounce of American processed cheese
- $1/4$ cup pudding made with whole milk
- $1/2$ cup chocolate ice cream

The protein in $1/6$ pound of raw chopped meat, cooked, equals approximately:

- $1/4$ small lamb chop
- $1/2$ egg
- $1/2$ slice Cheddar-type cheese (1 ounce)
- $1/8$ cup cottage cheese
- $1/2$ cup milk
- $1/4$ cup cooked, dried beans, peas, or lentils
- scant $1/8$ cup peanuts
- 1 tablespoon peanut butter

The iron contained in 2 ounces of liver is also found in:

- $1^1/2$ ounces of pork, beef, or veal
- $1/4$ cup prune juice
- $1/3$ cup oatmeal
- $1/2$ cup tomato juice
- $1/4$ cup spinach
- $1/4$ cup lima beans, soybeans, lentils, or split peas

Who would think that such a benign activity as shopping for groceries could turn your normally good-natured, reasonable child into an unrecognizable monster, throwing a full-fledged fit in the middle of the store? Usually junk food—sweet cereals, candy, soda, and chips—is the root of the problem. Mom says no, her mini-consumer, brainwashed by TV, says yes, and a battle of the wills is in full swing. Some ways to avoid these confrontations, short of leaving your child at home, are:

- You can eat lunch before you go shopping. A full belly won't be so interested in food.
- We purposely fed our kids lunch in the supermarket while we shopped, blithely paying for the empty containers of yogurt, etc., at the checkout. We'd start shopping in a section where there are healthy foods such as yogurt, cheese, and fruit, and we'd get our kids eating and occupied. Our children liked getting to pick out what they wanted to eat and were entertained and busily occupied while we were left to concentrate on filling a second cart with groceries.
- When they're big enough to reason with, let your child choose one item for the shopping basket. Close your eyes to the selection.

HALLOWEEN

"I can't wait to dress up Andy for his first Halloween and take him around trick-or-treating in the neighborhood. But how do I handle the gobs of candy? Of course, I don't want him to eat it all."

Parents deal with Halloween—Easter, Valentine's Day, and other candy holidays—in different ways. Here's one suggestion we found worked:

"I always let my children eat as much as they want of their Halloween loot the night they bring the candy home. Our understanding is that the rest gets thrown out—or given away if your child accepts that better. Although you might think this practice would give your child a colossal bellyache, you'd be surprised at how little most will really eat. They're usually too tired and too excited to consume more than a few pieces."

THE KITCHEN SLAVE

"Stephanie is two now and she's impossible at mealtime. Just yesterday at breakfast I prepared her favorite eggs. She ate three bites, then sweetly asked for cereal and milk, and I obliged. After a few spoonfuls, she wanted waffles. So I popped a frozen waffle in the toaster. She ate none of this. I want Stephanie to enjoy mealtime and look forward to it, but I'm beginning to dread the ordeal."

Asking your child what he wants to eat can be asking for trouble. Don't confuse your child with too many choices. Two are enough. But be sure these include something that's familiar and usually enjoyed. If it's breakfast, try cereal or pancakes, for example. Tell her firmly she makes the choice and if she picks other foods not suggested by Mom, tell her she can have them for lunch, dinner, or tomorrow's breakfast.

OBESITY AND CHILDREN

Almost all the parents who take our classes are very concerned about health and nutrition. They don't want their children to grow up to be fat adults. Obesity in our school-age children is alarming; in the last two decades it has risen almost 20 percent. Studies have shown that for the obese child, growing up fat is the worst thing that could ever happen to him.

Where does overeating begin and how do you avoid it? First of all, the latest research shows that there's a strong genetic component; if obesity isn't in your family, you probably don't need to give it another thought. But it's also a psychological problem. Most overeaters do so because their good memories about life's experiences are surrounded by food. All too frequently the pattern starts with a mom who is far too occupied with food. She communicates her fears and concerns to her child, who is likely to make the misconceived connection that food equals love. The child then sees food as a way to fill the void of a missing mom or to comfort him in times of stress. (How many adults do you know who pig out on ice cream and cookies when they are strung out?)

The best way to avoid obesity is not to put your child on a diet that could actually stunt his growth and impair his development, but to provide a well-balanced diet coupled with lots of fresh air and physical activity. Discourage your child from turning into a couch potato. Don't let him sit in front of the TV with a bowl of cookies or chips for hours on end! If you're not home when your child returns from school, give your caregiver instructions about this as well.

If your child becomes overweight, get some professional advice. Do *not* put him on a self-styled diet and do *not* criticize him about his weight. Both approaches can have harmful effects.

CHAPTER SIX

Preparing Your Very Own Baby Food

THE RATIONALE

In the introduction to this book we summed up the compelling reasons for making your own fresh baby food. There's no doubt that fresh baby food is healthier for your baby than commercial food. Besides being pure and additive-free, homemade baby food has more nutrients. Vitamin C, for example, is especially fragile and sensitive to oxygen. Even the simple act of juicing an orange reduces its C content. Orange juice from cardboard cartons contains up to 30 percent less vitamin C than freshly squeezed juice. And up to 40 percent of the C left is biologically inactive—of no use whatsoever.

But how about my baby? Will he care or sense the difference? We suggest that you conduct the same simple tasting we perform for our Mommy Made students: try a few spoonfuls of our freshly made product (using a recipe in Part II) next to its commercial, jarred counterpart. The results are always unanimous: fresh food not only tastes better but also looks and smells better than jarred. From our experience, if you can taste the difference, so will your baby—perhaps even more so. Although they have more taste buds than adults, what babies taste is relatively uncharted territory. Scientific studies have, however, demonstrated that babies are born with a preference for sugar, but without a bias for (or against) salt. As they get older, both sugar and salt appear to become acquired tastes if they are added to their diets.

Babies also like bright colors and enticing aromas as much as we adults do. The rich aroma of acorn squash or a sweet potato roasting in the oven is sure to sharpen the appetite. But like many of life's finer points, good taste is learned. And Mom and Dad have to educate baby's palate.

From our experience as parents, hunger seems to be the overriding issue with the littlest babies (under one year), and they will wolf down almost anything to satisfy this need. As babies get more mobile and into the oral stage, we've all observed that they will eat the most unlikely and even dangerous things, from caterpillars to dish detergent. Part of this behavior clearly has nothing to do with taste, but rather their tremendous curiosity. Texture, however, seems to be where some draw the line. We've found that some babies started on the very smooth, commercial baby food purees rarely accept Mommy Made's fresh counterpart with its denser body. So best to get baby started on the best from the beginning. Then, after reaching fickle toddlerhood and your baby's tastes narrow to small servings of a few favorites, at least you'll be sure that whatever he eats is packed with nutrition.

And the good news is that preparing your own baby food from scratch is less work than you might imagine. In one three-hour session on a quiet Sunday afternoon—while baby's napping or out in his stroller with the sitter—Mom or Dad can easily cook, puree, and stash in the freezer two weeks' worth of fresh fruits, vegetables, and meats for a hungry baby. If you cook dinner every night, you will probably find it easier to cook for your baby—especially as he gets older—while you are preparing meals for the rest of the family. The Mommy Made recipes in

Part II of this book show how to vary one basic recipe to satisfy the needs and tastes of the whole family from baby and toddler to Mom and Dad. And if you delay the introduction of solid food until the sixth month, the puree stage in your baby's diet will be greatly shortened. In no time at all, baby will be eating unseasoned, cut-up pieces of soft table foods alongside everyone else.

TAKING STOCK: THE BABY FOOD BATTERIE DE CUISINE

Before you begin cooking, check the contents of your kitchen cabinets against the list below. A few basic cooking pots and utensils will take the "task" out of preparing your own baby food and make it fun and fast. If you like to cook, you most likely own much of this cooking equipment already. If not, with the exception of one or two of the optional appliances, these items can be purchased inexpensively in the housewares section of any hardware or department store. (They also make nice baby shower presents.)

FOR FOOD PREP AND COOKING

- assorted kitchen gadgets and utensils, including a small, sharp paring knife, vegetable brush and peeler, measuring cups and spoons, slotted spoon, ladle, and spatula
- grater
- colander
- fine-meshed strainer
- cutting board (Recent tests have shown that both wood and plastic provide mediums for bacterial growth. Just make sure to clean your cutting board well, especially after cutting up chicken. Raw chicken is frequently infected with salmonella

bacteria. This bacteria is destroyed by the hot temperatures required to cook chicken, but traces of raw poultry on your cutting board can contaminate the next food prepared on its surface and make you and your baby quite sick.)

- medium-size saucepan with lid
- vegetable steamer (The inexpensive, three-legged metal steamers that expand to fit most cooking pots are our favorite. They are small, tuck away easily, and have traveled with us everywhere—even to the Caribbean! They're also nice because their expandability allows you to cook small or large amounts, depending on your need.)
- roasting pan
- ovenproof glass custard cups

FOR PUREEING, STRAINING, AND MASHING

- utensils, including a fork and potato masher
- food mill (excellent for straining fruits and vegetables cooked with the skin on)
- blender (good for pureeing small amounts of food, liquefying food, and making nutritious fruit/milk shakes, malts, smoothies, and frosties)
- food processor (The best all-around food-pureeing appliance. It chops, grates, purees, etc., to any desired consistency depending on the blade used.)
- a mini–food processor (optional, but indispensable for preparing small batches of purees; Martha's most prized possession)
- hand-cranked baby food grinder (great for fast food prep at the table when you and baby are dining out)

Microwaving is a popular way of cooking for many families. Parents often ask: "Is it safe?" "Am I exposing my child to nuclear waves?" To put your mind at ease, microwaves do not cook with nuclear waves, but with small radio waves emitted from a magnetron tube. These waves pass through the food and cause its molecules to vibrate, producing friction and subsequently heat. Technology has ironed out the problems of earlier ovens that sometimes "leaked" waves, and they are now considered quite safe. The real danger of microwave cooking is that it frequently heats unevenly. And although the food may feel tepid on the surface, hot pockets can lurk inside and burn your baby's mouth. To prevent this, be sure to thoroughly mix and taste all microwaved food before serving it to baby. Bottles of formula are particularly difficult to heat evenly. We don't recommend the common practice of "zapping" them in the microwave to take off the chill unless you shake them well and test them thoroughly.

FOR REFRIGERATOR AND FREEZER STORAGE

- cookie sheet
- ice cube tray with divider or individual plastic ice cube containers
- storage jars (recycled, commercial baby food jars, jelly jars, or small plastic food storage containers—Rubbermaid makes a perfect 4-ounce size)
- wax paper, plastic wrap, small freezer storage bags, freezer tape, marking pen

FOR THAWING AND REHEATING

- egg poacher
- custard cups

OPTIONAL APPLIANCES FOR EFFICIENT, FAST COOKING AND REHEATING

- microwave oven
- toaster oven

STRATEGIC PLANNING

Decide on what you are going to cook by factoring in the following as you leaf through the recipe section for ideas:

1. *The age appropriateness of the food for your baby:* This information is covered in Chapter Two, but reminders are noted in the margin next to each recipe.

2. *Food allergies and personal preferences:* Don't cook large quantities of new foods. You won't want to be left with a quart of mango puree that your baby is allergic to or won't touch with a 10-foot pole.

3. *The season:* Fruits and vegetables are not only at their tastiest and most nutritious in season but are your most cost-effective purchases. (Some of this menu decision-making may take place at the supermarket as you respond to a bumper crop of blueberries or asparagus.) Don't go looking for nectarines in December just because your baby's at the right age to try them.

TO MARKET, TO MARKET: FOOD SELECTION AND PESTICIDES

For a copy of *For Our Kid's Sake: How to Protect Your Child Against Pesticides in Food,* send a check for $7.95 (payable to Mothers and Others), P.O. Box 96641, Washington, D.C. 20090.

Healthy cooking really starts with your food source. There's been a lot of publicity on the widespread use of pesticides, hormones, and other chemicals by farmers throughout the world to perfect the ripening time, appearance, and productivity of their crops and herds. Much to the consumer's horror, these aggressive agricultural chemicals are affecting our health now and endangering it in the future. It's a chilling fact that most pesticides used today were registered either before modern testing requirements were in place or before the EPA (Environmental Protection Agency) even existed.

While we are truly concerned with these issues, we don't advocate a completely pesticide-free food chain. Simply because for farmers to produce enough food to feed the world's population at a price affordable for both rich and poor, the use of some pesticides and other chemicals is necessary.

We are very concerned with the effect of these substances on babies, however. (Proportionate to their weight, a baby's potential for consuming pesticides in fruits and vegetables, a mainstay of their diets, is four times greater than for adults.) But instead of banning them completely, we urge greater testing of chemicals before they are approved, less widespread use, and the use of organic methods whenever possible. We believe the food chain should be safe for all people.

In our Mommy Made classes we teach—and experts agree—that the health benefits of eating fresh fruit and vegetables far outweigh the risk of pesticides.

- Choose produce carefully. Avoid fruits and veggies with cuts, mold, decay, or insect holes.
- Wash all produce with water. Avoid soap unless it is meant for produce. Soap can leave its own inedible residue.
- Remove outer leaves from leafy vegetables.
- You can reduce superficial pesticide residue by peeling fruits and veggies, but you are giving up some nutrients and fiber.
- Eating a variety of foods not only gives nutritional benefits, but reduces the pesticide risks.

Canning: The Great Vitamin Massacre*	
VITAMIN A	39%
THIAMINE	69%
RIBOFLAVIN	55%
NIACIN	46%
VITAMIN B$_6$	54%
FOLATE	61%
PANTOTHENATE	61%
BIOTIN	51%
VITAMIN C	64%

*Editors of *Prevention Magazine, The Prevention Total Health System: Understanding Vitamins and Minerals.* Emmaus, Pennsylvania: The Rodale Press Inc., 1984.

The chart on page 95 shows that vegetables lose *lots* of vitamins when they're canned. (The percentages are averages of vitamin losses from canned asparagus, beets, carrots, corn, cowpeas, green beans, green peas, lima beans, mushrooms, spinach, and tomatoes.) The problem with canning is heat and water, both of which can destroy fragile nutrients. As you can see, thiamine (a must for steady nerves) and vitamin C (for a strong immune system) are the most sensitive to canning, but no vitamin escapes unscathed.

BACK HOME—PROPER PREPPING AND COOKING

The Mommy Made recipes in this book give directions for prepping and cooking each food in the most nutritious and healthful way. For your general information, however:

Wash all fruits and vegetables well, scrubbing them with a vegetable brush. Trim ends. Peel, pit, and seed as recipes direct, cutting out and discarding any soft, rotted, or sprouting parts. For better nutrient retention, do not soak fruits and vegetables, and keep chopping and peeling to a minimum. Cook fresh produce promptly after cleaning to prevent browning and to conserve nutrients.

Trim excess fat off meat and poultry.

Steaming fruits and vegetables, either in a steamer basket or in your microwave, is the most nutritious method of cooking them. (The Department of Agriculture evaluated the nutritional advantages of microwave cooking versus stove-top methods. So far, the data indicate that it all depends on the particular food cooked.) We have given the method for stove-top steaming fruits and vegetables in the main body of each recipe, since the equipment needed is cheaper and more widely available. Microwave directions, when applicable, follow, for those who own this extra appliance.

Ten Common Food Handling Mistakes

- Countertop thawing
- Leftovers left out
- Unclean cutting board
- Room-temperature marinating
- Store-to-refrigerator lag time
- BBQ blunder: same platter for raw and grilled meats
- Restaurant "doggie-bag" delay
- Stirring-and-tasting spoon
- Shared knife for trimming raw meat and chopping vegetables
- Hide-and-eat Easter eggs

From "Plating It Safe" a brochure developed by Association of State and Territorial Health Officials, Association of State and Territorial Public Health Nutrition Directors, National Association of County Health Officials Beef Board, and the Beef Industry Council of the Meat Board in Cooperation with: U.S. Department of Agriculture, Food Safety and Inspection Service/Extension Service

In stove-top steaming some of the food's vitamins and minerals are lost in the cooking process. But these can be recaptured by using the steaming liquid to thin pureed foods and by incorporating it into soups and sauces. Microwave cooking requires the least amount of water. (The little water that is used is pureed in or served with the food.) It is also the fastest method of cooking food. And microwave cooking also requires no additional fat to cook foods.

Other methods of cooking food, such as roasting, baking, and grilling, are also acceptable from a nutritional standpoint, especially for vegetables baked in their skins, such as potatoes, squash, and even beets. But steer away from boiling veggies and fruits, unless you are preparing soup—it leaches out their nutrients. And avoid deep frying or any cooking method that adds fats to food.

FOOD STORAGE AND NUTRITION

Even before you get home from the supermarket, you can affect the nutritional value of the food you purchase by how you handle it. For example, shopping last for perishable and frozen foods and taking them home right away—especially in warm weather—will preserve their nutritional content. When you get home, put the food away immediately, starting with the frozen items first, refrigerated second.

Fresh is best! Frozen is second, and canned is last. While freshly prepared food is most nutritious, this statement is not meant to be a guilt trip for busy parents, just a guideline for ranking the nutritional merits of each method of food storage. After all, as much as we love our children, life can't always revolve around them. With many moms working, convenience counts with a capital *C*. What makes the whole family's routine smooth and easy will in the end benefit baby more than a few extra vita-

Because your fresh Mommy Made baby food does not contain any preservatives or additives, you must store it in your refrigerator or freezer. *In the refrigerator, its shelf life is three days; in the freezer, one month.*

mins or minerals lost in freezing or canning. If you do use canned produce, look for fruits that are packed in their own juices with no sugar added and vegetables that are low in salt.

Package your baby food in quantities according to the appetite and age of your baby. Here are some suggestions:

For beginning eaters: Place cookie-sized dollops (a healthy tablespoon) of baby food purees or slices of cooked foods, such as squash, in rows on a baking sheet lined with wax paper. Freeze them until they're solid. Peel hardened food "cookies" and slices from wax paper and place them in tightly sealed plastic bags for continued freezer storage.

Filling sectioned ice cube trays or individual plastic (2-ounce) ice cube containers with pureed food is another option. Pop the hardened cubes out of the tray or individual ice cube molds and transfer them to tightly sealed freezer bags for continued freezer storage.

For bigger appetites: Recycled commercial baby food jars, small jelly jars, and plastic containers make good meal-sized freezer containers for older babies and toddlers. Be sure they are very clean and have tight-fitting lids. Don't fill the jars to the brim as the food needs room to expand as it freezes, especially when stored in glass.

FOOD STORAGE CAVEATS

Always carefully label all foods with contents and date. You would be surprised how similar acorn squash and apples can look after they have been pureed and frozen or how quickly you forget how long the food's been on hand. If in doubt about the age of any food (either refrigerated or frozen), throw it out! It's better to waste a little food than risk making your baby sick.

Never feed your baby directly from your refrigerator or freezer storage jars of baby food unless he will finish all of its contents at that meal. Bacteria in saliva transferred from the feeding spoon

Protect Yourself and Your Food from Plastic Wrap

Recent studies suggest that DEHA, the component that adds the clinginess to many plastic wraps, is a hormone disrupter that can cause problems with our endocrine systems, breast cancer, birth defects, low sperm count, and mental problems. DEHA in plastic wrap can leach into food on contact, especially foods with a high fat content like meat and cheese. Package labeling does not divulge which wraps contain DEHA. To protect your family:

- Remove plastic wrap immediately from cheese or meat and store it in a plastic bag or container.

- Remove the DEHA that has leached onto the surface of plastic wrapped cheese or meat by shaving or scraping off a thin slice.

- Purchase meat from a butcher and ask that it be wrapped in paper. Purchase cheese from a wheel. Ask that it be wrapped in paper or put in a plastic bag.

- Don't let plastic wrap covering bowls of food touch the food.

- Don't *ever* let plastic wrap touch food that is cooked in the microwave.

to the container will quickly spoil any remaining food. Instead, remove the portion for a single meal to a separate dish.

Hold any leftover food intended for the next meal in the refrigerator.

And just to be on the safe side, discard food that has been standing at room temperature for more than two hours.

Do not refreeze defrosted cooked food. (Uncooked frozen food that is then cooked can be frozen—such as pea puree made from frozen peas.)

A WORD ON CANNING

We don't recommend canning as a home method of preserving baby food. It's not only labor-intensive, but it's the least nutritious of the food storage methods. For the novice or for baby food use only, the investment needed for the proper equipment is hard to justify for the month or two your child will be eating purees.

Canning, however, can be a cost-effective method of food preservation. Canned foods have the longest shelf life with no associated energy expenses. It's a viable option for those who are old hands at this technique, already own the equipment, market or garden by the bushel, and/or don't mind the extra effort involved. One of the best books on this method of food storage is *Putting Food By* by Janet Greene et al.

TIME FOR DINNER: DEFROSTING AND REHEATING

Defrosting prepared baby food in the refrigerator is simplest. It requires no extra effort on Mom's part, and you don't have to worry about food left out on the counter turning. It does, however, require planning ahead.

To defrost frozen baby food in the refrigerator: Put frozen food cookies or cubes into a dish. Cover with plastic wrap. Place in the refrigerator. A small container of frozen food can be defrosted by simply transferring it to the refrigerator section. (Leave the lid on.) In approximately two to three hours cookies and cubes will be defrosted; small containers take three to four hours.

The egg poacher method: A faster method of defrosting disks and cubes of frozen food while warming them at the same time is to use an egg poacher. Place portions of food in the egg-shaped hollows of the poacher. Place the poacher in a shallow pan containing about 1 to $1^1/_2$ cups water. Bring to a boil. Cover and continue to heat until food is completely defrosted (about four to five minutes). Stir food occasionally to promote even heating. Depending on the number of sections in your poacher, a variety of foods can easily be reheated at once using this technique.

Microwaves are magic when it comes to one-step defrosting and reheating: Simply place frozen food cookies or cubes in a microwave-safe dish (small Pyrex custard cups and coffee cups are handy). Use a separate cup for each food if you wish. Do not cover. Microwave at LOW or DEFROST for one to two minutes.

To defrost and warm a small frozen container of baby food in your microwave oven, first be sure the container is suitable for microwave cooking. (Glass, most ceramics, and plastic are appropriate for microwave use. If in doubt, check your oven's manual.) Remove container cover. Microwave at LOW or DEFROST for two minutes. Stir. Continue to heat at same power level for two to three minutes more or until food is completely defrosted. Stir well and taste again before serving to baby. Microwave heating frequently causes hot pockets.

Small glass containers of food can also be defrosted and warmed in a water bath. (Plastic containers won't be able to take the heat.) Place the uncovered jar in a small saucepan. Fill the pan with water until the level reaches two-thirds the height of

Always test heated food served to your baby. Heated food should be stirred before serving to even out its temperature. Then place a dab of it on the sensitive inside skin of your wrist. (This is especially important for microwaved foods since they can overheat very easily.)

the jar. Heat over medium heat until the food is soft, stirring occasionally to promote even defrosting and warming.

FOOD TEXTURE STAGES

Your baby, even at an early age, will like his food prepared a certain way. (As he gets older, he may or may not want the peas touching the carrots, and he will definitely develop a preference for how his sandwich is cut—triangles or squares.) In the following Mommy Made recipes we suggest that you thicken or thin puree consistencies to the age and preference of your baby. Here are some guidelines on age-appropriate textures as well as thinners, thickeners, and smoothers to help you please his palate and match his stage of development.

Reheating already-cooked food destroys some of its nutritional content. So reheat as gently as possible, for as short a time as possible. If you can get your baby used to eating cool or even cold food, so much the better. He will not only benefit from its added nutritional value, but cutting out the warming step also means less work for Mom. And, when you're traveling together, baby will be easier to feed in inconvenient places.

AGE-APPROPRIATE FOOD TEXTURES

GRAVY, PLEASE

Baby's first solid foods should be soupy or, as one mom put it, the consistency of gravy. That way your baby can suck them down. If you start your baby on solid foods at six months, this very smooth, soupy puree stage is rather short-lived and won't last as long as for a baby who starts solids sooner. A slightly thicker consistency can be offered as soon as your baby has the hang of eating. But remember, babies do not like any food that is too pasty. And food that might stick to the roof of the mouth should be avoided.

TEXTURE NEXT

As baby's teeth begin to emerge, more texture can be added. However, even babies without teeth can begin to gum steamed fruit and vegetables as early as eight months. More texture can be created in your food processor by pulsing the steamed foods on and off briefly, as opposed to pushing the switch and letting the steel blade go at full tilt. Crusty teethers (page 250) and bagels will also stimulate sensitive gums before teeth appear.

FORGET THE GRAVY—WHERE'S THE MEAT?

A slightly textured sauce with some body is optimal by nine months. Not only will this thicker consistency give baby some experience with chewing, but the food will stick to the spoon better and make his self-feeding attempts more successful. In addition, babies who are not introduced to thicker textured purees may develop a strong preference for the soupy ones.

I'LL DO IT MYSELF

By ten months, many but not all babies are enjoying textures, sauces, and many steamed or naturally soft finger foods. If they are anything like our daughter Renée, they'll get the knack of it early on and won't let you even try to feed them one bite.

ALL GROWN UP

By one year of age—sooner for some, later for others—table food can become the mainstay of your baby's diet. However, certain purees and sauces can stay in the diet for a lifetime. We haven't met a grown-up yet who doesn't love fresh raspberry-applesauce (page 118) or our blueberry-applesauce oatmeal muffins (page 251).

THINNER, THICKER, SMOOTHER

Here's how to get those textures just the way your baby likes them.

THINNERS

- Breast milk and formula are good thinners for rice cereal and very first meals, since they combine a familiar, already accepted taste with a new one. Breast milk mixed with a puree can be safely stored in the refrigerator for 24 hours, in the freezer for one month. Formula keeps in the refrigerator about the same length of time, but does not freeze.
- Fruit juice, chicken and beef stock, liquid from steaming fruit and vegetables, and just straight tap water all keep well in the refrigerator and freezer when mixed with purees. Go easy on the fruit juice, though. You don't want your baby to develop a taste for sweets.

THICKENERS

As your baby begins to gum his food and really chew it with newly emerging teeth, rather than just sucking and swallowing it, you will want to thicken his purees in preparation for the next stage in eating, pieces of soft food.

- Baby cereals, especially rice, are great for tightening watery or overblended baby food.
- Mashed potatoes, particularly the usually well-received sweet potato, are good too.
- Even arrowroot starch can be used. It is highly digestible and rich in calcium and potassium as well.

SMOOTHERS

- Bananas are a great favorite and easy to use.
- Yogurt not only smooths, but cools as well.

PART II

The Recipes

▦ POULTRY ▦

▦ BEEF, LAMB, AND PORK ▦

▦ BAKED GOODS ▦

▦ SHAKES, SMOOTHIES, AND THIRST QUENCHERS ▦

■ DRESSINGS AND TOPPINGS FOR DIPPING, ■
DUNKING, AND SPREADING

Introduction

The following recipes include wonderful baby purees and toddler entrees that are both delicious and nutritious for the whole family. In each section the basic puree or preparation appropriate for baby's first taste of that food comes first. Following are variations and more sophisticated recipes suitable for bigger babies with teeth, toddlers, and even Mom and Dad. In practice—in the kitchen—you can jump ahead to these more advanced recipes, setting aside a portion of cooked, unseasoned food to puree for baby. This will eliminate the chore of cooking purees separately. The puree recipes are given for your convenience, however, in case you want to cook a batch of fresh baby food to keep on hand in your refrigerator and freezer. Suggestions and recipes are also included for turning extra purees into grown-up soups, milk shakes, fruit butters, ice cream, and other adult fare.

All the basic baby puree recipes give instructions for both conventionally steaming (with a basket steamer placed in a pot on your stove) and microwaving fruits and vegetables. As cooking methods, conventional steaming and microwave steaming are about equivalent nutritionally. Microwaved fruits and vegetables generally require only a tablespoon or two of water for cooking, and this liquid is usually served and consumed with the food. When conventionally steaming, to preserve the most vitamins and minerals, save the steaming liquid remaining in the bottom of the pot and use it to thin purees and in soups and sauces.

The *Primary Purees* labels in the following recipes are designed for baby's first encounter with solid foods—when Mom and Dad are doing the spooning in. *Spoon and Finger Foods for Bigger Babies* are for the eight- to ten-month-and-up set who are beginning to feed themselves with hands and spoons. *Table Food for Toddlers and Grown-ups Too* is one-pot cooking for the whole family. These recipes are geared for bigger babies—over one year—but the rest of the family will enjoy them too.

Age of introduction and notes on nutrition (including major vitamin and mineral contribution), selection, storage, and preparation of each food are given in the margin next to the recipes. For more detailed information on food introduction and nutrition, see Chapters Two and Three.

For the Best Results in the Recipes:

■ Always read the entire recipe before beginning.

● Set out everything you need before you start to cook.

▲ Make sure all ingredients for baking are at room temperature.

■ Tablespoons and teaspoons are level measures unless specified.

● Eggs are always large.

▲ 1 teaspoon dried herbs equals 1 tablespoon fresh.

■ Always use unsalted butter or unsalted margarine.

● Minimal salt is used in our recipes. It can be eliminated totally or used to taste. Remember to go slow in seasoning. It's easy to add a bit more, but difficult to correct an overseasoned food.

▲ Virgin olive oil is fine in these recipes. Corn oil can be substituted for vegetable oil.

■ Always use fresh vegetables when available.

● When using a hand food mill or baby food grinder, cook items a little longer to aid in pureeing.

▲ When using your food processor, remember to scrape down the work bowl at least once during processing.

■ Avoid cooking in thinly constructed pans, as they heat unevenly.

● Try whenever possible to center food heating or cooking in your oven.

▲ Turn pot handles inward so bigger babies can't pull them down and adults don't accidentally knock them over.

■ Always stir and test the temperature of foods before feeding baby, especially those heated in your microwave oven.

Fruits

My First Applesauce

■ ■ ■ ■ ■ ■ ■ ■ ■ ■ ■ ■ ■ ■ ■ ■ ■ ■

Primary Purees

We can't guarantee that an apple a day will keep the doctor away, but we do know this applesauce is delicious and contains lots of vitamins and minerals. We recommend using Golden Delicious apples in baby's first sauce, since this variety is the least acidic. If you can't find them, another all-purpose cooking apple such as Rome can be substituted. Just be sure to avoid the acidic green-skinned apples, such as Granny Smiths, in the first year. Leaving the peel on the apple during cooking makes for a more nutrient-rich and tastier sauce.

6 medium-size Golden Delicious apples, washed, quartered, and cored just before cooking

APPLES

Introduce the milder varieties—Golden Delicious has the least amount of acid—at 6 months. Save green-skinned apples, such as Granny Smiths, for over age 1.

▲

Nutritional Profile: vitamin C; potassium. Apples are also rich in pectin, which is soothing when your baby has an upset stomach or diarrhea.

●

Fall is the season for apples. The widest choice and the highest quality will be available to you then. Try to avoid apples coated with paraffin, which makes them shine. Wash this coating off with mild soap and water before consuming.

Place prepared apple quarters in a steamer basket set in a pot filled with a small amount of lightly boiling water. Cover tightly (for better nutrient retention) and steam for 10 to 12 minutes or until apples are tender, replenishing water during steaming if necessary. Check for doneness with a toothpick or fork; apples should pierce easily. Set apples and cooking liquid aside to cool. Strain cooked apples in a food mill to puree and remove skins. Or scrape the apple from the skin and puree in a food processor fitted with the steel blade. Add about 1 tablespoon reserved cooking liquid per apple to puree, adjusting consistency according to age and preference of your baby.

Makes 16 to 18 1-ounce or heaped tablespoon baby servings.

Microwave Directions: Place prepared apple quarters in microwave-safe dish. Add $1/4$ cup water and cover tightly with plastic wrap, turning back one corner to vent. Microwave on HIGH for 3 minutes, stir apples thoroughly, re-cover, and cook for 3 to 6 minutes or until tender. Check for doneness, cool, and proceed with recipe.

Serving Suggestion: Peel a few of the cooked apple quarters, slice thickly, and freeze for a soothing snack for teething babies or summertime finger food.

Smooth and/or Chunky Applesauce

Golden Delicious or other cooking apples, cooked as directed in preceding recipe

Puree cooked apples until smooth or chunky, depending on the age of your baby and tastes of your family.

Variations: Try one of the following for a change of taste, depending on the age of your baby:

- Puree uncooked berries with apples.
- Puree *ripe,* peeled, and pitted apricots with apples (to peel apricots easily, see Just Peachy recipe, page 123).
- Mix in a few drops of vanilla or almond extract.
- Dust with a little ground cinnamon.
- Mix in some lemon zest (finely grated yellow peel without the white pith).
- Mix in a few ground walnuts and a little maple syrup.
- Mix in a handful of raisins plumped in apple juice.
- Top individual servings with a dollop of yogurt; marbleize by running a knife through it once in a zigzag pattern.

Apples are good keepers. Store them for 2 weeks in refrigerator in a plastic bag to prevent apples from losing moisture and from picking up odors from other foods.

Basic Baked Apple

4 large baking apples (Rome, Cortland, Stayman, or Winesap)
$1/2$ cup water
$1/2$ cup apple juice

Table Food for Toddlers
and Grown-ups Too

Preheat oven to 350 degrees. Wash apples and core from stem end to within $1/2$ inch of bottom. With a vegetable peeler, remove skin from top half of apple. Place apples, peeled end up, in 8-inch square baking dish with water and juice. Cover with aluminum foil and bake 30 to 50 minutes or until tender, basting occasionally with cooking juices. Remove from oven and baste one last time. Serve warm or chilled.

Makes 4 grown-up portions.

Microwave Directions: Place prepared apples in microwave-safe dish. Use only $1/4$ cup water and $1/4$ cup juice. Cover with plastic wrap, venting back one corner. *(Do not* cover with aluminum foil.) Microwave on HIGH until apples are tender, approximately 10 to 14 minutes.

For Bigger Babies (over 10 months): Remove skin and mash apple with a fork.

Variations: Before baking, fill the apple cavity with one or more of the following:

- $1/2$ ripe banana
- pureed sweet potato or carrot
- whole blueberries or raspberries
- sliced strawberries
- peanut butter, honey, and raisins
- chocolate chips
- ham and cheese
- cooked couscous
- cooked rice and vegetables

Walnut-Raisin Baked Apples

**Table Food for Toddlers
and Grown-ups Too**

4 apples, peeled and cored as directed in preceding recipe
1/2 cup raisins
1/2 cup chopped walnuts
1/2 cup water
1/2 cup apple juice
1/4 cup honey
1 tablespoon unsalted butter

Fill cavities of prepared apples with raisins and chopped walnuts. Place apples in 8-inch square baking dish. Pour water and apple juice over all. Brush apple tops with honey and dot with butter. Bake according to directions in previous recipe.

Makes 4 grown-up servings.

For Grown-ups: For a romantic touch, pour 1/4 cup warmed Calvados or applejack over baked apples and ignite with a match. Serve with vanilla ice cream or frozen yogurt.

Banana

Babies are big on bananas, for good reason—they're tasty, easy to swallow, and very digestible. Bananas make very handy prepackaged snacks. Never leave home without tucking one into your diaper bag. Everyone knows how to mash a ripe banana, but here are some other ways to serve this popular fruit. Bananas turn brown when mashed, but that doesn't affect their nutritional value or flavor. If desired, add a touch of lemon juice (at 10 months and up) to keep the banana from browning.

1 ripe banana, peeled

Mash banana with a fork and add a little formula, juice, or water to adjust consistency if desired.

Makes 4 to 6 1-ounce or heaped tablespoon baby servings.

Serving Suggestion: Frozen, peeled banana spears make a soothing teething food and are a good way to preserve a bunch of bananas that all ripen at once.

Variations for Bigger Babies: Bananas blend wonderfully with other fruits:

- banana-butternut puree
- banana-prune puree
- banana-strawberry puree
- banana-blueberry puree
- banana-orange puree
- banana-raspberry puree
- banana-papaya puree
- banana-mango puree
- And, for an instant dessert, whip up bananas—and banana puree combos—with yogurt in your food processor.

Primary Purees

BANANAS

Introduce bananas at 6 months.

Nutritional Profile: vitamins C and B complex; potassium.

Purchase bananas by the bunch. Select those with smooth, unbruised skins and firm, unbroken stems. Serve only ripe bananas (the skin should be nicely speckled with brown). Cut out any rotted or soft spots.

Never store bananas in the refrigerator or in a plastic bag. If bananas are purchased green, place them in a brown paper bag overnight to hasten ripening.

In addition to the ordinary banana, you might see short, stubby ones in your supermarket. These make excellent eating too. The large green plantains are used for cooking.

Pear Puree

Primary Purees

Fruits and Vegetables That Brown When Cut or Bruised

- Apples
- Apricots
- Artichokes
- Avocados
- Bananas
- Cherries
- Eggplant
- Mushrooms
- Nectarines
- Peaches
- Pears
- Potatoes

PEARS

Introduce pears, another first fruit after apples, at 6 months.

Nutritional Profile: vitamin C; potassium.

Pears ripen from the inside out. Select pears that are firm to the touch but not too hard. Pears that are too hard when picked become mealy as they ripen. Ripe pears should give a bit at the stem end when pressed and have a faintly sweet scent. Store pears in the refrigerator when ripe; they'll keep 3 to 5 days in a plastic bag.

Bartlett, Anjou, and Bosc are the most common pears in supermarkets. All make good-tasting sauce, but Bartletts stay the whitest when cooked.

4 medium-size Bartlett, Anjou, or Bosc pears, washed, peeled, quartered, and cored just before cooking

Place pear quarters in a steamer basket set in a pot filled with a small amount of lightly boiling water. Cover tightly (for better nutrient retention) and cook for 8 to 12 minutes or until pears are tender, replenishing water during steaming if necessary. Test for doneness with a toothpick or fork; pears should pierce easily. Set pears aside to cool. Strain pears in a food mill or puree in a food processor fitted with the steel blade. Discard the cooking liquid or save for another use. No additional liquid is needed.

Makes 12 to 14 1-ounce or heaped tablespoon baby servings.

Microwave Directions: Place prepared pear quarters in a microwave-safe dish. Add ¼ cup water and cover tightly with plastic wrap, pulling back one corner to vent. Microwave on HIGH for 3 minutes, stir thoroughly, re-cover, and cook for 3 to 6 minutes or until tender. Check for doneness, cool, and proceed with recipe.

Just Peachy

Most kids are peachy keen on peach puree. Ripe peaches—as well as ripe apricots, plums, and nectarines need a quick steam to soften them up a bit and break down the fiber. Peaches tend to brown when cooked and pureed, but this is not harmful, nor does it affect their flavor or nutritional value. The freestone variety is easiest to pit.

4 medium-size ripe peaches, washed, peeled,* halved, and pitted

Place prepared peach halves in a steamer basket set in a pot filled with a small amount of lightly boiling water. Cover tightly (for better nutrient retention) and steam for 2 to 4 minutes or until tender (cooking time will depend on ripeness of peaches), replenishing water during steaming if necessary. Check for doneness with a toothpick or fork; peaches should pierce easily. Strain cooked peaches in a food mill or puree in a food processor fitted with the steel blade. Usually no additional liquid is required to correct consistency.

Makes 12 to 14 1-ounce or heaped tablespoon baby servings.

Microwave Directions: Place prepared peach halves in a microwave-safe dish. Add $1/4$ cup water and cover tightly with plastic wrap, pulling back one corner to vent. Microwave on HIGH for 1 minute, stir peaches thoroughly, re-cover, and cook for 1 to 2 minutes. Check for doneness as above, cool, and proceed with recipe.

To peel easily: immerse peaches in boiling water for a few seconds to loosen skin. Cool slightly. Skin should slip off easily with a little help from fingers and/or a paring knife.

Primary Purees

Short of cooking the fruits and vegetables listed on page 122 immediately, you can slow the browning process by two means. Immersing the cut fruit and vegetable pieces in cold water will slow the process. The best way, however, is to toss the pieces with the juice of a freshly squeezed lemon or to add the juice to the cooking water. (It's not necessary to add lemon juice to potato water. But if you're making potato salad, a quick toss with lemon juice after the potatoes are boiled and drained really brightens them up—in addition to providing extra flavor.) Lemon juice should not be used on food served to babies before age 10 months.

PEACHES

Introduce peaches at 7 months.

Nutritional Profile: vitamin A; potassium.

Select firm, but ripe peaches with good color and a fragrant scent. Green peaches will not ripen on the kitchen counter, no matter what your grocer promises. Avoid cracked, shriveled, or bruised fruit. Store peaches in plastic bags in a cold, moist spot in the refrigerator; they'll keep 3 to 5 days.

A Plum of a Puree

The yield in this recipe will vary depending on the size and type of plum. Stanley, Burbank, and Santa Rosa are the most common plums. To peel plums, see Just Peachy recipe, page 123.

6 plums, washed, peeled, halved, and pitted

Place prepared plums in a steamer basket set in a pot filled with a small amount of lightly boiling water. Cover tightly (for better nutrient retention) and steam for 1 to 3 minutes or until plums are soft (cooking time may vary depending on ripeness of plums), replenishing water during steaming if necessary. Check for doneness with a toothpick or fork; plums should pierce easily. Set plums aside to cool, reserving cooking liquid. Strain plums in a food mill or puree in a food processor fitted with the steel blade. Usually no additional liquid is required, but if needed, use a little of the steaming liquid.

Makes 12 to 14 1-ounce or heaped tablespoon baby servings.

Microwave Directions: Place prepared plums in a microwave-safe dish. Add ¼ cup water and cover tightly with plastic wrap, pulling back one corner to vent. Microwave on HIGH for 45 seconds, stir plums thoroughly, re-cover, and cook for 15 to 75 seconds. Check for doneness, cool, and proceed with recipe.

PLUMS

Introduce plums at 7 months.

Nutritional Profile: vitamins A and C; potassium.

Select plums that are full-colored, have a sweet fragrance, and are firm but not rock-hard. (Do not judge ripeness by color as variety dictates hue.) Ripen plums at home at room temperature until soft. Store ripe plums in refrigerator. Keep plums moist by placing a moist paper towel in storage bin; they'll keep 3 to 5 days.

Fresh Apricot Puree

Like peaches, apricots will tend to brown when cooked and pureed, but this is not harmful, nor will it affect their delicate flavor or nutritional content. To peel apricots, see Just Peachy recipe, page 123. If your apricot puree is too tart, add unsweetened, undiluted apple juice concentrate, 1 teaspoon at a time, or a spoonful or 2 of banana puree, until baby likes the taste.

6 fresh apricots, washed, peeled, halved, and pitted

Place prepared apricot halves in a steamer basket set in a pot filled with a small amount of lightly boiling water. Cover tightly (for better nutrient retention) and steam for 2 to 4 minutes or until tender (cooking time may vary, depending on ripeness of the apricots), replenishing water during steaming if necessary. Check for doneness with a toothpick or fork; apricots should pierce easily. Set apricots aside until cool enough to handle. Strain apricots in a food mill or puree in a food processor fitted with the steel blade. Usually no additional liquid is required.

Makes 10 to 12 1-ounce or heaped tablespoon baby servings.

Microwave Directions: Place prepared apricots in a microwave-safe dish. Add $1/4$ cup water and cover tightly with plastic wrap, pulling back one corner to vent. Microwave on HIGH for 1 minute, stir apricots thoroughly, re-cover, and cook for 1 or 2 minutes. Check for doneness, cool, and proceed with recipe.

APRICOTS

Introduce fresh apricots at 8 months. Hold off on dried apricots until after age 1.

Nutritional Profile: vitamins A and C; potassium. (Dried apricots are particularly rich in iron.)

Select firm, plump, ripe apricots with good color and size. Pass up greenish ones. Store fresh apricots in a moist spot in your refrigerator. A damp paper towel in your storage bin will do the trick. Use within 2 or 3 days of purchase. Fresh apricots have a short season. They are generally available in June and July in the East and May to August in the West.

Purely Papaya

The papaya is a large, oblong tropical fruit with a thick green or yellow skin. It has soft orange flesh with black seeds in the center. Papayas are mild-tasting and smooth-textured and can be eaten like melons. Grown-ups (and babies over 10 months) can add a squeeze of fresh lemon or lime.

2 ripe papayas, halved, seeded, and cut lengthwise into thirds just before cooking

Place papaya thirds in a steamer basket set in a pot filled with a small amount of lightly boiling water. Cover tightly (for better nutrient retention) and steam for 6 to 8 minutes or until papaya is tender. Check for doneness with a toothpick or fork; papaya flesh should pierce easily. Set papaya aside to cool. Using a spoon, scrape the cooked papaya from its skin and strain flesh in a food mill or puree in a food processor fitted with the steel blade. No additional liquid is needed.

Makes 12 to 14 1-ounce or heaped tablespoon baby servings.

Microwave Directions: Place prepared papaya thirds in microwave-safe dish. Add $1/4$ cup water and cover tightly with plastic wrap, pulling back one corner to vent. Microwave on HIGH for 3 minutes, rearrange papaya thirds in the dish, re-cover, and cook for 3 to 6 minutes or until tender. Check for doneness, cool, and proceed with recipe.

PAPAYAS

Introduce papaya at 9 months.

Nutritional Profile: vitamins A and C; potassium. Papayas are also very high in natural digestive enzymes.

Select smooth, unbruised fruit. Ripe papayas are soft to the touch, have yellow skins, and are heavy. Ripen at room temperature and refrigerate to hold. Fully ripe fruit will keep up to 2 weeks stored in a plastic bag in the refrigerator.

Prune Puree

When you need to get things going, sweet prunes are a natural. They are among the highest in fiber of all the fruits. A little goes a long way, so we've reduced the yield in this recipe.

8 pitted dried prunes

Place prunes in a small saucepan. Bring to a boil over high heat, reduce heat, and simmer for 10 to 12 minutes or until tender. Check for doneness with a toothpick or fork; prunes should pierce easily. Drain prunes, reserving cooking liquid. Set both aside to cool. Strain prunes in a food mill or puree in a food processor fitted with the steel blade. A little cooking liquid may be needed to adjust consistency. Serve any leftover cooking "juice" to baby in cup or bottle.

Makes 4 to 6 1-ounce or heaped tablespoon baby servings.

Microwave Directions: Place prunes in a microwave-safe dish. Add 3 tablespoons water and cover tightly with plastic wrap, pulling back one corner to vent. Microwave on HIGH for 1 minute. Puree cooked prunes with $1/3$ cup water in food processor fitted with the steel blade.

Variations: Try these tasty ideas:

- Add a mashed ripe banana to half the prune puree for a wonderful treat.
- prune and sweet potato puree
- prune and carrot puree
- prune and apple puree
- Try this recipe with raisins instead of prunes.

Primary Purees

PRUNES

Introduce prunes at 10 months, or earlier if your doctor advises.

Nutritional Profile: vitamin A; iron. Some species contain B vitamins.

Select plump, soft, shiny prunes that have been naturally sun-dried and are not treated with paraffin and sulphur dioxide. Store prunes in a well-sealed container in a cool, dry place.

Nifty Nectarines

To peel nectarines, see Just Peachy recipe, page 123.

4 medium-size nectarines, washed, peeled, halved, and pitted

Place nectarine halves in a steamer basket set in a pot filled with a small amount of lightly boiling water. Cover tightly (for better nutrient retention) and steam for 2 to 4 minutes or until tender (cooking time may vary, depending on ripeness of nectarines), replenishing water during steaming if necessary. Check for doneness with a toothpick or fork; nectarines should pierce easily. Set nectarines aside until cool enough to handle. Strain nectarines in a food mill or puree in a food processor fitted with the steel blade. Usually no additional liquid is required.

Makes 12 to 14 1-ounce or heaped tablespoon baby servings.

Microwave Directions: Place nectarine halves in a microwave-safe dish. Add 1/4 cup water and cover tightly with plastic wrap, pulling back one corner to vent. Microwave on HIGH for 1 minute, stir nectarines thoroughly, re-cover, and cook for 1 to 2 minutes. Check for doneness, cool slightly, and proceed with recipe.

NECTARINES

Introduce nectarines, a fuzzless relative of the peach, at 10 months.

Nutritional Profile: vitamins A and B complex; potassium.

Select smooth, plump, highly colored, mature fruit with a sweet fragrance. These will become riper and juicier on your kitchen counter. Nectarines with considerable green won't. Store ripe nectarines in a plastic bag in the refrigerator; they'll keep 5 days or longer.

Kiwifruit

Kiwifruit, or Chinese gooseberry, is an adorable, brown, furry-skinned fruit with sweet-tasting, bright green flesh speckled with dramatic, edible black seeds. Kiwifruit is good for you too! It contains more vitamin C than orange juice. Although its thin skin is digestible, always peel it off for baby, since he could choke on it.

1 ripe kiwifruit, peeled

Mash kiwifruit with a fork as you would a banana. If the flesh is tart, add a little ripe banana to the puree. If the kiwi is large, mash only half for baby and slice the other for Mom and Dad's fruit salad, cereal topping, or dinner plate garnish.

Makes 4 tablespoons.

For Toddlers (over 1 year): Peeled kiwifruit can be cut into spears, slices, or cubes for bigger babies.

For Younger Toddlers: Toddlers will enjoy spooning theirs right out of the ripe, unpeeled fruit. Simply cut off the top and present in an eggcup or place in the toddler's hand with a demitasse spoon.

KIWIFRUIT

Introduce kiwifruit at 11 months.

Nutritional Profile: vitamin C; potassium.

Select unblemished fruit. Ripe kiwifruit gives slightly when pressed. Hard ones can be ripened at room temperature. Store ripe kiwis in the refrigerator up to 1 week.

Cantaloupe Puree

Primary Purees

Ripe cantaloupe spears make wonderful finger food for the older baby.

1 medium-size ripe cantaloupe, cut into eighths, rind removed, and seeds discarded

Place prepared cantaloupe wedges in a steamer basket set in a pot filled with a small amount of lightly boiling water. Cover tightly (for better nutrient retention) and steam for 3 to 5 minutes or until fruit is soft, replenishing water during steaming if necessary. Check for doneness with a toothpick or fork; fruit should pierce easily. Set cantaloupe aside to cool. Strain cantaloupe in a food mill or puree in a food processor fitted with the steel blade. No additional liquid is required.

Makes 12 to 14 1-ounce or heaped tablespoon baby servings.

Microwave Directions: Place prepared cantaloupe wedges in a microwave-safe dish. Add $1/4$ cup water and cover tightly with plastic wrap, pulling back one corner to vent. Microwave on HIGH for $1^{1}/_{2}$ minutes, rearrange wedges, re-cover, and cook for 30 seconds to $2^{1}/_{2}$ minutes. Check for doneness and proceed with recipe.

CANTALOUPE

Introduce cantaloupe and all other melons at 12 months.

Nutritional Profile: vitamins A and C; potassium.

Ripe cantaloupes take on a yellow appearance, have a sweet, fragrant scent, and give slightly when pressed at the blossom end. Avoid cantaloupes with soft spots and mold on the stem end or elsewhere. Unripened cantaloupes will ripen on your kitchen counter in a day or two. Seal ripe cantaloupes in a plastic bag and store in the warmest part of the refrigerator. (The bag keeps the melon from exchanging odors with other foods.) Cantaloupes are generally available all year but are sweetest and cheapest during their peak season, May through September.

Vegetables

Acorn Squash Puree

1 medium-size acorn squash

Preheat oven to 350 degrees. Pierce squash with a fork 3 or 4 times. Bake on a foil-lined pan for 45 minutes to 1 hour, turning squash over after 25 minutes. Check for doneness with a toothpick or fork; squash should pierce easily. Cut squash in half to cool and remove seeds with a spoon. When squash is slightly cool, peel off outer skin, scraping any remaining pulp with a spoon. Puree in a food processor fitted with the steel blade or strain in a food mill. Usually no additional liquid is needed.

Makes 12 to 14 1-ounce or heaped tablespoon baby servings.

Microwave Directions: Cut squash into quarters, scoop out seeds, and place skin-side down in a microwave-safe dish. Add 1 tablespoon water and cover tightly with plastic wrap, pulling back one corner to vent. Microwave on HIGH for 10 to 12 minutes. Check for doneness and proceed with recipe.

Serving Suggestion: Chunks of cooked squash, peeled and seeded, make great finger foods.

Primary Purees

ACORN SQUASH

Introduce acorn squash, a first vegetable, at 6 months.

Nutritional Profile: vitamins C and B complex; calcium and potassium.

Select firm-skinned, heavy, brightly colored acorn squash. This is a winter squash and best (and cheapest) in the late fall and winter months. The squash will keep on a cool pantry shelf 7 to 10 days or in a cooler place (55°F) 2 to 4 weeks.

Sweet Potatoes and Yams Too

Yams and sweet potatoes are not one and the same. But in U.S. supermarkets the names are used interchangeably for the commonly cultivated sweet potato. One cooks yams the same way as sweet potatoes, so we've included a reference to them in this recipe, even though they are rarely available. Cut into chunks, sweet potatoes and yams make great finger food.

1 large sweet potato or yam, scrubbed and pierced a few times with a fork

Preheat oven to 350 degrees. Bake sweet potato (or yam) on a foil-lined pan for 1 hour, turning after 30 minutes. Check for doneness with a toothpick or fork; the sweet potato should pierce easily. Cook another 15 minutes or so if necessary. Set aside until cool enough to handle. Peel off outer skin and strain cooked potato in a food mill or puree in a food processor fitted with the steel blade. Add about 5 tablespoons water to puree, adjusting consistency according to age and preference of your baby.

Makes 12 to 14 1-ounce or heaped tablespoon baby servings.

Microwave Directions: Place prepared sweet potato in a shallow microwave-safe dish. Microwave on HIGH for 7 to 9 minutes or until tender. Check for doneness; potatoes may still feel firm to the touch but should pierce easily with a fork. Proceed with recipe.

Variations: Sweet potato or yam puree is particularly tasty mixed with other fruit purees such as apple, apricot, pineapple, and orange.

SWEET POTATOES

Introduce sweet potatoes and yams at 6 months.

Nutritional Profile: vitamin A; potassium.

Sweet potatoes are at their peak in fall and midwinter. Select small ones with smooth skins. Avoid any with soft spots. (Discard any sweet potatoes on hand that have bad spots. The whole vegetable will have started to decay and will have an off flavor.) Store dry; do not refrigerate. Yams will keep 3 to 4 days on a cool pantry shelf or 4 to 6 weeks at 55°F.

Sweet potatoes and yams make good windowsill houseplants. Help your toddler plant a sweet potato in a glass, suspending half the potato above the water line with toothpicks. He can water and watch it grow.

For Toddlers (over 1 year): The above calls for 1 large potato. To feed a toddler and the rest of the family, bake 2 to 3 sweet potatoes as above. Add 1 to 2 minutes to the microwave cooking time. Serve hot (cool your toddler's potato to a safe temperature), split and topped with a pat of unsalted butter.

Cinnamon-Honey Acorn Squash

1 medium-size acorn squash, halved, seeds discarded, stem and blossom end trimmed flat
3 tablespoons honey
1 tablespoon unsalted butter
1/4 teaspoon ground cinnamon

Preheat oven to 350 degrees. Place squash halves on foil-lined baking sheet. Brush cavities and tops with honey, dot with butter, and sprinkle with cinnamon. Bake for 45 minutes or until tender when pierced with a toothpick or fork.

Makes 2 grown-up servings.

Variations: Brush squash with maple syrup instead of honey or only with melted butter. (Skip the cinnamon.) When cooking is nearly completed, fill cavity with one of the following. Garnish with chopped parsley and bake for 15 minutes more.

- applesauce
- sautéed mushrooms and onions
- sautéed seasonal vegetables
- navel orange sections

Table Food for Toddlers and Grown-ups Too

Fruit and Vegetable Puree Combinations from the Mommy Made Professional Kitchen That You Can Make at Home

- apple-raspberry
- apple-strawberry
- apple–acorn squash
- apple–sweet potato
- apple-carrot
- pear–butternut squash
- pear-cauliflower
- pear-blueberry
- pear-zucchini
- pear-carrot
- pear-broccoli
- banana-nectarine
- banana-raspberry
- banana-tangerine
- banana-papaya
- peach-raspberry
- strawberry-papaya

Butternut Squash Puree

Primary Purees

A light tan winter squash 8 to 10 inches long with a fat, round end. Its bright orange flesh is good eating.

1 medium-size butternut squash (about 1 pound)

Preheat oven to 350 degrees. Pierce squash with a fork 3 to 4 times. Bake on a foil-lined pan for 45 minutes to 1 hour, turning squash after 25 minutes. Check for doneness with a toothpick or fork; squash should pierce easily. Cut squash in half to cool and remove seeds with a spoon. When slightly cool, peel off outer skin, scraping any remaining pulp with a spoon. Strain in a food mill or puree in a food processor fitted with the steel blade. Usually no additional liquid is needed.

Makes 16 to 18 1-ounce or heaped tablespoon baby servings.

Microwave Directions: Cut squash into quarters, scoop out seeds, and place skin-side down in a microwave-safe dish. Add 1 tablespoon water and cover tightly with plastic wrap, pulling back one corner to vent. Microwave on HIGH for 10 to 12 minutes. Check for doneness and proceed with recipe.

Acorn and butternut squashes and sweet potatoes taste best when baked in your oven. Baking caramelizes their natural sugars. Winter squashes—acorn and butternut—retain the most vitamin A cooked this way.

Butternut Squash Variations

1 medium-size butternut squash, baked as directed in preceding recipe

Puree peeled and seeded squash or cut into chunks as desired. Liven up with one of the following:

- sautéed onions and/or mushrooms
- sour cream
- grated peeled fresh ginger
- chopped walnuts and plumped raisins
- a pinch of allspice
- chopped spinach
- chopped ham or crumbled bacon
- crushed pineapple
- chopped pimiento
- chopped fresh herbs, such as parsley

Table Food for Toddlers
and Grown-ups Too

BUTTERNUT SQUASH

Introduce butternut squash, a first vegetable, at 6 months.

Nutritional Profile: vitamins A, C, and B complex; calcium and potassium.

This winter squash should be hard and heavy with smooth, unblemished skin. Butternuts mature in the fall but will keep for months in a cool, dry place. Once the skin is cut, cook squash immediately.

Green Beans

Primary Purees

String or green beans are fibrous and do not puree easily. You'll need a blender to make them smooth—and be sure to start with beans that are well cooked.

6 ounces green beans, washed, tops and tails snapped off

Put cleaned beans in a steamer basket set in a pot filled with a small amount of lightly boiling water. Cover tightly (for better nutrient retention) and steam for 12 to 15 minutes or until *very* tender, replenishing water during steaming if necessary. Have ready a bowl of ice water. Check for doneness with a fork; the beans should pierce very easily. Immediately transfer steamer basket with beans to sink, reserving steaming liquid. Plunge the beans into the ice water. Run cold water over all until green beans are completely cool, 2 to 3 minutes. Puree beans in a blender with 2 tablespoons steaming liquid until smooth, scraping down sides of bowl once or twice.

Makes 10 1-ounce or heaped tablespoon baby servings.

Microwave Directions: Place prepared beans in a microwave-safe dish. Add 1/4 cup water and cover with plastic wrap, pulling back one corner to vent. Microwave on HIGH for 13 to 15 minutes or until tender. Cool and proceed with recipe.

For Bigger Babies (over 10 months): Green beans make great finger food. Serve whole, either plain or with one of our dipping sauces, pages 273–283.

For Toddlers (over 1 year): For a refreshing, eye-catching side dish, toss whole steamed green beans with a little vinaigrette (see A Vinaigrette for All Seasons recipe, page 274.) Garnish with chopped tomato.

GREEN BEANS

Introduce green beans at 7 months.

Nutritional Profile: vitamins A and C; iron and potassium.

Select smooth, unbruised, crisp, young pods. (They should readily snap in two!) Green beans are available all year. Store in a plastic bag in your refrigerator for up to 4 days.

Peas, Please!

Green peas are a favorite with babies. They love their bright color and naturally sweet taste. Older babies will love the way peas bounce, squish, and roll on the high chair tray. Fresh peas are tastiest and most nutritious—especially tender early peas. But their season is short and the supply limited. Frozen peas are almost as good for you, almost as tasty, and easy to come by. Cook them the same way as fresh peas for approximately the same time.

1 pound fresh peas, shelled and washed just before cooking

Place shelled peas in a steamer basket set in a pot filled with a small amount of lightly boiling water. (Depending on your steam tray, you may have to place peas in a shallow dish first, so they don't drop through the steam tray holes into the water.) Cover tightly (for better nutrient retention) and steam for 7 to 10 minutes or until peas are tender, replenishing water during steaming if necessary. Check peas for doneness with a fork; they should mash easily. Immediately transfer steamer basket with peas to sink, reserving steaming liquid. Cover peas with ice and run cold water over all until the peas are completely cool—2 to 3 minutes. Strain peas in a food mill or puree in a food processor fitted with the steel blade. Add 2 tablespoons reserved cooking liquid to the puree, adjusting consistency according to age and preference of your baby.

Makes 8 to 10 1-ounce or heaped tablespoon baby servings.

Microwave Directions: Place prepared peas in a microwave-safe dish. Add ¼ cup water and cover tightly with plastic wrap, pulling back one corner to vent. Microwave on HIGH for 3 minutes, stir peas thoroughly, re-cover, and cook for 2 to 4 minutes or until tender. Check for doneness, cool, and proceed with recipe.

Primary Purees

PEAS

Introduce peas at 7 months.

Nutritional Profile: high in protein; vitamins A and C; iron.

Fresh peas are in season from March through May. Select peas with small, shiny green pods. Store fresh peas, unshelled, in a plastic bag in refrigerator and cook as soon as possible. Held at room temperature, fresh peas quickly lose their natural sugar and tenderness.

Carrot Puree

Primary Purees

We're not sure who loves carrots more: babies or rabbits. Too many carrots, however, will turn your baby's skin yellow. This harmless but unattractive condition is caused by their high carotene content. Your baby's rosy complexion will return naturally once you stop serving too many carrots. (Once or twice a week is a safe limit.) Cooked carrots are a great finger/teething food.

1 1-pound bag or bunch of carrots, trimmed, peeled, and cut into ¼-inch
  rounds just before cooking

Place carrot rounds in a steamer basket set in a pot filled with a small amount of lightly boiling water. Cover tightly (for better nutrient retention) and cook for 12 to 14 minutes or until carrots are tender, replenishing water during steaming if necessary. Check for doneness with a toothpick or fork; carrots should pierce easily. Set carrots and cooking liquid aside to cool. Strain carrots in a food mill or puree in a food processor fitted with the steel blade. Add about 1 tablespoon cooking liquid per carrot to puree, adjusting consistency according to age and preference of your baby.

Makes 12 to 14 1-ounce or heaped tablespoon baby servings.

Microwave Directions: Place prepared carrot rounds in a microwave-safe dish. Add ¼ cup water and cover tightly with plastic wrap, pulling back one corner to vent. Microwave on HIGH for 5 minutes, stir carrots thoroughly, re-cover, and cook for 3 to 6 minutes or until tender. Check for doneness, cool, and proceed with recipe.

For Toddlers (over 1 year): Double the amount of carrots, increase cooking time slightly, and puree half for baby. Serve remaining carrots to the rest of the family topped with a pat of unsalted butter and a sprinkle of chopped parsley.

CARROTS

Introduce carrots after yellow squashes and vegetables, at 7 months.

Nutritional Profile: very high in vitamin A—a single carrot far exceeds the adult minimum daily requirement of vitamin A and potassium.

Select bright orange carrots that are firm and not cracked. Slender carrots tend to be sweeter and have a smaller fibrous core. Carrots with hairy rootlets are old. If you buy carrots with their greens attached—these are fresher than trimmed, bagged carrots—chop the tops off immediately. Carrots will keep nicely in a plastic bag in your refrigerator for up to 2 weeks.

Cooked carrots are also good with:

- grated orange zest and raspberries
- a sprinkle of cumin seed and sautéed onion
- a dollop of yogurt and chopped chives

Yellow or Summer Squash Puree

In general all thin- or edible-skinned squashes are considered summer squash, and despite their seasonal name they are generally available year-round—although their peak season is summer.

2 medium-size yellow summer squash, washed and cut into ¼-inch rounds just before cooking

Place yellow squash rounds in a steamer basket set in a pot of lightly boiling water. Cover tightly (for better nutrient retention) and steam for 7 to 10 minutes or until tender, replenishing water during steaming if necessary. Check for doneness with a toothpick or fork; the squash should pierce easily. Set aside to cool. When cool, strain squash in a food mill or puree in a food processor fitted with the steel blade. No additional liquid is required.

Makes 10 to 12 1-ounce or heaped tablespoon baby servings.

Microwave Directions: Place yellow squash rounds in a microwave-safe dish. Add ¼ cup water and cover tightly with plastic wrap, pulling back one corner to vent. Microwave on HIGH for 3 minutes, stir thoroughly, re-cover, and cook for 2 to 4 minutes or until tender. Check for doneness and proceed with recipe.

For Bigger Babies (over 10 months): Steamed summer squash rounds (and spears) make great finger foods.

Primary Purees

SUMMER SQUASH

Introduce summer squash at 8 months.

Nutritional Profile: vitamins A and C; potassium.

Select summer squash that are small to medium-size and firm, with shiny, tender, unblemished skins. (Some varieties have a bumpy surface.) Store in refrigerator in a plastic bag and use within a few days.

Zucchini Puree

Primary Purees

2 medium-size zucchini, washed and cut into ¼-inch rounds just before cooking

Place zucchini rounds in a steamer basket set in a pot filled with a small amount of lightly boiling water. Cover tightly (for better nutrient retention) and steam for 7 to 10 minutes or until tender, replenishing water during steaming if necessary. Check for doneness with a toothpick or fork; zucchini should pierce easily. Immediately transfer steamer basket with zucchini to sink. Cover with ice and run cold water over all until the zucchini is completely cool—2 to 3 minutes. Strain zucchini in a food mill or puree in a food processor fitted with the steel blade. No additional liquid is required.

Makes 12 to 14 1-ounce or heaped tablespoon baby servings.

Microwave Directions: Place zucchini rounds in a microwave-safe dish. Add ¼ cup water and cover tightly with plastic wrap, pulling back one corner to vent. Microwave on HIGH for 3 minutes, stir thoroughly, re-cover, and cook for 2 to 4 minutes or until tender. Check for doneness and proceed with recipe.

For Bigger Babies (over 10 months): Steamed zucchini rounds (and spears) also make great finger foods.

ZUCCHINI

Introduce zucchini at 8 months.

Nutritional Profile: vitamins A and C; potassium.

Select firm, small to medium-size zucchini with bright, shiny, unblemished green skins. Store in refrigerator in a plastic bag and use within a few days.

Zucchini with Garlic and Parmesan

1 tablespoon virgin olive oil
2 garlic cloves, peeled and minced
2 medium-size zucchini, sliced and steamed as directed in preceding recipe
$\frac{1}{4}$ cup freshly grated Parmesan cheese

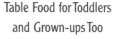

Table Food for Toddlers
and Grown-ups Too

Place olive oil in a sauté pan over medium heat. Add garlic and stir until aroma of garlic is pronounced, but don't let the garlic burn. Add zucchini to pan and continue cooking for 3 minutes or until heated through. Sprinkle with Parmesan cheese and serve.

Makes 4 grown-up servings.

Avocado Puree

Primary Purees

Avocado flesh browns when exposed to the air. But if it's consumed within a reasonable amount of time (2 hours), browning does not affect its nutritional value. When your baby is big enough (10 months), a squeeze of lemon juice will keep it bright. The following guacamole recipe makes use of the leftover avocado half.

½ ripe avocado, peeled and pitted

In a small bowl, mash avocado flesh with a fork, adding a little formula or other liquid to adjust consistency.

Makes about ½ cup puree or 4 1-ounce baby portions.

For Bigger Babies (over 10 months): Avocado spears make great finger food. (This shape makes its slippery flesh easier for baby to hang on to.)

Variations: High in nutrients, avocado is a good fortifier. Mix it with butternut or acorn squash purees, any fruit puree, or yogurt.

AVOCADO

Introduce avocados at 9 months.

Nutritional Profile: vitamins A and C; potassium.

Select avocados with unbroken skins that are heavy for their size. Ripe avocados are soft to the touch and fragrant. Ripen hard ones at room temperature on your windowsill. Store ripe avocados in your refrigerator. Although the shiny green avocados look inviting, try the bumpy, thick-skinned black Haas variety from California; they have more flavor. Avocados will keep in the vegetable drawer of the refrigerator from 10 days to 2 weeks.

Avocados grow into handsome houseplants. Help your toddler plant an avocado pit in a glass, suspending half the pit above the water line with toothpicks. He can water and watch it grow.

Guacamole

When mashing up half an avocado for your baby, turn the other half into a quick avocado dip for everyone else. This dip is so popular in our house, we always add another avocado to the bowl—just to be sure there's enough to go around.

Table Food for Toddlers
and Grown-ups Too

1^1/$_2$ ripe avocados, peeled and pitted
1^1/$_2$ tablespoons freshly squeezed lemon juice
^{1}/$_2$ teaspoon minced onion
1 small garlic clove, minced
1 4-ounce can green chilies, drained and chopped (optional)
Tabasco sauce to taste (a few drops go a long way)
^{1}/$_8$ teaspoon salt
^{1}/$_4$ cup yogurt or sour cream (optional)
1 small tomato, diced
Corn chips or vegetable dippers

Mash avocado flesh with a fork until smooth. Add lemon juice, onion, garlic, chilies, Tabasco sauce, and salt. Mix well, adjust seasonings to taste, and let sit, covered, for 30 minutes in your refrigerator to blend flavors.

To serve: Garnish with a large dollop of yogurt or sour cream, if using, and chopped tomatoes. Accompany with corn chips or vegetable dippers.

Makes 2 cups.

Asparagus

Dining on asparagus may make your baby's diaper smell of this veggie. Don't be alarmed; it's perfectly natural.

Primary Purees

1 bunch asparagus (about ³/₄ pound), washed, and tough ends cut or snapped off, lower stalks peeled

Put prepared asparagus in a steamer basket set in a pot containing a small amount of lightly boiling water. Cover tightly (for better nutrient retention) and steam for 6 to 8 minutes for thin asparagus or 10 to 11 minutes for thick, replenishing water during steaming if necessary. Have ready a bowl of ice water. Check asparagus for doneness with a fork; they should pierce very easily. When cooked, immediately remove steamer basket with asparagus and plunge into ice water, reserving steaming liquid. Run cold water over all until asparagus are completely cool—2 to 3 minutes. Strain asparagus in a food mill or puree in a food processor fitted with the steel blade. Add 2 to 4 tablespoons steaming liquid to the puree, adjusting consistency according to age and preference of your baby.

Microwave Directions: Place prepared asparagus in a microwave-safe dish. Add ¹/₄ cup water and cover tightly with plastic wrap, pulling back one corner to vent. Microwave on HIGH for 6 to 7 minutes or until tender. Cool and proceed with recipe.

Makes 8 to 10 1-ounce or heaped tablespoon baby servings.

For Bigger Babies (over 10 months): Asparagus make great finger food when they are cooked slightly *al dente*. To achieve this, subtract 2 minutes from the stove-top steaming time above and 1 minute from the microwave directions.

ASPARAGUS

Introduce asparagus at 9 months.

Nutritional Profile: vitamins A, B complex, and C; potassium and iron. (White asparagus, considered a delicacy, has not been exposed to sunlight and is thought to contain fewer vitamins.)

April is asparagus month. Although the season stretches on, this is when the shoots are most tender. Select asparagus with tightly closed tips and fresh, firm, dark green stalks with no shriveling at the base. Like most stem vegetables (green beans and broccoli included), asparagus loses its natural sugar quickly after being picked, so consume it as soon as possible. Refrigerate in a plastic bag until cooking time.

Sweet Beets

Beets come out the same color as they go in, so don't be alarmed if they stain your baby's diaper.

1 bunch of beets (approximately 6) with 1 inch of tops left on, washed

Place whole beets in a steamer basket set over a full pot of lightly boiling water. Cover tightly (for better nutrient retention) and steam for 45 to 60 minutes or until beets are tender, replenishing water during steaming if necessary. Check for doneness with a toothpick or fork; beets should pierce easily. Remove beets from heat. Cool slightly and slip skins off with fingers or a paring knife. (Wear rubber gloves for this last step, or you're in for crimson fingers.) Finish cooling. Strain beets in a food mill or puree in a food processor fitted with the steel blade.

Makes 16 to 20 1-ounce or heaped tablespoon baby servings.

Oven Method: Beets can be baked in their jackets just like potatoes. Preheat oven to 350 degrees. Scrub, trim, and pierce beets. Rub lightly with vegetable oil and wrap in aluminum foil, leaving stem ends showing. Place beets on a pan in the oven. Bake until tender, about 45 minutes, depending on size. Check for doneness. Remove skins and proceed with recipe.

Variation: Pair pureed beets with applesauce or sweet potato. They're unbeatable combinations.

For Bigger Babies (over 10 months): Cooked beet slices or spears make great finger foods. If they're lush and beautiful, don't throw the beet greens away. They're both delicious and nutritious. Rinse and roughly chop stems and leaves, then cook and season as you would spinach.

Primary Purees

BEETS

Introduce beets at 10 months; beet greens at 11 months.

Nutritional Profile: vitamin C; potassium. Beet greens and stalks are a great source of vitamin A.

Choose smallish firm beets with smooth skins and, if attached, fresh-looking (unwilted) green leaves. Cut off stalks (2 inches above beet, so red color doesn't bleed out during cooking) and store beets and leaves in plastic bags in your refrigerator. Use beet greens immediately. The beetroots will keep for about 3 weeks.

Broccoli Puree

Primary Purees

BROCCOLI

Introduce broccoli at 10 months.

Nutritional Profile: vitamins C and A; calcium.

Choose broccoli that is firm with a compact, dark green top. Flowerets should not be opened or yellow. Stalks and greens should show no signs of withering. Broccoli is available all year but is at its peak from fall through spring. Store in a plastic bag in your refrigerator for up to 4 days.

Broccoli is a great source of nutrition! One medium stalk provides 20 percent of your child's daily requirement of vitamin C and 15 percent of vitamin A (in the form of betacarotene). Broccoli is also an excellent source of potassium and calcium and sulphoraphane, a phytochemical that may potentially reduce the risk of cancer.

Broccoli can cause gas in babies.

Steamed broccoli flowerets make great finger food and good "dunkers" for dips and sauces. You don't have to discard the stalks in this recipe. Instead you can peel them, slice them into rounds, and steam and puree them with the flowerets. If the stems are thick, halve them lengthwise first, then slice them for more even cooking.

1 bunch of broccoli, stalks removed and head separated into medium-small flowerets

Place broccoli flowerets in a steamer basket set in a pot filled with a small amount of lightly boiling water. Cover tightly (for better nutrient retention) and cook for 8 to 11 minutes or until the flowerets are tender, replenishing water during steaming if necessary. Have ready a large bowl of ice water. Check for doneness with a toothpick or fork; stem section of floweret should pierce easily. Immediately remove steamer basket with broccoli and plunge into ice water. Run cold water over all until the broccoli is completely cool—2 to 3 minutes. Puree broccoli in a food processor fitted with the steel blade. (Broccoli does not puree well in a food mill. If used, you will need to pass it through the mill a few times to achieve a smooth consistency.) Usually no additional liquid is required.

Makes 14 to 16 1-ounce or heaped tablespoon baby servings.

Microwave Directions: Place prepared broccoli flowerets in a microwave-safe dish. Add $1/4$ cup water and cover tightly with plastic wrap, pulling back one corner to vent. Microwave on HIGH for 3 minutes, stir thoroughly, re-cover, and cook for 3 to 5 minutes or until tender. Check for doneness as above and proceed with recipe.

For Toddlers (over 1 year): Use any leftover broccoli puree to make Basic Cream Soup (page 214).

Stuffed Spudniks

For the littlest eaters, simply mash plain baked potato with a bit of formula and serve. For bigger babies, after the potato halves are stuffed, make potato faces with steamed carrot strip smiles, frozen green pea eyes, and parsley hair before final heating.

Table Food for Toddlers
and Grown-ups Too

1 baking potato, baked* and halved
2 slices Black Forest ham, chopped
¼ cup grated Swiss cheese
¼ cup sour cream or yogurt
1 teaspoon chopped fresh parsley
garnish: steamed carrot strips, peas, parsley (optional)

Preheat oven to 350 degrees. Scoop potato flesh carefully out of skin, leaving it intact. Set skins aside and mash potato in a small bowl. Add ham, cheese, sour cream, and parsley and mix well. Stuff back into potato halves and chill. Decorate the potatoes as described above with the optional garnishes. To serve, heat for 5 to 7 minutes in the oven. (Or microwave on HIGH for 1 or 2 minutes.)

Makes 2 grown-up servings.

*To bake potato, scrub, puncture in a few places with a fork, and place in a preheated 350-degree oven for 1 hour or until potato pierces easily with a fork.

Variations: Instead of ham and Swiss, try these stuffing suggestions:

- chopped broccoli flowerets
- grated Cheddar cheese
- chopped spinach
- corn niblets, peas, and red pepper cubes
- chopped asparagus and freshly grated Parmesan cheese
- crumbled bacon and chopped hard-cooked eggs
- sautéed onions and mushrooms
- steamed zucchini
- sautéed ground beef, shredded green pepper, and diced onion

Potato Pancakes

These are the very best potato pancakes. Serve them hot with home-made applesauce, pages 116–18, or sour cream. Purists grate the potatoes and onions by hand, but a food processor is quicker and the results just as tasty. For a little variety, add grated carrot and/or zuc-chini.

4 large potatoes, peeled and eyes removed
1 large onion, peeled
2 eggs, beaten
Kosher salt to taste
2 tablespoons flour
Vegetable oil for frying

Cut potatoes and onion in large chunks (eighths) and grate in a food processor. Place in a large bowl. Add eggs, salt, and flour and mix together. Immediately fry by the generous spoonful in a little oil. (The potatoes will turn black if you let the mixture sit too long.)

Makes 4 grown-up servings.

POTATOES

Introduce potatoes at 11 months.

Nutritional Profile: vitamin C and B_6; potassium.

Select unblemished potatoes. Avoid spongy, greenish, or sprouting ones; they will be bitter. It is not necessary to refrigerate potatoes. In a cool, dry place, most varieties will keep for about 3 weeks. (New potatoes are an exception. Buy them in small quanti-ties and use as soon as possible. They will lose their sweet flavor after a few days.)

Potato-Parsnip Puree

Parsnips are root vegetables with a unique but very pleasing flavor due in part to their high sugar content. Parsnips make a great addition to almost any soup. And freezing does not injure them. In fact, some growers believe it improves their flavor. Try parsnips alone or as a side dish or decorative "frosting" for Marvelous Meat Loaf (page 178).

3 medium potatoes, peeled and quartered
2 small parsnips, peeled and quartered
salt and freshly ground pepper to taste
2 tablespoons unsalted butter
$1/2$ to $3/4$ cup warm milk

Place potatoes and parsnips in a medium saucepan. Cover with cold water and bring to a boil over high heat. Reduce heat to medium and simmer for 15 to 20 minutes or until vegetables are tender. Drain and, while still hot, rice parsnips and potatoes by passing through a food mill or mash by hand in a large bowl. Add salt and pepper to taste and butter. Mix well, adding $1/2$ to $3/4$ cup warmed milk in three stages, whipping after each addition, until desired consistency is reached. (Milk can be warmed quickly in your microwave oven.) Check seasoning and adjust if necessary. Serve puree immediately or use to cover or pipe around meat loaf.

Makes 3 to $3^1/2$ cups to serve 10.

Spoon and Finger Food
for Bigger Babies

PARSNIPS

Introduce parsnips at 11 months.

Nutritional Profile: vitamin C; potassium and calcium.

Select small, smooth parsnips. Parsnips will keep in a plastic bag in your refrigerator for up to a month. They are at their peak from October through January.

Spinach

■ ■

Spoon and Finger Food
for Bigger Babies

Fresh spinach can be gritty, especially if it is harvested after a heavy rain. To clean, soak leaves in cold water and carefully remove them so sand remains in bottom of bowl or sink. You may have to repeat the process. This recipe can be enjoyed as is or creamed. To cream, finely chop the cooked spinach and mix tablespoon-for-tablespoon with plain yogurt.

$2/3$ pound fresh spinach, picked over, stalks removed, and leaves carefully
washed in cold water, *or* 1 10-ounce package frozen

Place wet (the water clinging to the leaves is sufficient), cleaned spinach in a pot. Cover and cook over medium heat, just until leaves are wilted—2 to 3 minutes. Drain spinach and squeeze out excess moisture. Finely chop in the food processor fitted with the steel blade or with a knife on the cutting board.

Using frozen spinach: thaw in the microwave, in a steam tray, or at room temperature. Drain and squeeze out excess moisture. Finely chop and cook as above.

Makes 10 1-ounce or heaped tablespoon baby servings.

Microwave Directions: Place prepared spinach in a large microwave-safe dish. Add $1/4$ cup water and cover tightly with plastic wrap, pulling back one corner to vent. Microwave on HIGH for 3 to 4 minutes or until leaves are wilted. Cool slightly and proceed with recipe.

SPINACH

Introduce spinach at 11 months.

▲

Nutritional Profile: vitamins A and C; potassium. (Popeye to the contrary, spinach is not tremendously high in iron.)

●

Look for loose, unpackaged spinach with dark green, unblemished leaves. Fresh spinach is available year-round. Refrigerate in a plastic bag, and use within 2 to 3 days.

Cauliflower Puree

Steamed cauliflower flowerets make great finger food for older babies and handy dunkers for dips and sauces.

½ head of cauliflower, separated into medium-small flowerets

Place cauliflower in a steamer basket set in a pot filled with a small amount of lightly boiling water. Cover tightly (for better nutrient retention) and cook for 10 to 12 minutes or until flowerets are tender, replenishing water during steaming if necessary. Check for doneness with a toothpick or fork; stem section should pierce easily. Immediately transfer steamer basket with cauliflower to sink and run cold water over all until cauliflower is completely cool—2 to 3 minutes. Puree cauliflower in a food processor fitted with the steel blade. (Cauliflower does not puree well in a food mill.) Usually no additional liquid is required.

Makes 10 to 12 1-ounce or heaped tablespoon baby servings.

Microwave Directions: Place cauliflower flowerets in a microwave-safe dish. Add ¼ cup water and cover tightly with plastic wrap, pulling back one corner to vent. Microwave on HIGH for 4 minutes, stir thoroughly, re-cover, and cook for 4 to 6 minutes or until tender. Check for doneness and proceed with recipe.

Primary Purees

CAULIFLOWER

Introduce cauliflower at 12 months.

Nutritional Profile: vitamins C and B complex; potassium.

Look for cauliflower with creamy white, clean, firm, compact curds. (The flowered ends are called *curds.)* Avoid spotted or speckled heads with brown areas, indicating bruises. Cauliflower is available year-round but is at its peak in late fall through spring.

Keep cauliflower cold and humid—place in a plastic bag with a damp paper towel in your refrigerator. Use within 5 days.

Steamed Artichokes

Artichoke leaves with a flavorful dipping sauce (see pages 273–283) make a fine finger food for toddlers who are old enough to mimic Mom and Dad pulling the fleshy end of the leaf between their front teeth. Even smaller children can enjoy the pureed heart. With a spoon, clean choke and thistle from cooked heart and place in the food processor with a little of the steaming liquid. Puree until the desired consistency is reached. The very small artichokes, if they are available in your supermarket, can be eaten whole.

2 large artichokes, washed, stem trimmed level with base, and small leaves
    around stem removed
1 lemon, halved

With a knife, cut about 1 inch off the artichoke top. Then, using scissors, cut the spiked tips off the remaining leaves. (This will prevent a toddler or an adult from getting pricked.) Run cold water into the artichoke to spread leaves apart. Rub all cut parts with cut lemon to prevent discoloration. Set prepared artichokes upright in a steamer basket set in a pot containing a small amount of lightly boiling water. Cover tightly (for better nutrient retention) and steam for 35 to 45 minutes, depending on size of artichokes, replenishing water during steaming if necessary. Check for doneness with a knife; the artichoke base should pierce easily. Remove artichokes from steamer basket. If you want to serve them cold, allow to cool at room temperature.

Makes 2 artichokes or 6 to 8 heaped tablespoon baby portions.

ARTICHOKES

Introduce pureed artichoke heart at 12 months; artichoke leaves at 2 years or older.

Nutritional Profile: vitamins A and C; potassium and calcium.

When purchasing, look for unblemished, heavy, grayish-green globes with fresh, crisp leaves on tightly closed heads. Artichokes are in season from March through May. A later fall crop has purple-tinged leaves, which is natural. To store, sprinkle artichokes lightly with water or wrap in a damp towel and place in a plastic bag in your refrigerator. They will keep for approximately 1 week.

Fresh Lima Bean Puree

If you're lucky enough to find good, fresh limas in your market, you'll love this puree. If not, frozen limas work equally well. Just follow the package directions for stove or microwave preparation and proceed with the recipe. Teamed with rice, mushrooms, or sesame seeds, lima beans become a complete protein and a healthy substitute for red meat.

1 pound fresh lima beans, washed and hulled just before cooking

Place hulled lima beans in a steamer basket set in a pot filled with a small amount of lightly boiling water. Cover tightly (for better nutrient retention) and steam for 9 to 12 minutes or until limas are tender, replenishing water during steaming if necessary. Have ready a large bowl of ice water. Check for doneness with a toothpick or fork; limas should pierce easily. Immediately remove steamer basket with limas and plunge into ice water. Run cold water over all until lima beans are completely cool—2 to 3 minutes. Set cooking liquid aside to cool. Strain limas in a food mill or puree in a food processor fitted with the steel blade. Add about 1/4 cup reserved cooking liquid to puree, adjusting consistency according to age and preference of your baby.

Makes 8 to 10 1-ounce or heaped tablespoon baby servings.

Microwave Directions: Place washed and hulled limas in a microwave-safe dish. Add 1/4 cup water and cover tightly with plastic wrap, pulling back one corner to vent. Microwave on HIGH for 3 minutes, stir lima beans thoroughly, re-cover, and cook for 3 to 5 minutes or until tender. Check for doneness, cool, and proceed with recipe.

Primary Purees

LIMA BEANS

Introduce lima beans at 12 months.

Nutritional Profile: vitamin B complex; magnesium, iron, and zinc.

Fresh lima beans are in limited supply and are highly perishable. Select well-filled pods with bright skins. (Avoid the shelled, packaged fresh limas that are sometimes available. They are usually dyed and have little flavor.) Store fresh lima beans in the refrigerator and use as soon as possible.

Tomato Sauce

■ ■

Basic marinara, plain and simple, to top your pizza or favorite pasta. For added dash, try the herb, meat, and sweet and savory variations that follow.

Table Food for Toddlers and Grown-ups Too

2 tablespoons virgin olive oil
1 medium onion, finely chopped
1 large garlic clove, minced
2 tablespoons tomato paste
1 28-ounce can crushed tomatoes
1 15-ounce can tomato sauce
1 small bay leaf
$\frac{1}{2}$ teaspoon salt (optional)
$\frac{1}{2}$ teaspoon freshly ground pepper (optional)

Heat olive oil in a $2\frac{1}{2}$-quart sauce pan over medium heat for 1 minute. Add onion and cook, stirring occasionally, for 5 to 6 minutes or until onion is translucent. Add garlic and cook, stirring constantly, for 1 minute longer or until garlic aroma is evident. Reduce heat to low, add tomato paste, and cook for 4 to 5 minutes, stirring frequently. Add crushed tomatoes, tomato sauce, bay leaf, and salt and pepper if desired. Bring to a boil. Reduce heat to low and simmer for 30 minutes, stirring occasionally.

Makes 1 quart.

Variations: To make tomato sauce with herbs, add the following to the sauce during last 30 minutes of cooking:

1 tablespoon chopped fresh parsley *or* 1 teaspoon dried
2 teaspoons chopped fresh basil *or* $\frac{1}{2}$ teaspoon dried
1 teaspoon chopped fresh oregano *or* $\frac{1}{4}$ teaspoon dried

To make meat sauce, which is great on wagon wheel noodles or in lasagne, add the following:

TOMATOES

Tomatoes are high in acid; introduce after 1 year and watch for signs of gastric irritation.

Nutritional Profile: vitamin C; potassium.

Store tomatoes at room temperature until they reach desired degree of ripeness, then refrigerate. Out of season, fresh tomatoes are disappointing, to say the least, which is why our basic sauce specifies canned tomatoes.

2 tablespoons virgin olive oil
1 pound ground beef (preferably round)

Sauté beef in olive oil until no longer pink and fat is rendered. Drain. Add cooked beef with herbs to basic sauce during last 30 minutes of cooking.

To make sweet and savory tomato sauce, especially good on meat loaf, add the following:

1 medium carrot, diced
½ cup chicken broth
¼ cup golden raisins
½ teaspoon dried marjoram

Add above to basic sauce during last 30 minutes of cooking.

Sweet Red Pepper Puree

Although the consistency of this puree is suitable for little ones, sweet red pepper puree is quite intense and should be combined with other foods. It's delicious and pretty on pasta, makes a bright dipping sauce, and Teddi at 3 loved it spread on her egg salad sandwich. And, most important, it's the base for the terrific tomatoless marinara sauce that follows. If you're not used to peeling peppers, it may seem like a fuss, but actually it's very easy to do and gives the pepper flesh a wonderful deep taste.

2 large red bell peppers, washed and dried

Preheat broiler for 8 to 10 minutes with rack set 6 to 7 inches from heat. Line roasting pan with aluminum foil. Put peppers on pan and place under broiler. Roast peppers for 12 to 15 minutes or until skin is charred and begins to split. (Be sure to turn frequently to ensure even roasting.) Remove pan from broiler and carefully loosen foil from pan. Wrap peppers loosely in foil and allow to cool. (Steam trapped by the foil wrapping will make the peppers easier to peel.) When cool, remove skin by peeling off with your fingers. Cut skinned peppers in half. Remove stem and seeds. Cut into 1- to 2-inch pieces and puree in a blender, or small food processor fitted with the steel blade, for 45 seconds or until smooth, scraping down sides of container once or twice.

Makes 1½ cups.

Spoon and Finger Food for Bigger Babies

BELL PEPPERS

Introduce bell peppers at 12 months.

Nutritional Profile: vitamins A and C; iron and potassium.

Sweet bell peppers are available in a variety of bright hues: green, red, yellow, and purple. The Spanish pimentos—which have pointed tips—are the sweetest; green ones the least sweet. The red, yellow, and purple shades are simply allowed to ripen longer on the "vine," and you pay dearly for this in the market. Select firm, crisp peppers without dark or soft spots. Store in your refrigerator in perforated plastic bags for 2 to 3 weeks. Peppers peak May through December.

No-Tomato Marinara Sauce

Table Food for Toddlers
and Grown-ups Too

We developed this recipe for a family whose members love tomato sauce but are terribly allergic to tomatoes. On tasting, they couldn't believe there were no tomato products in this sauce—then they couldn't believe how good it is. We think you'll agree. This sauce can be used in place of tomato sauce in almost any recipe except stuffed peppers. Try it in our Chickpea and Spinach Casserole (page 201).

2 tablespoons virgin olive oil
1 medium onion, finely diced
1 garlic clove, minced
3 cups Sweet Red Pepper Puree (double preceding recipe)
1 tablespoon finely chopped fresh parsley
$1/4$ teaspoon dried oregano
$1/4$ teaspoon dried basil
$1/4$ teaspoon salt
$1/4$ teaspoon freshly ground pepper

Heat olive oil in a saucepan over medium-high heat for 2 minutes. Add onion and sauté, stirring frequently, until very soft—8 to 9 minutes. Add garlic and cook for 1 minute or until garlic aroma is pronounced. Add red pepper puree and herbs. Season with salt and pepper. Bring to a simmer, stirring frequently. Then reduce heat to low and partially cover pot to allow steam to escape. Continue cooking for 15 to 20 minutes, stirring frequently. (Be careful when stirring sauce; it tends to spurt.)

Makes $2^{1}/_{2}$ cups.

Garden Variety Pizza

This makes 1 large 16-inch pizza for sharing or 4 individual 6-inch pizzas that you can customize for your customers. For example: if the acidity in tomato sauce irritates your baby, any vegetable puree is a delicious substitute. Vary the vegetables by adding steamed chopped broccoli, sliced onions, mushrooms, etc. Tired of garden-variety pizza? Try beefing it up with sautéed ground beef, cooked shrimp, shredded roast turkey, or grated Cheddar cheese.

1 recipe Pizza Crust dough (page 159) or store-bought

1 cup Tomato Sauce (page 154) or store-bought

1 red bell pepper, cored, seeds removed, thinly sliced

1 small zucchini, trimmed, cut into rounds, and steamed (see page 140)

1 4-ounce square of very cold cream cheese, cut crosswise into thin strips

1 1/2 cups grated mozzarella cheese

2 tablespoons freshly grated Parmesan cheese (optional)

1/4 cup chopped fresh herbs such as basil and oregano *or* 1/2 teaspoon dried (optional)

Preheat oven to 425 degrees. Punch down dough, form into a ball, and roll into a 1/2-inch-thick circle on a floured surface. With your fingertips, press dough from center to outside edge, leaving it thicker at the outside edge. Place in a 16-inch-diameter pizza pan and additionally stretch and press to fit into pan. Top with tomato sauce, vegetables, cheeses, and herbs if desired. Bake for 25 to 30 minutes or until crust is browned and cheese is melted. Let pizza sit for 10 minutes before serving.

Makes 1 16-inch pizza or 4 6-inch pizzas.

Pizza Crust

For a heartier, healthier crust, substitute 1 cup whole-wheat flour for 1 cup of the white flour. If using all white flour, be sure to purchase the more nutritious unbleached product.

3/4 teaspoon salt
2 tablespoons virgin olive oil plus 1 scant teaspoon more to oil the bowl
1 teaspoon sugar
1 cup lukewarm water
2 1/4 teaspoons active dry yeast (one envelope)
2 1/2 cups unbleached all-purpose flour

In a medium bowl, combine salt, 2 tablespoons olive oil, sugar, and water. Sprinkle yeast on surface and let stand until yeast is dissolved. Add flour and mix with a wooden spoon or hands until a soft ball is formed. (You may have to add a few more drops of water if dough is too stiff.)* Turn out dough on a lightly floured work surface and knead until smooth and elastic—about 5 minutes. Place in a large bowl lightly coated with remaining oil. Cover with plastic wrap and put in a warm place to rise. (The top of an unlit gas stove, your clothes dryer, or even a sunny window on a warm day is a good spot.) Allow dough to double in size. This will take about 30 minutes or longer.

Punch dough down. Roll into a ball** and return to bowl, re-cover with plastic wrap, and store in refrigerator for up to 8 hours. Remove from refrigerator 30 minutes before using.

Makes enough dough for 1 16-inch or 4 6-inch pizzas.

*The dough can be prepared in work bowl of your food processor up to this point, using the steel blade.

**If making individual pizzas, cut ball into quarters and store separately on a covered cookie sheet in the refrigerator.

FRESH, COOL, AND EASY—SALAD

Salad makes a great, quickly prepared meal or snack for baby once he gets his back teeth. (Molars are needed to break down fibrous lettuce leaves.) Nutritionally, lettuce contains good amounts of vitamin C and A and some vitamin B. Its composition is mostly water, but 1 percent is protein. Lettuce is an aid to the digestive system too. (It helps clear the intestinal tract.) Greens are also an excellent source of folic acid.

Salad can be more than just greens. Sprouts mixed with cottage cheese was our younger daughter's favorite first raw green. Another popular salad with both of our girls and many of our customers is Cool Cukes with Yogurt, Dill, and Sour Cream (page 162). And leftover steamed peas in a nest of shredded carrots make everyone in our family smile.

Choose bright, fresh-looking greens that are young and tender. Avoid dry or wilted leaves that are yellowed or have brown edges. Store greens in the crisper drawer of your refrigerator in separate plastic bags. We don't wash our lettuce until we are ready to use it. But if you do, be sure the leaves are completely dry before bagging, as moisture on them will cause rot. Salad spinners are great for removing moisture clinging to greens. Spreading the leaves on paper towels or a clean dish towel and patting them dry also works.

There's more to salad than iceberg lettuce. Although it's a good keeper, here are some fresh ideas to get you going:

- arugula
- Belgian endive
- Bibb lettuce
- Boston lettuce
- chicory
- curly endive
- dandelion greens
- escarole
- limestone lettuce
- red leaf lettuce
- romaine
- spinach
- watercress
- Chinese cabbage

Toss your greens with any of the following for more interest and excitement:

- asparagus (leftover, steamed)
- avocado (slices)
- artichoke hearts
- cucumbers (peeled and sliced)
- canned water chestnuts (drained and sliced)
- onion (thinly sliced and soaked in cold water for 15 minutes)
- celery (sliced or chopped)
- carrot (sliced or shredded)
- sprouts (any type)

- radishes (sliced)
- mushrooms (sliced)
- zucchini (thinly sliced)
- yellow squash (thinly sliced)
- bell peppers, any color (thin strips)
- tomatoes (diced or quartered, depending on size)
- hard-cooked eggs (quartered)
- orange or grapefruit sections
- seedless grapes (halved)
- pickles (chopped)
- raisins
- dates (diced)
- tofu (cubed)

- pitted olives (halved or chopped)
- cooked beets (sliced)
- cooked beans (chickpeas, kidney, etc.)
- peas (steamed fresh or frozen)
- corn niblets (steamed fresh or frozen)
- cheese (cubes, strips, or grated)
- cabbage (shredded)
- cauliflower and broccoli flowerets (steamed, leftover)

Cool Cukes with Yogurt, Dill, and Sour Cream

Table Food for Toddlers and Grown-ups Too

A cooling salad with crunch that's appropriate for toddlers and the rest of the family. The salt in this recipe is used to draw out the natural moisture from the cucumber. If desired, this recipe can be prepared without salt. Just omit the salting and subsequent weighting and rinsing steps.

1 large cucumber
1 tablespoon kosher or sea salt
1 tablespoon snipped fresh dill
$\frac{1}{4}$ cup sour cream
$\frac{1}{4}$ cup plain yogurt

Peel cucumber. Halve lengthwise and remove all seeds with a spoon. Cut each half crosswise into $\frac{1}{8}$-inch slices. Place in medium-sized bowl. Sprinkle evenly with salt. Place plate on top of cucumbers and weight plate down with a heavy can or brick (at least 2 pounds). Let rest in refrigerator for 1 hour. Rinse slices thoroughly in a strainer under cold running water. Drain well. Add dill, sour cream, and yogurt. Mix well and chill.

Makes 4 grown-up salad servings.

CUCUMBERS

Introduce cucumbers at 12 months.

Nutritional Profile: vitamin C; iron and potassium.

Select firm green cucumbers with un-waxed skins—if you can find them. (The wax does not wash off readily, but it is edible.) Store in your refrigerator and use as soon as possible.

Vitamin C "See You When You're Feeling Better" Salad

1 papaya, peeled, seeded, and cut into small chunks
½ cantaloupe, skinned, seeded, and cut into small chunks
2 oranges, peeled, seeded, and sectioned
2 kiwifruits, peeled and sliced
1 pint strawberries, hulls removed, halved
6 tablespoons frozen unsweetened pineapple juice concentrate, thawed
2 cups plain or vanilla yogurt

Combine all of the fruit in a large bowl. (Set aside a few slices of kiwifruit and strawberries for garnish.) Mix juice and yogurt together to make a sauce. Divide mixed fruits among serving dishes and spoon some sauce over each. Top each serving with a strawberry and kiwifruit slice.

Makes 6 grown-up servings.

Variations: For even more vitamin C, add any of the following:

- grapefruit sections
- blackberries
- blueberries
- cherries (halved and pitted)

Table Food for Toddlers
and Grown-ups Too

Poultry

Chicken Little

Primary Purees

When you need just a little chicken puree. For a nice creamy texture, use a generous hand when adding poaching liquid to the puree.

1 whole boneless chicken breast (about ³/₄ pound)

Bring a pot of water to a rolling boil. Remove any remaining skin, bones, and fat from the chicken breast and cut the meat into ³/₄-inch pieces. Add chicken to pot. Lower heat and simmer gently for approximately 8 minutes or until chicken is cooked through. Strain and reserve cooking liquid. Puree chicken dry in food processor fitted with the steel blade for 1 minute, then slowly add enough of the reserved cooking liquid until a smooth, creamy texture is achieved. (The longer you puree, the smoother the texture.)

Makes 12 to 14 1-ounce or heaped tablespoon baby servings.

Microwave Directions: Place prepared chicken in microwave-safe dish. Add ¹/₄ cup water and cover dish with plastic wrap, pulling back one corner to vent. Microwave on MEDIUM-HIGH for 6 to 8 minutes or until the chicken is cooked through.

Variations: For a complete dinner in a dish, mix 1 or 2 table-spoons of any of the following with ¹/₄ cup chicken puree:

- $^1/_2$ cooked carrot, pureed
- cooked pea puree
- cooked pasta puree
- cooked brown or basmati rice or kasha puree

Or, for one-pot cooking: Cut into chunks 1 skinned and boned chicken breast. Place in a pot with 1 carrot, peeled and cut into rounds. Add 2 cups water. Cover and cook for 8 minutes over medium heat. Add a handful of frozen peas and a handful of pre-cooked, frozen noodles (see Oodles of Noodles, page 193) to the pot and continue cooking for 4 minutes. Puree contents (with liquid) in a food processor fitted with the steel blade. Add water or chicken broth to thin if necessary.

Tarragon Roast Chicken with Root Vegetables

Table Food for Toddlers
and Grown-ups Too

A household favorite that we all enjoy. (A version for the littlest one is included.) It's the easiest way to get our chicks to eat chicken; the aroma is irresistible! The chicken skin on this roast is golden, crisp, and tempting, but for health reasons we don't serve it to anyone but our cat. And be sure to thoroughly wash the cutting board on which chicken was prepared to avoid infecting other foods with salmonella bacteria.

1 roasting chicken (about 4 to 5 pounds)
10 whole garlic cloves, peeled
4 fresh tarragon sprigs *or* a good pinch of dried
2 medium onions, peeled and quartered
6 to 8 carrots, peeled, halved, and quartered
3 medium potatoes, peeled and quartered
1/4 teaspoon salt (optional)
1/2 teaspoon freshly ground pepper (optional)
1 teaspoon paprika (optional)

Preheat oven to 450 degrees. Remove neck and giblets; rinse chicken inside and out with cold water. Drain cavity and pat dry with a towel. (Refrigerate raw liver for baby's dinner tomorrow; see recipe for Chicken Liver and Avocado puree; page 167.) Stuff chicken with garlic and tarragon and, if desired, truss with butcher's twine. Place chicken in a shallow roasting pan and arrange cut-up vegetables around it. Sprinkle with salt, pepper, and paprika if desired. Place chicken in the oven and immediately reduce the heat to 350 degrees. Roast for approximately 20 minutes per pound, being sure to briskly shake the roasting pan occasionally so the vegetables don't stick to the bottom and brown nicely on all sides.

Makes 6 grown-up servings.

For Babies (Under 1 year): A slice or 2 of chicken breast from the family's bird is perfect for baby's dinner too. Roasted breast meat, however, tends to be drier than poached, so be sure to use enough liquid (low-salt stock, water, or formula) to achieve a nice creamy consistency (see Chicken Little recipe, page 164, for technique). Puree or mash roasted carrots and potatoes and swirl in. Bigger babies will enjoy chunks of roasted vegetables and finely diced chicken as finger foods.

Chicken Liver and Avocado Puree

This recipe makes use of the leftover liver from the Tarragon Roast Chicken with Root Vegetables recipe (page 166). If you use store-bought stock in this recipe, be sure it's low-salt. One mother's trick to get her child to eat liver was to put it on crackers and to present it as an hors d'oeuvre. This is a loving deceit for encouraging your child to eat foods she dislikes or is wary about.

1 chicken liver
2 cups chicken soup (page 216), vegetable stock, or water
1/4 ripe avocado, peeled and pitted

Carefully remove any fat, connective tissue, skin, etc., from the chicken liver. Place in small pot of boiling stock or water. Immediately reduce heat to simmer and cook until tender, about 7 minutes. Do not overcook or cook over too high heat, or the liver will toughen. Drain, reserving cooking liquid. Pass the liver and avocado through a food mill or puree in a small food processor fitted with the steel blade. Add a little cooking liquid or water to achieve a smooth consistency.

Makes 3 to 4 1-ounce or heaped tablespoon baby servings.

Primary Purees

CHICKEN LIVER

Introduce chicken liver at 10 months.

Nutritional Profile: very rich in vitamins A, B complex, and C; protein; iron and copper. Do not serve chicken liver more than once a week; vitamin A is stored by the body and in excess can be toxic.

If purchasing separately, choose plump, shiny, bright livers.

COMMON HERBS AND SPICES AND FOODS THEY ENHANCE

Allspice: beef and lamb roasts and stews; chicken fricassee as well as pot pies; root vegetables and winter squash; pumpkin pie; gingerbread

Anise: beef and veal stews, roast duck, apple pie, baked apple, coffee cake, cookies

Basil: pizza, tomatoes any style, seafood, eggplant, cucumbers, asparagus, eggs, tomato and vegetable juices, pasta

Bay Leaf: beef and lamb stews, chicken fricassee, fish stock, tomato sauce

Caraway: beef and pork stews and roasts, eggs, coleslaw, turnips, potatoes, onions, cabbage, cheese, bread, apple pie, barbecue sauce

Cardamom: curried foods, winter squash, apples

Cayenne: dips, eggs, barbecue sauce, broiled/boiled shellfish, macaroni and cheese

Celery Seed: tomato juice, cheese spreads, eggs, coleslaw, chowders, meat loaf

Chervil: cottage cheese, eggs, shellfish, tomatoes, beets, broiled chicken

Cinnamon: French toast, coffee cake, pumpkin pie, baked apples, rice pudding, winter squashes, sweet potatoes, cranberry juice, raisins

Cloves: corned beef, pork, ham, spiced fruit, beets, carrots, gingerbread

Adding Spice to Baby's Life

Seasonings and seasoned foods can be introduced slowly and sparingly at the end of baby's first year. (We suggest in our classes that parents begin at 10 months.) Herbs and spices are a good way to boost the flavor of food in lieu of salt and sugar. Add herbs and spices to your baby's diet only after solid foods have been introduced systematically and accepted. Delaying seasonings and spices slightly allows your baby's digestive tract to mature enough to tolerate them.

Most spices and herbs work well with mixed greens, salad dressings, eggs, rice, cottage cheese, and vegetables. Be careful not to put flavors together that just don't work because of their uniqueness. Curry, cardamom, mace, turmeric, mint, and saffron are

Coriander: curried foods, mixed greens, spinach, gingerbread, eggs

Cumin: curried foods, meat loaf, cheese spreads

Curry Powder: cheese spreads, eggs, chicken, beef, shellfish, parsnips, carrots, winter squash

Dill: cheese spreads, eggs, fish (salmon) and shellfish, lamb chops or stew, mixed greens, cucumbers

Fennel Seed: Italian sausage, baked and poached fish, shellfish, beef, lamb, pork, cabbage, onions

Ginger: fruit, Asian dishes, carrots, sweet potatoes, baked puddings, chicken, all meats, cantaloupe, gingerbread

Mace: spice cakes; winter squash; lemon, lime, and orange desserts

Marjoram: chopped liver, herb spreads, eggs, cheese spreads, chicken, fish and shellfish, pot roasts and stews, collard greens, turkey, duck

Mint: fruit, lamb, whipped cream, peas, carrots, coleslaw, melon balls

Nutmeg: custard, puddings, pumpkin pie, apple pie, eggnog, beans, corn, spinach

Oregano: pizza, broiled fish, tomato sauce, pork dishes, eggs, cheese spreads, broiled shrimp

Paprika: primarily used as a garnish, fish stuffing, chicken and beef paprikash

Parsley: biscuits, cheese spreads, eggs, chicken dishes, fish and shellfish, stocks, beets, carrots, cauliflower, potatoes, tomatoes, beef, lamb

examples of herbs and spices that don't readily mix with others. Remember too that not all spices are hot; in fact, very few are. Use spices sparingly, but at the same time do not use too little. Great cooking is the result of delicacy, control, and restraint. Experiment and use your imagination. Spices do not change the chemistry of cooking.

In season, fresh herbs are best. Store sprigs and leaves in your refrigerator in plastic bags. Keep dried herbs and spices in a cool, dark spot in your kitchen—away from sunlight and the oven—in well-sealed containers. Check your spices and herbs every season to be sure they have not lost their bouquet. Fresh herbs are less potent than dried, so triple the quantity in recipes when substituting fresh for dried.

Pepper, black: all meat dishes, all egg dishes, all poultry dishes, all seafood dishes, most vegetables

Pepper, white: same as black pepper—use when black specks are not appropriate

Rosemary: eggs, lamb, chicken, stuffings, fish, turkey, scallops, chopped liver

Saffron: chicken, turkey, duck, all fish and shellfish, rice, eggs

Sage: pork, chicken, turkey, stuffing, summer squash and zucchini, corn bread, Cheddar cheese spreads

Tarragon: all egg dishes, chicken, turkey, mixed greens, lamb, tomatoes, carrots, green beans, summer squash

Thyme: all roasts and stews, meat loaf, chicken, fish and shellfish, chowders, eggs, cheese, beets, carrots, potatoes, mushrooms

Turmeric: curried foods, some fish

The Basic Spice Shelf

basil
bay leaf
black pepper
cayenne
celery seed
cinnamon
marjoram
nutmeg
oregano
rosemary
tarragon
thyme

Chicken Pesto Pizza

For pronto pizza, use shredded chicken (or turkey) from yesterday's roast and pesto from the freezer.

Table Food for Toddlers
and Grown-ups Too

1 recipe Pizza Crust dough (page 159) or store-bought
2 tablespoons Summer or Winter Pesto (pages 279–280)
$1/4$ cup cooked chicken, shredded
$1/4$ cup diced tomato
$1/4$ cup grated Jarlsberg cheese
2 teaspoons freshly grated Parmesan cheese

Preheat oven to 425 degrees. Flour work surface and roll dough $1/2$-inch thick. With your fingertips, press dough from center to outside edge, leaving it thicker at outside edge. Place in a 16-inch-diameter pizza pan and additionally stretch and press to fit into pan. Spread pesto evenly over pizza dough and arrange chicken pieces on pesto. Sprinkle on tomatoes, Jarlsberg, and Parmesan and bake for 25 to 30 minutes or until crust is browned and cheese is melted. Let pizza sit for 10 minutes before serving.

Makes 1 16-inch pizza or 4 6-inch pizzas.

Stir-Fry for Small Fry

Table Food for Toddlers
and Grown-ups Too

Children love the bright colors, textures, and bite-size pieces of stir-fried foods. This recipe calls for chicken, but it can also be made with beef. Just use any tender cut of beef (boneless rib eye, strip steak, or top round), cut into thin strips. Reduce cooking time by 1 minute and use only 1 tablespoon of peanut oil to cook the beef. (The chicken absorbs more oil in the cooking process.) This recipe is prepared in a frying pan, but use a wok if you own one.

2 scallions, thinly sliced
1 garlic clove, minced
1 teaspoon minced fresh gingerroot
2 tablespoons soy sauce
2 tablespoons hoisin sauce
2 tablespoons water
$1/4$ teaspoon light sesame oil
3 tablespoons peanut oil
$3/4$ pound (1 large) skinless, boneless chicken breast, cut into $1/4$-inch strips
4 cups steamed vegetables (carrots, broccoli, zucchini, celery, snow peas, etc.)
$1/2$ medium red bell pepper, cut into thin strips

Combine scallions, garlic, ginger, soy sauce, hoisin sauce, water, and sesame oil in a small bowl. Heat 2 tablespoons of the peanut oil in a large nonstick frying pan over high heat for 2 minutes. Add chicken strips, taking care not to crowd pan. (Cook in 2 batches if necessary.) Cook for approximately 2 minutes, stirring frequently. Do not overcook as chicken will get very dry. Remove chicken from pan and keep warm. Add last tablespoon of peanut oil to pan, then add steamed vegetables and red pepper strips. Cook over medium heat for 2 minutes, stirring constantly, just to heat vegetables through.

Return chicken to the pan and add reserved scallions, garlic, ginger, sauces, water, and sesame oil. Toss in pan to blend flavors and reheat chicken. Remove ingredients with a slotted

CHICKEN AND TURKEY

Introduce chicken and turkey at 8 months.

Nutritional Profile: protein; vitamin B complex; zinc and magnesium.

spoon or tongs to a serving platter. Cook juices remaining in pan for 1 minute or until slightly reduced, stirring gently with a wooden spoon. Pour sauce over stir-fry and serve immediately with rice, pasta, or Lo Mein with Sesame and Peanuts (page 197).

Makes 4 grown-up servings.

Free-range hens available from a butcher or health food store are best. Supermarket chickens vary in color, but this is not an indication of their flavor or freshness—only of their diet. Look for chickens with smooth, soft skin. Avoid chicken with an off smell and slimy or dry, unevenly colored skin. Be sure to buy the right chicken for the right dish—roasting chickens for roasting, stewing chickens for soup, broilers and fryers for grilling, and so on.

Turkeys are best freshly killed. They are plump and have nice white, smooth skin. But frozen turkeys are most readily available in supermarkets. If you purchase a frozen turkey, read the label. Self-basting turkeys are injected with oils and other chemicals. You won't want to pay extra for these additives. To defrost a frozen turkey, let it sit in your refrigerator for a day or two. In general larger turkeys are a better buy. They are meatier and juicier than small ones, and you get more meat for your money.

Turkey Puree

■ ■ ■ ■ ■ ■ ■ ■ ■ ■ ■ ■ ■ ■ ■ ■ ■ ■ ■ ■

Primary Purees

Adding carrots, sweet potato, celery, or onion to the cooking liquid will boost the flavor and nutritional value of the turkey. Use the leftover poached turkey in Turkey Pot Pies (page 175) for the whole family's dinner, turkey salad sandwiches for lunch, etc. Cooked turkey also freezes well. Roast turkey from the family table purees nicely too. Use the following technique. But since it's drier, use a little more liquid to achieve a creamy puree.

1 whole boneless turkey breast (about 7 ounces)

Bring a large pot of water to a rolling boil. Remove any remaining skin and fat from the turkey breast and cut the meat into $3/4$-inch pieces. Add turkey to pot. Lower heat and simmer gently for 8 minutes or until turkey is cooked through. Strain and reserve cooking liquid. Puree 1 cup cooked turkey (without liquid) in food processor fitted with the steel blade for approximately 2 minutes, then slowly add reserved broth until a smooth, creamy texture is achieved. (Like the chicken, the longer you puree, the smoother the texture.) Unless the turkey is very creamy, baby will hit the reject button.

Makes 10 to 12 1-ounce or heaped tablespoon baby servings.

Microwave Directions: Place skinned, cut-up turkey in a microwave-safe dish. Add $1/4$ cup water and cover with plastic wrap, pulling back one corner to vent. Microwave on MEDIUM-HIGH for 6 to 8 minutes or until turkey is cooked through.

Turkey Pot Pie

A great way to get babies and grown-ups alike to gobble up leftovers. Chicken can be used in place of turkey in this recipe. And individual, unbaked pies freeze nicely. (Disposable individual foil pie pans make great containers.) If you use store-bought broth for this recipe, be sure it's low-salt. The broth from the "Just What the Doctor Ordered!" Chicken Soup recipe (page 216) or leftover poaching liquid from Chicken Little (page 164) or Turkey Puree (page 174) also works wonderfully.

Table Food for Toddlers
and Grown-ups Too

2 cups cooked turkey, cut into bite-size pieces
$^1\!/_4$ cup green peas (thawed if frozen)
2 cups chicken broth
1 medium carrot, scrubbed and diced
1 celery stalk, diced
$^1\!/_4$ medium rutabaga, peeled and diced
$^1\!/_2$ small onion, diced
1 medium Idaho potato, peeled and diced
$^1\!/_4$ cup corn niblets (thawed if frozen)
1 tablespoon unsalted butter
2 tablespoons unbleached flour
2 tablespoons milk, half-and-half, or cream
$^1\!/_2$ recipe Easy as Pie Crust (page 263)

Place turkey and peas in a large bowl and set aside. Bring chicken broth to a boil in a 2-quart saucepan and add diced vegetables. Return to a boil, reduce heat to low, and simmer for 5 to 6 minutes or until vegetables are tender but retain some crunch. (Their cooking will be completed in the oven.) Remove vegetables from broth and add to bowl with turkey, saving broth to make sauce. Toss well to distribute meat and vegetables evenly.

To make sauce: Melt butter in a small saucepan over low heat. Add flour and cook for 1 minute, stirring constantly. Add reserved broth and cook for 18 to 20 minutes, stirring occasionally, until sauce is slightly thickened. Remove from heat, add milk, stir, and pour over turkey and vegetables, gently lifting ingredients so all get thoroughly coated with sauce. Preheat oven to 375 degrees. Pour into a 9-inch pie pan and top with vented piecrust. Bake for 35 to 40 minutes or until mixture is bubbly and crust is golden brown. Let pie sit for 10 minutes before serving.

Makes 1 9-inch pie, serving 4 to 5 grown-ups or 4 individual pies.

Beef, Lamb, and Pork

Here's the Beef

For a complete dinner, add any of the vegetables or grains suggested in the Chicken Little recipe (page 164).

½ pound lean ground beef

Place beef in a small saucepan and cover with cold water. Cook over medium heat for about 4 to 5 minutes or until beef is cooked. Strain and reserve cooking liquid. Place beef in food processor fitted with the steel blade or blender and puree for 2 minutes, slowly adding enough of the reserved cooking liquid to make a smooth and creamy texture.

Makes 12 to 14 1-ounce heaped tablespoon or baby servings.

Primary Purees

BEEF

Introduce lean beef at 9 months.

Nutritional Profile: protein; vitamins A, B complex, and C; iron and copper.

The leanest cuts are tenderloin (the most expensive but with the least flavor), top sirloin, and top round. (Chopped meat is usually ground round.) In general tender cuts, such as sirloin, require less cooking and remain tender while tougher cuts, like shoulder and chuck, must be cooked slowly to tenderize them. Tougher cuts, however, are more flavorful than tender cuts.

Marvelous Meat Loaf

We all eat with our eyes as well as our mouths. If you think of meat loaf as workaday fare, then check out some of the tricks that follow. They will transform this basic mix into a party entree sure to make your child smile and clean up his plate.

1 tablespoon virgin olive oil
1 small onion, finely chopped
1 celery stalk, finely chopped
1 small garlic clove, finely minced
1/4 cup seasoned dried bread crumbs
1/4 cup milk
1 1/2 to 2 pounds lean ground beef
2 eggs
2 tablespoons freshly grated Parmesan cheese
1 tablespoon Worcestershire sauce
1 tablespoon minced fresh parsley *or* 1 teaspoon parsley flakes
1/4 teaspoon salt
1/4 teaspoon freshly ground black pepper

Warm olive oil in a small frying pan over medium heat. Add onion, celery, and garlic and sauté for 4 to 5 minutes or until onion is translucent. Set aside to cool. In a large bowl, combine bread crumbs and milk. Stir and let sit for 4 to 5 minutes. Add remaining ingredients to bowl, including onion and celery. Mix lightly with a wooden spoon until just combined. Shape meat into a loaf and place in a shallow roasting pan or ovenproof dish, making sure meat does not touch the sides of the pan. Refrigerate, covered, for 1 hour or longer. Preheat oven to 375 degrees and bake meat loaf, uncovered, for 55 to 60 minutes. Allow meat loaf to rest for 10 minutes before serving.

Makes 4 to 5 grown-up servings.

Buy choice or prime beef with rich, bright color without water or blood pooled in the packaging. (Excessive blood will cause the meat to spoil quickly. Water is a sign that the meat may have been frozen.) The flesh should also spring back when pressed. A neighborhood butcher is a thing of the past in many parts of the country, but specialty butchers—as an adjunct to the packaged meat areas—are reappearing as "boutiques" in more upscale supermarkets. They will be able to provide aged beef, cut and trimmed to your specifications, as will some regular supermarket butchers with advance notice.

Variations—Special-Occasion Meat Loaf: Twenty minutes before baking is completed, spread $2^1/_2$ to 3 cups Potato-Parsnip Puree (page 149) over meat loaf and sprinkle 1 medium carrot, grated, over top, patting lightly so it sticks.

If baked in a large shallow roasting pan, the meat loaf mixture can be shaped, iced with Potato-Parsnip Puree, and decorated. Some fanciful examples:

- Teddy bear for a sleepover. Grate raw carrot over surface for fun fur just before serving.
- Snowman for a winter party. Add zucchini eyes, carrot nose, olive buttons, and red pepper mouth.
- Heart for Valentine's Day. Shape meat mixture into a heart and top with grated red bell pepper just before serving.
- Clover leaf for St. Patrick's Day. Garnish with steamed broccoli flowerets.

(If vegetable decorations look dry, drizzle them with pan juices or a bit of melted unsalted butter before serving.)

MEAT LOAF

Ketchup's always a favorite on meat loaf with kids, but for a change of taste, sauté red and green bell pepper strips with 1 cup Tomato Sauce (page 154) or use No-Tomato Marinara (page 157) and serve on the side with plain meat loaf or with meat loaf topped with Potato-Parsnip Puree.

One-Pot Beef Dinner

Serve the strained beef broth as a starter, then move on to the meat and vegetables for the second course. For a fancy fillip, float slices of toasted French bread on the broth surface, top with mozzarella, and run under a preheated broiler until cheese melts and begins to brown. Beef Dinner for under one year is included.

1 2½- to 3-pound beef roast (brisket, rump, or chuck)
6 to 7 cups beef broth
6 to 7 cups water
3 to 4 leeks, trimmed and cleaned*
2 to 3 medium carrots, washed, scrubbed, cut in half, and quartered
2 to 3 medium parsnips, peeled, cut in half, and quartered
6 medium new potatoes, scrubbed
1 bouquet garni**

Place beef in a large pot and cover with beef broth and water. Bring to a boil, reduce heat to a simmer, and cook beef for 2½ hours. Skim surface of pot occasionally during cooking as fat and other impurities rise to the surface. Add vegetables and bouquet garni and cook beef for 35 to 40 minutes longer or until tender. (If liquid is evaporating too quickly, replenish with water and partially cover pot with lid.) Meat is done when it is fork-tender or tines are easily inserted into the meat. Discard bouquet garni. Transfer meat to a platter, slice thickly, and surround with cooked vegetables. Keep warm until ready to serve. (The Horseradish Sauce, page 278, is perfect on the side.) Strain broth and serve as first course.

Makes 4 grown-up servings.

For Bigger Babies (over 10 months): Cut a well-trimmed slice of beef into small pieces and puree, dry, for 1 minute in food processor fitted with the steel blade. Add 1 piece of carrot, 1 potato, and 1 piece of parsnip and process for approximately 1 minute more, adding 4 to 5 tablespoons of cooking broth, 1 tablespoon at a time, until texture reaches desired consistency.

*To clean leeks: Trim root ends sparingly and cut off most of the green tops. (The tops can be saved and used for stocks.) Then split the leeks in half lengthwise, leaving root end intact. Soak in cold water for 20 minutes to loosen sand and dirt. Gently rinse under running water, separating leaves without breaking them off.

**To make bouquet garni: Cut a long celery stalk in half crosswise. In the hollow of the larger half, place a bay leaf, a pinch of thyme, 2 crushed garlic cloves, and 2 sprigs parsley. Place the smaller celery half on top and tie together with string to secure.

Monster Meatballs

Table Food for Toddlers
and Grown-ups Too

Meatballs and sauce over pasta are a natural. Stuff any leftover meat-balls and sauce into a hard roll for meatball sandwiches or slice them for pizza topping. Occasionally dipping hands in cold water while shaping raw meat into balls will keep them from sticking to you. These meatballs are large, but the bigger the meatball, the more tender the product. Just dice one for baby's dinner.

1 recipe Marvelous Meat Loaf (page 178), minus celery and onions
1/4 cup virgin olive oil
1 recipe Tomato Sauce with herbs (page 154)

Follow recipe for meat loaf, omitting celery and onions. Shape 1/2 cup meat mixture into a round ball. Place on a plate and re-peat until all meat is used. Chill meatballs for 1 hour. In a large nonstick frying pan, heat olive oil over medium-high heat. Add 6 to 7 meatballs, taking care they do not touch. Cook on all sides until browned. Remove from pan and cook remaining meatballs in same manner.

Heat tomato sauce over low heat in a pot large enough to ac-commodate all the meatballs. Add meatballs to sauce, bring to a simmer, and cook for 30 to 35 minutes.

Makes 10 to 12 large meatballs.

Mustard-Pecan Pork Medallions

You can easily cut the pork medallions yourself from a whole pork tenderloin, readily available in the meat department of your supermarket. Leave out the pecans if anyone is allergic to them. And for kids with plain tastes, dip their portion in a beaten egg and bread crumbs only and cook along with the rest.

5 tablespoons coarse-grain mustard (Pommery style)
1/4 cup Dijon-style mustard
1/4 cup dry white wine
1 cup coarsely chopped pecans
1/4 cup unseasoned dried breadcrumbs
2 to 3 tablespoons finely chopped fresh parsley
1 medium garlic clove, minced
1/4 cup virgin olive oil
8 1/2-inch-thick pork tenderloin medallions
2 teaspoons freshly ground black pepper

Preheat oven to 375 degrees. Mix mustards and white wine in a small bowl and set aside. Mix nuts with bread crumbs, parsley, and garlic, place in a flat dish or shallow pan, and set aside. Place a heavy frying pan over medium-high heat and add 2 tablespoons of the olive oil. Sprinkle pork medallions with black pepper and sear them 4 at a time for 1 to 2 minutes on each side. When seared, remove from pan with tongs and dip into mustard mixture, being sure to coat both sides. Place each medallion in the pecan-breadcrumb mixture and, using the palm of your hand, press the mixture into the pork. Repeat searing and coating until all medallions are prepared. Place in a large baking dish and bake for 20 minutes or until toasty brown and crusty on the outside but cooked through and juicy on the inside.

Makes 4 grown-up servings.

Table Food for Toddlers
and Grown-ups Too

PORK

Introduce pork at 12 months.

Nutritional Profile: protein; vitamin B complex; iron.

Select firm, light pink or reddish meat that is lean; tenderloin is ideal.

Grilled Lamb Chops with Savory Herb Sauce

Table Food for Toddlers and Grown-ups Too

Babies love to gum and suck lamb chop bones. One bone with a bit of meat clinging to it will keep most contentedly occupied while Mom and Dad enjoy a leisurely dinner. (After he has gummed the bone clean, your baby will beat it on his tray like a drumstick.) Cut meat from the chop in tiny, tiny pieces and strew them on the high chair tray for bigger babies to pick up. For younger ones, puree meat with a touch of sauce in your food processor. Check bone for sharp edges and remove fat before giving the bone to baby.

This recipe is not only a yummy way to prepare lamb chops but is an equally delicious preparation for other meats such as small steaks, veal chops, etc. (Rib eye lamb chops have just the right-size bones for baby, but to serve 2 adults and 1 baby, since these are generally smaller than shoulder or loin chops, count on 2 chops per adult and 1 for baby.)

SAVORY HERB MARINADE

2 garlic cloves
1 teaspoon dried rosemary
$\frac{1}{8}$ teaspoon dried thyme
$\frac{1}{8}$ teaspoon dried oregano
$\frac{1}{4}$ teaspoon dried marjoram
$\frac{1}{2}$ bay leaf
$\frac{1}{4}$ teaspoon freshly ground black pepper
$\frac{1}{4}$ cup virgin olive oil
2 tablespoons dry vermouth or dry sherry (optional)
5 rib lamb chops *or* 3 loin lamb chops
1 cup tomato sauce

LAMB

Introduce lamb at 10 months.

Nutritional Profile: protein; vitamin B complex; iron.

Look for pink to light red meat, with firm texture and little fat. Baby or spring lamb is most tender.

Combine marinade ingredients in a shallow dish that will hold all the chops in 1 layer. Arrange chops in dish, turning meat to coat all sides with marinade. Cover with plastic wrap and marinate for 2 hours or longer in the refrigerator.

Preheat broiler or grill for 10 minutes on high. While oven or grill is preheating, make sauce. Remove chops from marinade, scraping any onions and garlic into a small saucepan and adding remaining marinade. Heat marinade over low heat for 4 to 5 minutes or until onion is translucent. Add tomato sauce and simmer for 10 minutes longer. Keep sauce warm on low until needed.

To cook chops: Broil on tray or directly on grill for 2 ½ to 3 minutes per side for ½-inch-thick chops. For thicker chops, adjust cooking time. Serve with savory herb sauce.

Makes 5 rib chops or 3 loin chops.

Ham and Spinach Silver Dollars

Table Food for Toddlers
and Grown-ups Too

These little cakes are great with yogurt or sour cream and with any fruit puree for spreading or dunking. When we entertain, we serve them with dressed-up toppings such as melted horseradish Cheddar cheese, a whole shrimp sautéed in garlic, and apple puree sprinkled with chopped walnuts.

1 cup unbleached flour
$1/2$ teaspoon salt
2 eggs
1 cup milk
1 tablespoon unsalted butter, melted
$1/2$ cup finely chopped boiled ham
$1/2$ cup cooked spinach, finely chopped and squeezed dry
vegetable oil for brushing pan

Combine flour and salt in a medium bowl. Create a well in the center and add eggs. Blend together with a fork. (The mixture will be very thick.) Slowly add milk, stirring thoroughly. Add melted butter and mix again. Chill mixture for 2 to 3 hours or overnight in your refrigerator. Just before cooking, add ham and spinach, mixing well to incorporate.

To cook pancakes: Heat a large nonstick frying pan or griddle over medium heat for 1 to 2 minutes. Lightly brush cooking surface with oil and spoon 1 tablespoon of batter into pan or onto griddle for each silver dollar-size cake. (Leave enough space between cakes for spreading and easy turning.) When top of pancake begins to dry around edges, flip and cook for 1 minute more or until lightly browned on bottom side.

Makes 24 2-inch silver dollar-size pancakes.

Fish

One Fish, Two Fish, Easy-to-Do Fish

1 4- to 6-ounce piece of flounder fillet (or any mild, firm-fleshed white fish)

Place fish fillet in a steamer basket set in a pot filled with a small amount of lightly boiling water. Cover tightly (for better nutrient retention) and steam for 5 to 7 minutes or until fish is opaque and flakes easily with a fork, replenishing water during steaming if necessary. Set fish aside to cool, reserving steaming liquid. When cool, flake fish with a fork, discarding any bones, then mash to desired consistency. If necessary, thin fish with water or a bit of the steaming liquid.

Makes 4 to 6 1-ounce or heaped tablespoon baby servings.

Microwave Directions: Place the fillet on a microwave-safe dish. Add 3 tablespoons water and cover tightly with plastic wrap, pulling back one corner to vent. Microwave on HIGH for 3 to 5 minutes. Test for doneness and proceed with recipe. (To adjust consistency, use liquid left in cooking dish.)

Primary Purees

FISH

Introduce white-fleshed fish (not shellfish) at 12 months.

Nutritional Profile: protein; vitamins B complex, A, and D. Soft, edible bones of small fish (canned salmon, sardines, etc.) are an excellent source of calcium.

Fresh fish has:
- scales that adhere firmly to the skin
- gills that are reddish
- flesh that is firm to the touch
- no offensive odor
- bulging eyes
- Most fresh fish float in cold water.

Fish Chowder

This is an easy chowder with variations suitable for babies under one, toddlers, and grown-ups too. Depending on your preference, you can finish it with milk, cream, or half-and-half. To make this chowder Manhattan-style, substitute 1 cup chopped tomato and 1 tablespoon chopped parsley for the milk.

2 celery stalks, diced
1 medium onion, diced
2 tablespoons virgin olive oil
2 tablespoons unbleached all-purpose flour
6 cups fish stock (recipe follows)
½ small bay leaf
Pinch of dried thyme
2 medium Idaho potatoes, finely diced
¾ pound firm-fleshed white fish such as haddock, halibut, or scrod
½ cup milk, cream, or half-and-half

Sauté celery and onion in olive oil in a large heavy-bottomed pot over medium heat for 4 to 5 minutes or until celery is tender-crisp and onions are transparent. Sprinkle flour over vegetables and stir to coat. Cook, stirring frequently, for 2 to 3 minutes or until lightly browned. While stirring, gradually add fish stock. (Use a whisk if necessary to blend thoroughly.)

Add the bay leaf and thyme and bring to a boil. Add potato and cook for 15 minutes or until tender. Add fish and cook for 2 to 3 minutes more or until fish turns white and flesh flakes. Finish soup by adding milk, cream, or half-and-half and serve immediately.

Makes approximately 6 cups chowder and 6 1-ounce or heaped tablespoon baby servings.

For Bigger Babies (over 10 months): Remove approximately 1 cup of fish, potato, and vegetable mixture and 1 to 2 tablespoons of broth. Cool and strain through a food mill or puree in a food processor fitted with the steel blade until smooth. Adjust consistency with additional broth if needed.

Variations: For a heartier chowder, add before the milk:

- $1/4$ pound uncooked shrimp, peeled and deveined, and $1/4$ pound scallops, cut into quarters. Cook for 3 to 4 minutes and finish with milk.
- 10 to 12 littleneck or cherrystone clams, well scrubbed. Cook for 2 to 3 minutes or until the shells open. Then finish with milk.

Remember no shellfish, only fin fish in this chowder. Babies can be allergic to shellfish.

Store fish in an airtight container in your refrigerator. Fish may be kept directly on ice, if drainage is provided to prevent fish from absorbing water. Use all fish as soon as possible. If well wrapped, fish freezes nicely.

Fish Stock

Unlike chicken stock, fish stock is not available in your supermarket and takes less than an hour to prepare. Make a big batch and freeze the surplus. Use fish stock for poaching fish, fish chowder, or any other recipe that calls for fish stock.

2 pounds fish bones from firm-fleshed white fish such as halibut, flounder, or scrod
Pinch of salt
2 celery stalks with leaves, coarsely chopped
1 medium onion, quartered
Pinch of dried thyme
$\frac{1}{2}$ small bay leaf
$\frac{1}{2}$ teaspoon whole peppercorns
2 to 3 parsley sprigs

Rinse fish bones well under cold running water. Place in a large stockpot with remaining ingredients and cover with 3 to $3\frac{1}{2}$ quarts cold water. Bring to a boil over high heat. Skim surface. Reduce heat to low and simmer for 30 to 40 minutes or until fish taste is evident in stock. Turn off heat and allow stock to sit for 10 to 15 minutes. Strain through a fine-meshed strainer. Cool and refrigerate or use immediately.

Makes 5 to 6 cups.

Noodles, Dried Beans, and Peas

Pasta Pronto

In a hurry? Add any one or a combination of the following to $1/2$ cup of cooked pasta. Start with 1 healthy tablespoon of these toppings and adjust to suit your child's taste.

- yogurt
- cottage cheese
- ricotta cheese
- sour cream
- mashed banana
- any fruit puree
- any vegetable puree

Spices, herbs, and seasonings can be added, but be careful not to go overboard. Try these combinations:

- dill or grated cheese with sour cream
- cinnamon with banana
- vegetable puree and basil with yogurt
- oregano with ricotta
- fruit puree and cinnamon with cottage cheese

And when time permits, try one of the following Mommy Made recipes for sauces and toppings:

- Summer Pesto, page 279
- Winter Pesto, page 280
- Chickpea Puree, page 200
- Tomato Sauce, page 154
- Tahini Dressing, page 275

Macaroni and Cheese with Broccoli

If "Mama-Americana" ever becomes a legitimate cuisine, then this dish will surely be a star. It's quick, easy, economical, and can be enjoyed by the whole family.

½ pound egg-free elbow macaroni, cooked according to package directions
3 cups grated sharp Cheddar cheese (about ¾ pound)
1 cup milk
salt to taste
¼ teaspoon freshly ground black pepper
1½ cups broccoli flowerets, steamed
3 tablespoons freshly grated Parmesan cheese

Preheat oven to 350 degrees. Drain macaroni and toss with Cheddar cheese. Heat milk over medium heat until hot, add to macaroni and cheese, season with salt and pepper, and mix to blend. Add broccoli flowerets and mix carefully. Pour into 8-inch square glass or ceramic baking dish. Sprinkle Parmesan cheese over top and bake for 15 minutes or until bubbling. Allow casserole to sit for 5 to 10 minutes before serving.

Makes 4 grown-up servings.

Variations:

- Fold in 1 cup diced ham.
- Sprinkle top with ¼ cup crumbled cooked bacon.
- Layer top with slices of garden-ripe tomatoes (sprinkle Parmesan over tomatoes).
- Mix in assorted cut-up steamed vegetables.

NOODLES

Introduce egg-free noodles at 10 months: egg-enriched after 1 year.

Nutritional Profile: carbohydrates; vitamin B complex; iron.

The best dried noodles (pasta) are made from hard or durum wheat called *semolina*. (These products also contain the most protein, since semolina is virtually all protein.) Both domestic and imported brands containing this flour are available. Check labels before purchasing. Keep pasta stored in a sealed container or package in a cool, dry place for about 1 year (egg-enriched pasta for 6 months). Vegetable pastas and fresh pastas are also widely available. Fresh pastas should be stored in your refrigerator and used immediately. For longer storage, place in your freezer. Vegetable pastas add color to the plate. Their vegetable flavors can be pronounced or mild.

Egg Noodles with Cottage Cheese and Chunky Fruit

With a crispy salad and a loaf of warm bread, this is a comfortable meal for babies over one year. (Use egg-free pasta for those under one.) It's especially nice for Sunday brunch.

¹/₂ cup cottage cheese
1 cup Chunky Applesauce (page 118)
¹/₂ pound egg noodles, cooked according to package directions
¹/₄ teaspoon ground cinnamon

Mix cottage cheese and fruit sauce in a large serving bowl. Drain noodles, add to bowl (half at a time), and gently toss until well coated with cheese and fruit. Serve warm with a dusting of cinnamon.

Makes 4 grown-up servings.

Table Food for Toddlers and Grown-ups Too

Oodles of Noodles

Most of the kids we know—and particularly our own girls—have absolutely loved pasta from the very first day they tasted it! There is no question in our minds that the first word Renée spoke was not *mommy* or *daddy* or even *no;* it was *noodle.* (The second word she spoke was *more.*)

We have often wondered why so many of Teddi's visiting friends *always* sat down to a plate of noodles. In fact, with some of Teddi's playmates, we suspect this may have been their favorite part of the play date. We don't have a single answer as to why children adore noodles, but here are a few logical thoughts:

- The varied shapes and sizes make for great fun, visually and in the mouth.
- When cooked, they are naturally moist and therefore easy to chew and swallow.
- Other than spaghetti, pasta shapes make terrific finger food and are popular with the "I will feed myself!" age group.
- They cling to and taste good with myriad sauces and other toppings.

Lasagne with Meat Sauce

Table Food for Toddlers
and Grown-ups Too

Draining the hot water from the cooked lasagne noodles and replacing it with cold will not only cool the noodles but will also keep them from sticking together.

1 15-ounce container ricotta cheese
1 egg
1 teaspoon minced fresh parsley
$\frac{1}{8}$ teaspoon dried oregano
$\frac{1}{4}$ teaspoon dried basil
$\frac{1}{8}$ teaspoon freshly ground black pepper
5 cups Tomato Sauce with meat (page 154)
$\frac{3}{4}$ pound lasagne noodles (16 to 20 pieces), cooked according to package directions
$\frac{1}{2}$ pound mozzarella cheese, grated
$\frac{1}{2}$ cup freshly grated Parmesan cheese

Combine ricotta, egg, parsley, oregano, basil, and pepper in a small bowl. Mix well and chill.

Assemble lasagne: Spread 1 cup of sauce in bottom of 9 x 13-inch pan or ovenproof baking dish and top with a layer of cooked noodles. Next, cover the noodles with one half the seasoned ricotta mixture and sprinkle with one third of the grated cheeses. Add a second layer of lasagne noodles followed by 2 cups of sauce. Top with a third layer of noodles, the remaining ricotta, and one third of the grated cheeses. Add a final layer of noodles, the remaining 2 cups of sauce, and last one third of grated cheeses. Cover with aluminum foil and refrigerate for 2 hours before baking.

To bake: Preheat oven to 375 degrees. Bake foil-covered lasagne for 45 to 50 minutes. Remove foil and continue baking for 20

Pasta supplies the stick-to-your-ribs carbohydrates needed to fuel the energy your child expends daily. Pasta is also a good source of protein and is usually enriched with iron and B vitamins.

While pasta is easy to prepare and generally takes less than 12 minutes to cook, we always cook extra and freeze the drained noodles in portions in airtight plastic bags or containers. When ready to use, simply drop the frozen portion into boiling water until the noodles separate. The time saved is usually 7 minutes or more. And as we all know, "When it's time to eat, it's time to eat!" Better yet, just reheat it in the microwave.

If your child is allergic to wheat, there are a number of wheat-free pastas on the market that are delicious, just as easy to prepare, and come in a reasonable variety of shapes. These include corn, rice, and even artichoke noodles. Be sure, however, to read the labels on these vegetable and grain pastas to see if there is any wheat in the product.

minutes or until cheese topping is lightly browned and lasagne juices are bubbling. Remove from oven and allow lasagne to sit for 20 minutes before cutting and serving.

Makes 8 grown-up servings.

Buckwheat and Bows

Kasha or buckwheat is one of the best nonanimal sources of protein. Despite the wheat in its name, it's gluten-free and appropriate for babies who have wheat-related allergies. Kasha with bows (short for bow tie noodles) can also be served cold, tossed with a few tablespoons of vinaigrette dressing. Bow tie-shaped pasta is traditional in this recipe, but wagon wheels or other shapes taste just as good.

1 tablespoon unsalted butter
1 medium onion, diced
6 to 8 mushrooms, sliced
1 cup kasha (roasted buckwheat), cooked according to package directions and kept warm
1/3 pound bow tie noodles, cooked according to package directions and kept warm

Melt butter in medium-size sauté pan over medium-low heat. Add onions and cook slowly, stirring often, until edges of onions begin to brown. Add mushrooms and continue to cook until mushrooms begin to brown. Mix mushrooms and onions with cooked kasha, toss with drained noodles, and serve.

Makes 6 to 8 grown-up side-dish servings.

Table Food for Toddlers and Grown-ups Too

Egg noodles are also a nice alternative, but since the manufacturers use the whole egg in their preparation, do not introduce these until after age one.

Creating meals with noodles is easy. Use corkscrew twists, elbows, bow ties, or any other noodle that is easy for little fingers to pick up and will hold the sauce or topping nicely. For babies (10 to 14 months) try alphabet noodles, stars, tiny seashells, pastina, or couscous. These are what we call *spoon* or *soup pastas*. When loaded onto a spoon, they usually make it to the mouth, even with the worst of navigators.

The Vegetable Twist

Pasta twists and hard-cooked eggs intertwined with carrot ribbons and other fresh vegetables make a tasty and colorful salad for lunch or snack for those over one. Make carrot ribbons by cutting cleaned carrot in long strips with a vegetable peeler. Other fresh vegetables such as zucchini, summer squash, parsnip, celery, and even jicama can be cut into ribbons and used in this salad too. The elbow twist pasta called for in this recipe is a new shape. If you can't find it in your supermarket, use any larger pasta that will hold the dressing in its folds and be easy for your baby to pick up.

$1/2$-pound elbow twist pasta, cooked according to package directions
2 tablespoons cider vinegar
$1/4$ cup virgin olive oil
$1/2$ cup thinly sliced scallions
$1/4$ teaspoon salt
$1/4$ teaspoon freshly ground pepper
1 medium carrot, cut into ribbons
$1/2$ medium red bell pepper, cut into $1/8$-inch strips
1 celery stalk, thinly sliced
2 hard-cooked eggs, chopped
$1/4$ cup mayonnaise
2 tablespoons freshly grated Parmesan cheese

Drain cooked pasta. Rinse with cold water and drain again.

Whisk vinegar, oil, scallions, salt, and pepper in a large bowl. Add warm pasta and toss to coat with dressing. Allow to cool completely and add remaining ingredients, mixing well. Chill for 2 to 3 hours before serving.

Makes 8 cups.

Lo Mein with Sesame and Peanuts

Any bright vegetables on hand—a little grated carrot, strips of red bell pepper, snow peas, etc.—will add color and crunch to these Asian-inspired noodles. Prepared with whole-wheat pasta, this recipe provides complete protein. Any pasta shape can be used, but linguine or spaghetti is traditional.

Table Food for Toddlers
and Grown-ups Too

3 tablespoons peanut oil
¼ teaspoon light sesame oil
2 tablespoons chunky or smooth peanut butter
2 tablespoons soy sauce or tamari
4 tablespoons water
1 medium garlic clove, crushed
½ pound whole-wheat or regular linguine or spaghetti, cooked according to
    package directions
3 scallions, trimmed and thinly sliced
½ cucumber, peeled, seeded, and thinly sliced

Combine peanut and sesame oils in a large bowl. Add peanut butter, soy sauce, water, and garlic and mix well with a whisk to blend. Drain pasta well and toss with dressing. Garnish with scallion and cucumber.

Makes 5 cups.

Apple-Raisin Couscous

**Spoon and Finger Food
for Bigger Babies**

Couscous is a North African specialty usually made from wheat semolina. When cooked, it looks like a thousand large grains of sand but has a soft pastalike texture. Couscous is a great baby food! Like rice, it's a wonderful "carrier" for other foods and spices. You can combine any cooked vegetables and seasonings with it, add chicken stock, vegetable broth, etc., for extra flavor, or serve plain with stews. (Omit the raisins for babies under one year.)

1 medium Golden Delicious apple, peeled, cored, and finely diced
¼ cup raisins
1 tablespoon unsalted butter
1½ cups apple juice
1 2-inch piece of cinnamon stick
1 cup quick-cooking couscous

Combine apple, raisins, butter, juice, and cinnamon in a medium saucepan and bring to a boil over medium-high heat. Add couscous, stir, cover, and remove from heat. Allow to sit, undisturbed, for 5 minutes. Uncover, remove cinnamon stick, fluff with fork, and serve immediately.

Makes 4 adult portions, 8 baby servings.

PERFECT PAIRS: MAKING COMPLETE PROTEINS BY COMBINING PLANTS

Any food from the left-hand column can be combined with your choice in the right-hand column to form a complete protein. One and a half cups of combined plant-source food equals 7 grams of protein.

Whole-wheat bread (and flour)	Legumes (chickpeas,
Brown rice	soybeans, etc.)
Millet	Lentils
Bran	Wheat germ
Barley	
Oatmeal	

Brazil nuts	Leafy greens (spinach,
Sesame seeds	collards, etc.)
Millet	Brussels sprouts
Mushrooms	Lima beans
Rice	Green beans
	Cauliflower

Legumes	Wheat
Black beans	Rice
Lentils	Millet
Kidney beans	Bran
Navy beans	Corn (only with soybeans
Chickpeas	or black beans)
Soybeans	Barley

Peanuts	Spinach
Brazil nuts	Soybeans
Pistachios	Sesame seeds
Cashews	Legumes (not with peanuts)
	Wheat germ

Cooking Dried Peas and Beans

There are two primary methods for cooking legumes—chickpeas, kidney beans, navy beans, black beans, fava beans, and red beans, but *not* lentils, which don't need to be soaked: (1) the old-fashioned method and (2) the short method. In the old-fashioned method the beans are soaked overnight prior to a fairly short cooking. In the short method the soaking step is eliminated, but the cooking time is considerably longer. The taste and nutritional differences between the two methods are not dramatic. In the first the soaking liquid is discarded and along with it some vitamins and minerals. In the second the longer cooking time probably destroys an equivalent amount of nutrients. We think the old-fashioned method produces a better-tasting dish, but if you forget to put your beans and peas out to soak the night before, it's nice to know the fallback technique.

The Old-Fashioned (or Longer) Method: Place rinsed and picked-over dried beans or peas in a large container. Add cold water to cover and soak overnight. Just prior to cooking, drain peas and rinse again. Place in a small pot. Cover with fresh cold water and bring to a boil over medium heat. Reduce heat to low and simmer until beans or peas are tender. (Time varies from beans to peas; see individual recipes for guidelines.) Drain, reserving cooking liquid, and set beans or peas aside to cool. Strain the cooled, cooked beans or peas in a food mill or puree in a food processor fitted with the steel blade, adding cooking liquid a tablespoon at a time to adjust consistency to the age and preference of your baby.

Chickpea Puree

Primary Purees

Chickpeas are also called garbanzos and ceci. This recipe makes a lot. Use the leftovers, unpureed, in the Chickpea and Spinach Casserole (page 201) or for the Chickpea Dip (page 275). Cook chickpeas according to your taste and time constraints, using one of the two cooking methods described in the general directions (pages 199–200).

1 cup dried chickpeas, rinsed and picked over
3 cups water for soaking
4 cups water for cooking

Cooking Times: Old-fashioned method, $1^1/_2$ hours; short method, $1^1/_4$ hours

Makes 30 to 32 1-ounce or heaped tablespoon baby servings.

Soybean Puree

Don't turn the page—soybean puree is really yummy! Directions for cooking appear on pages 199–200.

1 cup dried soybeans
3 cups water for soaking
2 cups water for cooking

Cooking Time: Old-fashioned method, $2^1/_2$ to 3 hours; short method, 1 to $1^1/_2$ hours

Makes 28 to 32 1-ounce or heaped tablespoon baby servings.

Serving Suggestion: Add any smooth or chunky fruit or vegetable puree.

The Short Method: Place rinsed and picked-over dried beans or peas in a pot with water to cover. Bring to a rolling boil over high heat. Remove from heat. Cover with a tight-fitting lid and let sit for 1 hour. Return to high heat, bring to a boil, then reduce heat to low and simmer until tender (see recipes for approximate times), adding more water if required during cooking. Drain, cool, and puree as above.

One cup of dried beans or peas equals about 2 to $2^1/_4$ cups cooked.

Chickpea and Spinach Casserole

Try this with our No-Tomato Marinara Sauce (page 157). It's absolutely delicious.

1 medium onion, diced
1 tablespoon olive oil
1 garlic clove, minced
1 10-ounce package frozen spinach, thawed and drained
1½ cups Tomato Sauce (page 154) or No-Tomato Marinara Sauce (page 157)
2 cups cooked chickpeas (see preceding page or use drained and rinsed canned chickpeas)
salt and freshly ground pepper to taste
1 cup grated Monterey Jack cheese

Preheat oven to 350 degrees. Sauté onion in olive oil in a large frying pan over medium heat, stirring occasionally, until translucent—about 5 to 6 minutes. Add garlic and cook for 1 minute longer, stirring constantly. Add spinach and mix well. Fold in tomato sauce and chickpeas. Remove from heat and season to taste with salt and pepper. Transfer mixture to an 8-inch square or 9-inch round baking dish. Top with grated cheese and bake for 15 to 20 minutes or until bubbling and cheese is lightly browned.

Makes 4 to 6 grown-up servings.

Table Food for Toddlers and Grown-ups Too

DRIED PEAS AND BEANS

Introduce dried peas, beans, and lentils at 12 months.

Nutritional Profile: In general dried beans, peas, and lentils are excellent sources of protein, carbohydrates, vitamin B complex, and iron.

The freshest—and often cheapest—sources of dried beans, peas, and lentils are Asian markets and health food stores. Older dried legumes become stale and will not soften up when cooked. Avoid legumes with pinholes; they could be inhabited by parasites. Packaged supermarket legumes should be well sealed and dated. Store legumes in a cool, dry place. Be sure to rinse and pick over them to remove grit and small stones before cooking.

Lentil Stew

■ ■

Table Food for Toddlers and Grown-ups Too

A hearty one-pot supper/soup that will feed the whole family—perfect after a romp in the snow. Directions for under 1 year are included.

2 tablespoons virgin olive oil
2 celery stalks, diced
1 medium onion, diced
2 medium carrots, scrubbed and diced
$1/2$ small rutabaga, peeled and diced
2 small garlic cloves, minced
$1^{1}/_{2}$ cups dried lentils, picked over and rinsed
2 quarts chicken broth
$1/2$ bay leaf
$1/_{8}$ teaspoon dried oregano
$1/_{8}$ teaspoon dried basil
pinch of dried thyme
2 medium red bliss potatoes, scrubbed and diced
1 tablespoon cider vinegar
Sour cream or yogurt for garnish
Sliced scallion for garnish

Warm the olive oil in a $2^{1}/_{2}$-quart saucepan over medium-high heat. Add celery, onion, carrots, and rutabaga and sauté for 7 to 8 minutes, stirring frequently, until onions are translucent. Add garlic and lentils and cook for 2 minutes more, stirring constantly. Add chicken broth. Bring to a boil and reduce heat to low.

Simmer stew, uncovered, stirring occasionally, for approximately 1 hour, until lentils are tender.* Add herbs and potatoes and continue cooking for 20 minutes or until potatoes are tender. Stir in cider vinegar to finish. Serve steaming hot bowls of stew garnished with a spoonful of sour cream or yogurt and a sprinkling of sliced scallion.

Makes $2^{1}/_{2}$ quarts.

Variations: Add one of the following to the stew during the last 5 minutes of cooking:

- 1 cup cooked Polish or smoked sausage slices
- 1 cup cooked diced ham
- ¹/₂ cup cooked crumbled bacon

*For Babies Under 1: Remove a cup of stew at this point and puree until smooth in a food mill or food processor fitted with the steel blade. Continue with recipe for rest of the family.

Cereals and Breakfast Specials

Brown Rice Cereal

Spoon and Finger Food for Bigger Babies

Commercially prepared rice cereal will probably be your baby's first introduction to this grain. But once he can handle some texture, try this Mommy Made version. It calls for brown rice, which is not stripped of its outer hull of bran, making it richer in fiber and vitamins than white.

¼ cup brown rice
1 cup water, milk, or stock *or* ½ cup water and ½ cup apple juice

Place brown rice in a blender or small food processor and pulverize into fine powder—approximately 4 to 6 minutes at high speed. Bring liquid to a simmer in a small saucepan. Add pulverized brown rice and lower heat immediately. Cook for 4 to 6 minutes, stirring constantly (to discourage lumping). If mixture thickens too much, add a few tablespoons of water while cooking.

Makes 8 to 10 1-ounce or heaped tablespoon baby servings.

Serving Suggestions: Rice cereal can be mixed with any fruit or vegetable puree, including banana, peach, acorn squash, or peas. For toddlers, add chunks of steamed fruit such as apple, pear, peach, etc., a few raisins, a bit of maple syrup, or a sprinkle of ground cinnamon.

BROWN RICE

Introduce brown rice at 8 months.

Nutritional Profile: carbohydrates; vitamin B complex; iron and calcium; fiber.

Don't buy seasoned rice. The fresh seasoning and herbs you add will taste far better, and the rice will be additive-free. Try high proteins like quinoa and amaranth (available at health food stores) instead of rice.

Kasha Cream

For breakfast in short order, pulverize larger quantities of kasha in the food processor. Store ready-to-cook kasha in a tightly covered container on the shelf. Cooked Kasha Cream stores nicely for about a month in the freezer. This recipe works very well with oats too; just reduce the cooking time slightly.

¼ cup kasha (roasted buckwheat) or old-fashioned oats
1 cup water, milk, formula, or stock

Place kasha in a blender or small food processor and pulverize into a fine powder—approximately 3 to 5 minutes at high speed. Bring liquid to a simmer in a small saucepan, add pulverized kasha, and immediately lower heat. Cook for 3 to 5 minutes, stirring constantly. (Be sure there are no lumps.) If cereal is too thick, add a tablespoon or 2 of water to thin while cooking.

Makes 8 to 10 1-ounce or heaped tablespoon baby servings.

Serving Suggestion: Kasha Cream can be mixed with any fruit or vegetable puree—apple, pear, butternut squash, carrot, and so on.

For Bigger Babies (over 10 months):

- Add chunks of steamed fruit (apple, pear, peach, etc.) to cooked Kasha Cream
- Add a spoonful of dried raisins
- Top with a drizzle of maple syrup
- Dust with ground cinnamon

Primary Purees

KASHA

Introduce kasha (roasted buckwheat) at 8 months.

Nutritional Profile: carbohydrates; vitamin B complex; potassium and iron.

Buckwheat is a cereal made from the seeds of a variety of grass related to sorrel and rhubarb. Despite the wheat in its name, it is gluten-free and fine for babies who are allergic to wheat. Purchase only tightly sealed packages and store in a cool, dry place for up to 1 year.

Granola

■ ■

Homemade granola is delicious and good for you. Try it with milk as a breakfast cereal; sprinkled on yogurt for lunch; as a dessert topping on ice cream, rice pudding, and broiled grapefruit halves; and even stuffed into a baked apple or acorn squash. You can make it into a pie crust too (recipe follows).

5 cups old-fashioned rolled oats
1 cup wheat germ
1 cup wheat bran
$1/2$ cup unsalted sunflower seeds
$1/2$ cup slivered almonds
$1/3$ cup vegetable oil
$1/3$ cup honey
$1/3$ cup water
1 cup raisins
1 cup chopped dried apricots

Preheat oven to 250 degrees. Combine oats, wheat germ, bran, sunflower seeds, and almonds in a large bowl and stir to blend ingredients. In a separate small bowl, mix together oil, honey, and water. Pour over oat mixture and stir. (Mixture will be moist.) Spread in a roasting pan and bake for 1 hour, stirring occasionally. Granola is done when lightly brown and crisp. Remove from oven and allow to cool. Stir in raisins and apricots. Store in an airtight container in the refrigerator up to 3 weeks.

Makes $9 1/2$ cups.

Variations: Add to the mix before cooking:

- $1/3$ cup maple syrup in lieu of honey
- $1/2$ cup hazelnuts, walnuts, or pecans in place of almonds
- oat bran in place of wheat bran

OATS

Introduce oats at 6 months.

▲

Nutritional Profile: carbohydrates; fiber; vitamin B complex; potassium.

●

Uncut Irish or Scottish oatmeal is the richest-tasting, but the cut, quick-cooking Quaker brand is equally healthful and not as expensive. Store oatmeal in the refrigerator in a sealed container.

After roasting, add:

- ¹/₂ cup unsweetened shredded coconut
- dried apples, peaches, and/or pears
- 1 tablespoon ground cinnamon

GRANOLA PIE CRUST

Preheat oven to 350 degrees. Omit the fruit from the basic granola recipe. Grind 1¹/₃ cups of the mixture in a blender or food processor fitted with the steel blade. Mix well with ¹/₄ cup softened unsalted butter and press into a 9-inch pie plate. Bake for 6 to 8 minutes. Cool and fill.

Start the Day with a Great Breakfast

The vitamin-fortified dry baby cereals found on your grocer's shelf are wonderful, nutritious foods and should not be omitted from your baby's diet until he finally refuses to eat another bite. But breakfast need not be limited to cereal and fruit. When breakfast time becomes boring, try these instant ideas.

Spread one of the following on rice cakes, fresh or toasted bagels, whole-wheat English muffins, or frozen waffles or pancakes (look for the varieties in your supermarket freezer that contain whole grains and no preservatives or additives):

- cottage cheese
- ricotta cheese
- cream cheese
- nut butter
- mashed banana
- any pureed fruit

Or try a bowl of:

- yogurt and any pureed fruit
- cottage cheese and any pureed fruit
- nut milk, page 270, with mashed banana or yogurt
- steamed tofu with fruit

Challah French Toast

French toast made with challah, a traditional Jewish loaf, is our favorite. Challah is a light textured, braided, egg-enriched yeast bread available in bakeries. If you can't find it, raisin bread is equally good in this recipe.

Thick-cut ³/₄- to 1-inch slices of bread that is slightly stale (a day or 2 old) make the best French toast. Keep the first batch warm in a single layer on a cookie sheet in a low oven (120 to 160 degrees) while you cook the rest. This French toast deserves only the best. Serve it topped with a ribbon of pure maple syrup and lots of freshly cut ripe peaches, pears, berries, bananas, grapes—any fruit that's in season. It's also good with homemade Strawberry-Apple Butter (page 282).

4 eggs
3 cups milk
1 teaspoon vanilla extract
8 thick slices of challah or raisin bread
1 tablespoon unsalted butter, approximately, for greasing skillet

Whisk eggs thoroughly in a medium bowl. Add milk and vanilla and mix well. Place 4 slices of bread in an 8-inch square pan and pour half the egg-milk mixture over them. Let bread soak for at least 3 minutes, flipping them once so mixture is absorbed evenly. Lifting carefully, place slices in a large buttered skillet or on a buttered griddle over medium heat. Cook until lightly browned on each side. Soak remaining slices and repeat.

Makes 4 grown-up servings.

Puffy 'Cakes

These are puffy oven-baked pancakes. Try this recipe with slices of peeled apple or pear or with fresh berries instead of banana. If you don't own individual 1-cup baking dishes, Puffy 'Cakes can also be baked in an ovenproof glass pie plate. Simply cut into wedges to serve. With a candle, Puffy 'Cakes make a festive birthday breakfast, lunch, or even supper.

2 tablespoons unsalted butter
2 eggs
6 tablespoons unbleached all-purpose flour
6 tablespoons milk
a healthy dash of ground cinnamon
1 ripe banana, peeled and sliced
maple syrup

Preheat oven to 425 degrees. Divide butter between 2 shallow 1-cup ovenproof dishes. Place dishes in oven for a minute or 2 to melt butter. Watch carefully so butter doesn't burn; remove. Place eggs, flour, milk, and cinnamon in a small bowl and stir until just combined. (Batter will be lumpy.) Divide batter between the 2 prepared dishes and top each with half the banana slices. Return dishes to the oven and bake for 15 to 20 minutes or until they are puffed and golden. Serve hot from the oven with a drizzle of maple syrup. Be sure to slip the pancake out of the hot individual baking dishes before serving them to your child.

Makes 2 grown-up servings.

Table Food for Toddlers and Grown-ups Too

Country Peasant Omelet

No fancy folding or flipping skills are needed for this easy entree when time is short and the refrigerator is bare.

4 to 6 eggs
1 tablespoon water
1 tablespoon vegetable oil
1 medium boiling potato, scrubbed and cut into small dice
$1/2$ medium onion, diced
1 tablespoon unsalted butter
1 tablespoon chopped fresh parsley
Salt and freshly ground black pepper to taste

Combine eggs and water in a small bowl and set aside. Warm vegetable oil in a medium-size nonstick frying pan over medium-high heat for 2 minutes. Add potatoes and cook, stirring frequently, for 10 to 12 minutes or until potatoes are almost tender. Add onion and cook, stirring frequently, for 2 to 3 minutes more or until onion is lightly browned. Remove potato and onion filling from pan and keep warm while cooking the eggs.

Reduce heat to low and melt butter in pan. Beat eggs and water until foamy and add to pan, letting cook undisturbed for 15 seconds. Then, with a wooden spoon, pull an edge of omelet toward center and tilt pan so raw egg runs and fills bottom of pan again. Repeat process all around the pan until egg no longer runs. Once omelet is almost set, turn off heat but leave pan on burner. Spread potato and onions on top of omelet, sprinkle with chopped parsley, and season with salt and pepper. Gently loosen omelet from pan and slide onto a round platter. Cut into wedges and serve immediately.

Makes 2 to 3 grown-up servings.

EGGS

Introduce egg yolks at 11 months; whole eggs—with the whites—at 12 months.

Nutritional Profile: Eggs are an excellent source of protein and cholesterol (which kids need). They also provide calcium; iron; fat; and vitamins A, D, and B_2.

Variations: Finish with these—with or without the potato and onion:

- ¹/₄ cup grated cheese
- ¹/₄ cup chopped tomato
- 2 scallions, thinly sliced
- about 1 tablespoon chopped fresh herbs

Or, for a heartier omelet, add a handful of leftover shredded cooked chicken or ham along with the onion.

Egg in a Hole

All the king's horses and all the king's men probably wouldn't have minded if they knew this was how Humpty Dumpty ended up. For an extraordinary hole, use a fanciful cookie cutter or cut your child's initial in the bread.

1 slice whole-wheat or whole-grain bread
2 teaspoons unsalted butter
1 egg

With a sharp knife (or cookie cutter), cut at least a 2¹/₂- to 3-inch piece out of the center of the slice of bread. Set cutout aside. Melt half the butter in a small nonstick skillet over low heat. Place bread in pan and crack egg into hole. Cook for 2 minutes. Place remaining butter on top of egg, turn over, and cook for 1 minute longer. Transfer from pan to serving plate and keep warm. Raise heat to medium and quickly toast reserved cutout for dipping into the yolk.

Makes 1 grown-up serving.

Table Food for Toddlers
and Grown-ups Too

Farm-fresh eggs from free-range chickens are best. Most eggs sold in our supermarkets are from 1 week to 1 month old and laid by cooped-up chickens. Select eggs with clean shells, as the shells are very porous and can absorb harmful bacteria. (There is no difference in taste between white and brown eggs.) Store eggs in your refrigerator; they'll stay fresh for about a month. They keep best in the carton in which they were purchased. As eggs age, the air pockets at their fatter ends become larger, making stale eggs lighter than fresh ones. A sure test is to place the egg in question in cold water. A fresh one sinks to the bottom; an old one floats. For baking, bring eggs to room temperature before beginning recipe.

SOME GREAT FLAVOR COMBINATIONS

Don't be afraid to be creative. Once a food is allergy-tested and accepted, mix it with any food you like. Taste the combination yourself before feeding it to your baby. Chances are if you like it, baby will too!

Apples and:

- sweet potatoes or yams
- pears
- any cereal
- tofu
- carrots
- yogurt
- custard
- Chicken Little (page 164)

Pears and:

- squash
- sweet potatoes or yams
- custard
- carrots
- peas
- cottage cheese
- bananas

Bananas and:

- yams
- yogurt
- tofu
- custard
- soft-cooked egg yolks

Beets and:

- yogurt
- cottage cheese
- ricotta cheese
- baked potato
- carrots
- Brown Rice Cereal (page 204)
- One-Pot Beef Dinner (page 180)

Squash and:

- apples
- pears
- peaches
- liver
- beef

Beef and:

- noodles
- potatoes
- peas
- carrots
- beets

Noodles and:

- chicken
- peas and carrots
- pears and beets
- apples and carrots
- ricotta and beets
- pot cheese and apples

Egg Custard (page 239) and:

- peaches
- pears
- apples
- plums
- squash
- yams

Super Soups for Sipping and Supping

Basic Cream Soup

You can make an infinite variety of very grown-up soups with any of baby's leftover vegetable or fruit purees. We've used broccoli here, but you can simply substitute 2 cups of any vegetable—or even fruit— puree for broccoli and follow this basic recipe, adjusting herbs and spices to taste. Some possibilities: cream of carrot with a touch of orange, cream of zucchini with parsley, pear and pumpkin with ginger.

2 celery stalks, cut into large dice
1 small onion, cut into large dice
1½ quarts chicken stock
2 large potatoes, peeled and thinly sliced
2 cups broccoli or any vegetable puree
pinch of dried thyme
1 small bay leaf
¼ cup milk, half-and-half, or cream

Combine all the ingredients except the milk in a large pot. Bring to a boil over high heat. Reduce heat to low and simmer, stirring occasionally, for 20 to 25 minutes or until potato is tender. Remove from heat and allow to cool. Discard bay leaf, and puree soup in a food processor fitted with the steel blade until smooth—approximately 30 to 40 seconds. (To prevent spills, puree in small batches.) Return pureed soup to the pot. Add milk and bring almost to a boil. Serve immediately with a cooked broccoli "tree"—a small branching stalk—for garnish.

Makes 2 quarts.

Warm Butternut Squash–Tangerine Soup

A very grown-up use for baby's puree that's suitable for baby too. The juice of any orange can be used in place of tangerine.

¹/₄ cup freshly squeezed and strained tangerine or orange juice
1 recipe Butternut Squash Puree (page 134)
¹/₂ cup plain yogurt
1 teaspoon grated tangerine or orange zest

In a saucepan, add tangerine juice to puree to thin. Heat slowly. If soup is too thick, add more juice until desired consistency is reached. Remember to add only a little juice at a time; it's easier to thin than thicken. To serve, garnish with a dollop of yogurt and a bit of grated tangerine zest.

Makes 2 cups.

Spoon and Finger Food
for Bigger Babies

"Just What the Doctor Ordered!" Chicken Soup

Table Food for Toddlers
and Grown-ups Too

The therapeutic qualities of a steaming bowl of chicken soup are beginning to receive some scientific support. In 1982 a research team at Mt. Sinai Medical Center in Miami, Florida, tested the sinus-clearing value of chicken soup over other hot and cold liquids. Chicken soup and its vapors proved far superior to any other liquid, even when the soup was cold and sipped through a straw inserted in a lid! But this soothing favorite of children and grown-ups is good anytime. And it freezes perfectly—including the vegetables—either in bulk or in individual portions.

1 large stewing or soup chicken, including the neck
1 tablespoon coarse (kosher) salt
1 large sweet potato, peeled and quartered
2 parsnips, peeled
4 carrots, peeled
1 large onion, peeled and halved
1 rutabaga, peeled and quartered
3 celery stalks including tops, cut lengthwise into quarters
2 fresh dill sprigs *or* a pinch of dried

Place chicken and chicken neck in a large pot. Cover with cold water and add salt. Bring to a boil and then lower heat to a simmer. Add remaining ingredients. Simmer for approximately 3 hours. (The chicken should fall off the bones, and the vegetables should be very tender.) Strain soup and carefully pick out the vegetables and return to the broth. Reserve chicken for other uses—chicken salad, finger food, pieces served with the soup. Discard the chicken skin, bones, celery tops, and dill sprigs. Adjust the seasonings and chill. When the soup is cold, the fat will form a layer at the top; discard it. To serve, reheat soup; place a piece of each vegetable in each bowl and cover with broth. Add a piece of chicken if you like.

This recipe is from Teddi and Renée's Grandma Miriam Kimmel, as taught to her by her mother.

Makes 6 to 8 grown-up servings.

For Bigger Babies (over 10 months): Mash or puree the vegetables (except the onion) with a little broth to achieve a smooth consistency. Also offer broth either at room temperature or slightly warmed by spoon, by cup, or even in a bottle.

Very Veggie Broth and Beverage

Here is a very nutritious "sick" soup/beverage for older babies and another way to get your child to eat vegetables. Because of the onion and tomato, this broth should not be introduced before 1 year. For the finicky eater, freeze the broth in ice cube trays and use as "ice" in apple juice. Or turn this broth into a soup by adding the cooked vegetables and/or some bite-size pasta.

2 large sweet potatoes, peeled and quartered
4 carrots, peeled and cut into chunks
1 medium red bell pepper, seeded, cored, and quartered
5 celery tops
1 medium tomato, quartered
1 medium onion, peeled and quartered
2 fresh dill sprigs
2 fresh parsley sprigs
2$\frac{1}{2}$ quarts cold water

Place vegetables and herbs in stockpot. Add cold water. Simmer over low heat (do not boil) until vegetables are very soft—approximately 1 hour. Strain well. Serve broth cold, at room temperature, or warm in a bottle, cup, or bowl.

Makes 2$\frac{1}{2}$ quarts.

Spoon and Finger Food
for Bigger Babies

Spell-Your-Name Soup

Table Food for Toddlers
and Grown-ups Too

Your child will love having his name spelled out in pasta. If he is feeding himself, keep the vegetables big enough so that he can pluck them out of the soup with his fingers. If you're out of alphabet pasta, any shape can be substituted. Chicken broth can also be used instead of water. If you're using canned broth, be sure to taste the finished soup before adding salt.

2 tablespoons virgin olive oil
2 medium carrots, sliced
2 to 3 celery stalks, sliced
1 medium yellow onion, chopped
½ small rutabaga, peeled and diced
1 garlic clove, minced
2 quarts water
1 bay leaf
pinch of dried thyme
1 cup green beans, cut into ½-inch pieces
1 cup frozen corn niblets
1 cup frozen green peas
½ cup uncooked alphabet pasta
salt and freshly ground black pepper to taste

Warm olive oil in a large pot. Add carrot, celery, onion, and rutabaga and cook over medium heat, stirring frequently, until onion is transparent—about 5 to 6 minutes. Add garlic and cook for 1 minute longer, stirring frequently. Add water, bay leaf, and thyme and bring to a boil. Reduce heat and simmer soup for 25 to 30 minutes. Add remaining ingredients except salt and pepper and cook until pasta is tender. (Use cooking time for pasta listed on box.) Remove bay leaf before serving* and season to taste.

Keep some precooked alphabet pasta in the freezer. It quickly defrosts in any hot soup and makes it special.

Makes 2$^1/_2$ quarts.

For Bigger Babies (over 10 months): At this point in the recipe, before seasoning soup with salt and pepper, strain a baby-sized amount of vegetables and pasta from broth and puree in a food mill or processor fitted with the steel blade. Add broth to adjust consistency to your child's taste.

Variations: Add one of the following:

- $^1/_2$ cup coarsely chopped tomato along with pasta
- miso bean paste to taste after pasta is cooked
- shredded spinach or kale or sliced mushrooms 5 minutes before pasta is finished cooking

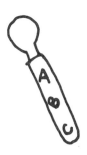

Calcium-Rich Broth

Spoon and Finger Food
for Bigger Babies

A great way to add calcium to the diets of milk-sensitive and lactose-intolerant babies and toddlers. In this recipe and the Iron-Rich Broth that follows, any particular vegetable can be omitted.

1 quart cold water
2 broccoli branches washed and cut into 1/4-inch rounds
1/2 cup collard or dandelion greens, rinsed well and roughly chopped
1/2 cup well-rinsed, roughly chopped kale
3 carrots, scrubbed, trimmed, and cut into 1/4-inch rounds

Place cold water in a medium-size pot with a close-fitting lid. Add all vegetables. Cover tightly (for better nutrient retention) and bring broth to a boil over high heat. Reduce heat to a simmer and cook for 1 hour. Strain broth, discarding vegetables. Serve warm or cool in a bottle or cup. (Leftovers freeze perfectly in ice cube trays. Pop a broth cube into your child's favorite juice to fortify with calcium.)

Makes about 3 cups.

Iron-Rich Broth

1 quart cold water
$^{1}/_{2}$ cup shelled fresh or frozen peas
$^{1}/_{2}$ cup well-rinsed, roughly chopped beet greens
$^{1}/_{2}$ cup endive or escarole, rinsed well and roughly chopped
1 large sweet potato, peeled and quartered

Spoon and Finger Food
for Bigger Babies

Place water in a medium-size pot with a close-fitting lid. Add all vegetables. Cover tightly (for better nutrient retention) and bring to a boil over high heat. Reduce heat until broth barely simmers and continue cooking for 1 hour. Strain liquid, discarding vegetables. Serve broth warm or cool in a baby bottle or cup. (Leftovers freeze perfectly in ice cube trays. Plunk a broth cube into your child's favorite juice to fortify with iron.)

Makes approximately 3 cups.

Snacks and Sandwiches

Curried Tuna Salad

Table Food for Toddlers
and Grown-ups Too

If your child is allergic to (or just doesn't like) raisins, nuts, scallions, celery, or even the curry in this recipe, just leave any or all out. In the summer curried tuna salad can star, stuffed in a whole garden-ripe tomato, or anytime as a filling for pita pockets or toasted whole-wheat or rye bread sandwiches. Using 1 cup diced chicken or turkey in place of the tuna in this recipe is also yummy.

1 6½-ounce can water-packed tuna, drained
1 small celery stalk, finely chopped
1 scallion, finely sliced
a medium handful of toasted whole almonds, coarsely chopped
2 tablespoons raisins
¼ cup mayonnaise (or less to taste)
2 teaspoons curry powder

Flake tuna in a small bowl with a fork. Add remaining ingredients and mix well. Serve immediately or chill until mealtime.

Makes enough to fill 3 sandwiches.

Variations: Omit raisins, almonds, and curry and add 1 hard-cooked egg, chopped, or ¼ cup chopped apple.

Egg Salad with Caramelized Onions

Try this special egg salad on a toasted roll, raisin bread, or stuffed into a pita pocket with sprouts.

1 tablespoon unsalted butter
1 cup minced onion
6 large hard-cooked eggs, chopped
1/3 cup mayonnaise
1/4 teaspoon salt
1/8 teaspoon freshly ground pepper

Melt butter in a small frying pan over very low heat. Add onions and cook slowly for 15 to 18 minutes or until golden brown (caramelized). Remove pan from heat and allow onions to cool. In a medium bowl, combine onion, chopped eggs, mayonnaise, salt, and pepper; mix well. Cover with plastic wrap and chill.

Makes 2 cups.

TASMANIAN DEVIL EGGHEADS

Any leftover hard-cooked eggs? Turn them into Tasmanian Devil Eggheads. We nicknamed our younger daughter and these goodies after this popular cartoon character, since they both go so fast. Great at parties. They can be made well ahead; keep covered in the refrigerator until serving time.

Cut peeled hard-cooked eggs in half lengthwise. Carefully remove yolks, reserving whites, and mash in a medium bowl with 1/2 teaspoon ketchup and 1/2 teaspoon mayonnaise per egg. Scoop a teaspoon of the mixture back into each egg white half. Decorate stuffed eggs with pea eyes, a carrot strip mouth, and fresh or dried dill or parsley hair.

Table Food for Toddlers and Grown-ups Too

Perfect Hard-Cooked Eggs

To hard-cook eggs without turning their yolks green: Place room-temperature eggs in a small pot and cover with water. (If they're very fresh, leave them at room temperature overnight so they'll shell easily.) Watching carefully, bring to a boil over medium heat. When the water boils, promptly cover pot with a tight-fitting lid and turn off heat. (If using an electric stove, move pot to a cool element.) Allow to sit for 14 minutes. Remove from stove, drain, and set pot under cool running water for 1 minute to cool eggs. Once eggs are cool enough to handle, gently tap fat ends against side of pot and return eggs to water to complete cooling. When ready to serve, tap eggshells thoroughly on any hard surface and peel off. Rinse shelled eggs under cold running water and set on paper or cloth towel to drain.

Inside-Out Sandwiches

These simple sandwiches take only seconds to prepare, don't fall apart on baby, and are a great traveling snack. They are best with freshly baked breadsticks. But if these are unavailable, the thick toasted ones commonly available in supermarkets will work too. Serve with baby's favorite dip for an extra treat: Horseradish Sauce (page 278), Summer Pesto (page 279), Winter Pesto (page 280), My First Salad Dressing (page 273), etc.

4 very thin slices lean ham (such as Black Forest)
4 very thin slices lean roast beef
4 very thin slices Swiss cheese
12 short, thick, sesame seed breadsticks

Lay out slices of ham, roast beef, and Swiss cheese. Place a breadstick at the end of each slice and roll up. To go: wrap the sticks tightly in foil.

Makes 12 sandwiches.

Lettuce Roll-Ups

When kids put together their own food, they're sure to eat it! Simply set out an assortment of fillings, garnishes, and lettuce wrappers and let them have fun—with Mommy and Daddy's supervision, of course. Place 2 to 3 tablespoons of any filling in a wrapper, garnish, roll up, and it's ready to eat. Dips and dunking sauces add yet another delicious dimension to this handy, eat-in-hand entree.

Table Food for Toddlers
and Grown-ups Too

Fillings and Garnishes: tuna salad, egg salad, chicken or turkey salad, Chickpea Dip (page 275), chopped tomatoes, shredded cheese (Swiss, Cheddar, Monterey Jack), chopped scallion, pickle slices, raisins, chopped olives, Summer or Winter Pesto (pages 279–280), nuts, shredded carrot, cucumber strands, capers, Lo Mein with Sesame and Peanuts (page 197), roasted and raw bell peppers, seasoned rice.

Wrappers: iceberg, romaine, bibb, or Boston lettuce leaves.

Dips and Dunking Sauces: My First Salad Dressing (page 273), Tahini Dressing (page 275), Yogurt Topping (page 276), hoisin sauce, assorted mustards, mayonnaise, and ketchup.

A Few of Our Favorite Roll-Up Combos

- Lo Mein with Sesame and Peanuts (page 197), hoisin sauce, and cucumber shreds
- Egg Salad with Caramelized Onions (page 223) with chopped tomatoes
- Curried Tuna Salad (page 222) with carrot shreds and chopped pickles
- Chickpea Dip (page 275) with roasted bell peppers and grated cheese

Grilled Cheese Triangles . . . and Squares and Rectangles

Table Food for Toddlers and Grown-ups Too

A geometry lesson in a sandwich, especially if you change the shape each day. Dust with pizza seasoning and/or tuck sliced tomato between the cheese slices and you have a "pizza sandwich."

2 slices whole wheat sandwich bread
2 slices American cheese
Pizza seasoning (optional)
Sliced tomato (optional)
1 tablespoon butter

Assemble sandwich, putting seasoning and tomato between cheese slices. Melt butter in a small frying pan. When hot add sandwich and heat over medium-low heat until bread is brown and crusted on one side. Flip, and continue cooking until the other side is toasty and cheese begins to melt. Cut, letting your child pick her shape of the day.

Makes 1 sandwich.

Stuffed Cucumber Logs with Raisin Ants

2 ounces cream cheese, left at room temperature to soften
1 cucumber, peeled, halved lengthwise, and seeded
a small handful of raisins, chopped

Table Food for Toddlers
and Grown-ups Too

Fill each cucumber half with softened cream cheese. Sprinkle on chopped raisins (the ants), gently patting them into the cheese with your hand. Cut logs in half or quarters. Chill or serve immediately.

Makes a snack for 2.

Variations: Jazz up the cream cheese filling by mixing in any of the following:

- $1/4$ steamed carrot, cut into small dice
- $1/4$ red bell pepper, cut into small dice
- 2 tablespoons crumbled crisp-cooked bacon
- 1 slice ham, chopped
- a few chunks of pineapple, chopped

Or try any of these log fillings instead of cream cheese:

- peanut butter
- Egg Salad with Caramelized Onions (page 223)
- Curried Tuna Salad (page 222)
- cottage cheese
- shrimp salad
- Chicken Liver and Avocado Puree (page 167)

Cone-u-Copias

Table Food for Toddlers
and Grown-ups Too

Ordinary ice-cream cones (the biscuit variety with the flat bottoms) become virtual horns of plenty when filled with any of the following. Although most cones found on your supermarket shelf contain some sugar, they make any meal special and will persuade babies and toddlers with the most finicky appetites to nibble away at their nutritious contents.

Here are some of our favorite fillings to get you started:

- egg salad dipped in shredded carrot
- tuna salad with a grape cherry
- a Monster Meatball (page 182)
- fruit salad sprinkled with coconut
- popcorn dusted with freshly grated Parmesan cheese
- chicken salad with raisins
- assorted vegetable sticks with Chickpea Dip (page 275) in bottom of cone
- cottage cheese mixed with melon chunks

CONE CAKES

Preheat oven to 350 degrees. Fill each cone half full with your favorite cake batter and bake cone upright on a cookie sheet until a toothpick inserted in center comes out clean—about 30 to 35 minutes. When cone cakes are cool, frost with your favorite icing and decorate.

Toasted Waffles with Peanut Butter, Jelly, and Fresh Fruit

Here's a twist on that perennial toddler favorite, peanut butter and jelly. In a pinch, use frozen waffles from the supermarket. Some brands are quite nutritious and additive-free; just check the fine print on the package. Waffles also make fun open-face sandwiches. They are good with almost anything spreadable, including tuna, cream cheese and jelly, and egg salad.

2 fresh or frozen waffles
1 tablespoon peanut butter
a small handful of sliced strawberries, whole blueberries, or whole raspberries
1 tablespoon sugar-free strawberry, blueberry, or raspberry jelly

Toast waffles. Spread one half with peanut butter. Arrange fruit on top and gently press in. Spread other waffle with jelly and make a sandwich. To serve, cut into quarters, triangles, or other shapes.

Makes 1 waffle sandwich.

Table Food for Toddlers and Grown-ups Too

PEANUTS

Introduce peanuts and peanut butter after 1 year and with care. Peanuts are a common allergen, and both peanuts and peanut butter are a common cause of choking in young children.

Nutritional Profile: protein; fat; fiber (roasted peanuts); vitamins E and B complex; iron and potassium.

Choose freshly roasted peanuts in their shells or tightly sealed jars or cans of processed peanuts. Freshly ground peanut butter made from just peanuts is best. It is usually available in health food stores and the deli department of some supermarkets. Commercial peanut butter can contain salt, sugar, and other oils. Read the label. Store commercial peanut butter in tightly sealed jar at room temperature. Freshly ground peanut butter should be kept in the refrigerator. It will need a quick stir to combine the oils before using.

From the Grocer's Shelf

Your local supermarket can be an excellent source of healthy, prepared food products for the whole family. These will save Mommy and Daddy time in the kitchen while adding instant variety to the menu. You should always read the labels when purchasing prepared foods: look for products that contain little or no salt, sugar, additives, preservatives, or artificial coloring.

Fruit Juice: Be wary of labels reading "juice cocktail," "juice punch," "juice drink," or "100 percent natural." The fine print will reveal that corn syrup or another sweetener has been added. Sugar is hard to escape. Although it's not listed as an ingredient, even the juice concentrates used to make bottled juices usually have some added sugar. Mix fruit juice with club soda or seltzer for a great low-sugar or sugar-free soda pop.

Jelly and Jam: We like the fruit-sweetened jams such as Polaner All Fruit and Smucker's Simply Fruit. They are not quite as sweet as the regular jams and jellies, which contain corn syrup and sugar.

Peanut Butter: A pantry essential. If freshly ground peanut butter is unavailable, some of the name brands such as Smucker's Natural contain only peanuts and are lightly salted. Read the fine print; much of the standard supermarket peanut butter contains sugar and hydrogenated oil.

Waffles: When we don't have time to make our own, we serve Kellogg's Eggo waffles. Our kids think they're the best of the lot. Eggo waffles come in different varieties—NutriGrain is our favorite. Try them toasted and topped with fruit puree and cottage cheese, yogurt and freshly cut-up fruit, or sandwiched with peanut butter and fruit-sweetened jam, a touch of honey (1 year old plus, only), or maple syrup. When every moment counts, these always seem to please.

Breakfast Cereals: Cheerios are the house favorite. And although they have a little sugar in them (the label lists 1 gram per 1-ounce serving), we offer them for breakfast and snacks. They're good finger food, and the "O" shape is popular.

Hot Cereals: Oatmeal is a breakfast staple for the kids, quick to make, and very satisfying—Mom and Dad usually end up eating some of it too. Quaker Oats are good, as is the H-O brand. Top a bowl of steaming oatmeal with freshly sliced bananas, fruit puree, yogurt, or milk and a drizzle of maple syrup, a handful of raisins, or a dusting of cinnamon. Instant Cream of Wheat (regular) is also good for a change of taste.

Pancake Mix: Another favorite that makes it to our table at least once a week is pancakes. We like Pepperidge Farm Homestyle. It's made from a blend of five flours and has a lot of character. All Pepperidge Farm pancake mixes are of high quality.

Buckwheat or Kasha: Wolff's is consistently good and available in different granulations—although we all seem to like medium-size the best.

Couscous: Near East brand is a great product. The line also includes other high-quality Middle Eastern specialties, including falafel, tabbouleh, and sesame tahini.

Pasta (dried): A most important food in our family, especially popular between one and three years. We serve it at least twice a week in a variety of ways. Some pasta is made only with wheat semolina; some is enriched with wheat germ, iron, and niacin. Some pastas are sodium-free. Egg noodles are made with whole eggs. (Don't worry about the cholesterol in the yolks for baby, but hold off on the whites until baby is over one year.) We use almost all of the available brands as they offer different shapes and sizes. Whenever noodles are on the menu, we always cook some extra to freeze for future quick meals. (See Oodles of Noodles, page 193, for more information.)

Pasta Sauces: We almost always make our own. But when in a pinch our toddler wanted it *now,* we would reach for a jar. In all fairness, some of the mass-produced sauces are not so bad. Read the labels and avoid products that list corn syrup, sugar, MSG, or other chemical additives as ingredients. Prego or Buitoni marinara is usually what we keep in the cupboard. Although a bit pricey, for more variety, try the fresh sauces found in the refrigerator section of your supermarket.

Rice: We almost always serve brown rice. Not only does it have more flavor and texture than white, but it contains more nutrients. Try River brand natural long-grain brown rice.

Rice Cakes: These make marvelously crunchy all-natural, wheat-free snacks and open-face sandwich bottoms. Spread them with just about anything—cottage cheese, jam, peanut butter, tuna. They hold together well, even after the first bite.

Soft, Spreadable Dairy Products, Including Cottage Cheese, Yogurt, Sour Cream, Ricotta Cheese, Cream Cheese, and Farmer's Cheese: These are all great in a hurry and mix well with fruit purees, serve as toppings for eggs or cooked vegetables, and can be spread on bread, bagels, and English muffins, to mention a few possibilities.

Cheese: While most mild cheeses are very popular with our kids, Muenster, Swiss, and mozzarella head the list. And Polly-O string cheese sticks made of 100 percent part-skim-milk mozzarella is their absolute favorite.

Tuna: Always pick water-packed. Tuna is very versatile. Use it for tuna noodle casseroles, tuna salad, etc. However you enjoy it, just be sure the preparation is moist enough for baby to chew and swallow easily.

Frozen Vegetables: Fresh is always our first choice, but sometimes it's just not practical. Frozen is always our next consideration and quite good, especially whole peas, lima beans, and corn niblets. Choose a brand that has no butter, sauce, or other topping and use as if fresh. Avoid thawing frozen vegetables before cooking.

Frozen Fruits: As with vegetables, fresh fruit is best too. But when necessary, frozen fruit is a good second. Choose frozen fruit with no added sugar. (By law added sugar must be listed near the product name.) Avoid packages with heavy frost on the outside, which indicates some improper handling along the way. Big Valley brand frozen fruit is of high quality and contains no added sugar.

Canned Pineapple: Don't want to cut a whole fresh pineapple for just a little for baby? Dole packages pineapple in its own unsweetened juice. Serve in chunks as finger food or top with vanilla yogurt for dessert. Our girls would have us doling it out every day if they had their way.

Tapioca: Minute brand quick-cooking tapioca is widely available and good.

Riding-the-Range Trail Mix

Table Food for Toddlers
and Grown-ups Too

Don't leave home without it! Trail mix doesn't spoil, and when the hungries strike—in the park, at the supermarket, in the doctor's office—you can beat them to the draw. It's also a good lunch box treat.

1/4 cup dried banana chips
1/2 cup Corn Chex
1/4 cup chopped dried fruit (apricot, peach, apple)
1/4 cup raisins
1/4 cup shelled peanuts
1/4 cup sunflower seeds

Mix all ingredients together in a bowl and store in an airtight container; it will keep 2 weeks.

Makes 1³/₄ cups.

Variations: The key to a good trail mix is variety in the colors, shapes, textures, and tastes. Almost anything that doesn't need refrigeration can work, such as:

- pretzel sticks
- Ritz Bits (mini Ritz crackers)
- hazelnuts, walnuts, pecans, almonds, and cashews
- popcorn
- low-sugar cold cereal in interesting shapes
- granola
- dates
- prunes
- rice or corn chips
- even chocolate chips

Bagel and English Muffin Melts

Here are three possibilities using toasted bagel halves or torn English muffin halves as a base. Vary the toppings to suit your family and the contents of your refrigerator: blue cheese, pears, and walnuts for the gourmets; chili, diced tomato, chopped onion, and grated Cheddar for the bigger kids. Raisin or whole-wheat bagels and muffins will add another dimension. Make and serve melts while everyone waits. They take only minutes to prepare and should be eaten piping hot.

VEGGIE MELT
$1/4$ medium tomato, chopped
1 tablespoon sliced scallion
2 tablespoons chopped red bell pepper
1 large, thin slice of Jarlsberg, halved

Combine tomato, scallion, and red pepper in a small bowl. Cut bagel or tear muffin and toast halves lightly. Divide mixture and top bagel or muffin halves with it and the cheese. Heat halves in toaster oven or under preheated oven broiler until cheese melts, bubbles, and begins to brown. Serve immediately.

PESTO-TUNA MELT
2 tablespoons Summer or Winter Pesto (pages 279–280)
$1/4$ medium tomato, chopped
$1/4$ cup drained and flaked water-packed tuna
1 slice mozzarella, diced

Spread 1 tablespoon pesto on each toasted bagel or muffin half. Combine tomato and tuna, divide equally, and mound on each bagel or muffin half. Top with diced mozzarella and heat in toaster oven or under preheated oven broiler until cheese melts, bubbles, and begins to brown. Serve immediately.

Table Food for Toddlers and Grown-ups Too

For the wee ones, plain bagels make tasty teething rings. When you're out for a walk or cooking in the kitchen, loop a short ribbon through the hole and tie it to baby's stroller or high chair so he can retrieve it if it falls.

COTTAGE MELT
½ cup cottage cheese
½ cup steamed fruit, cut into chunks

Spread each toasted bagel or muffin half with ¼ cup cottage cheese and top with fruit. Lightly brown in toaster oven or under preheated oven broiler. Serve immediately.

Each of the above toppings makes enough for 2 bagel or muffin halves—1 grown-up serving.

Cinnamon Toast

Table Food for Toddlers and Grown-ups Too

Cinnamon toast is a cinch to make and nice for an afternoon snack when the cookie jar is empty. Chopped walnuts can be added to the cinnamon sugar.

2 slices white bread
1 tablespoon butter
1 teaspoon cinnamon
2 tablespoons sugar

Toast bread and butter. Mix sugar and cinnamon and sprinkle some on buttered toast. (Save any leftover cinnamon sugar for seconds, French toast, or pancakes.) Cut toast in triangles and serve.

Make 2 grown-up servings.

Popcorn Plus

This is our low-sugar, but still sweet, version of the popular commercial popcorn-and-peanut snacks. Popcorn is high in fiber and the perfect all-natural treat/snack food for bigger babies with lots of teeth. (Smaller ones can choke on popcorn.) Pop it dry in a hot-air popper for the purest product. Then add your own embellishments.

Table Food for Toddlers
and Grown-ups Too

$1/2$ cup unpopped corn, popped
2 tablespoons molasses
$1/4$ cup light corn syrup
$1/4$ cup peanuts

Combine popped corn with remaining ingredients in a large bowl and toss to mix well. Form into balls, use to fill ice cream cones, or just let dry for a few hours and eat as is.

Variations: Also try on plain popped corn:

- 1 tablespoon ground cinnamon
- 3 tablespoons freshly grated Parmesan cheese
- any no-salt vegetable seasoning

Fruit Leather

Table Food for Toddlers
and Grown-ups Too

This is a delicious, naturally sweet, take-anywhere snack. Although this recipe contains only fruit puree, feed fruit leather only to bigger babies with teeth.

2 cups fruit puree (apple, pear, papaya, peach, apricot; see recipes in "Fruits" section)

Line a cookie sheet with waxed paper. Spread fruit puree evenly over wrap (about $1/4$ inch thick) and place in oven.

Electric oven: Preheat oven to its lowest setting (120 to 140 degrees) and place tray on middle shelf. Leave door ajar (3 to 5 inches) and allow to dry for 6 to 8 hours or until leather is dry to the touch.

Gas oven: The pilot light usually provides enough heat to dry fruit. Place tray on middle shelf. Open door for a few moments every few hours to let moisture escape. Drying can take from 1 to 2 days.

To store: Roll up fruit leather in the waxed paper. Mommy Made fruit leather will hold for about 3 to 4 weeks at room temperature, 3 months in the refrigerator, or 6 months frozen.

Makes 1 large piece, the size of your cookie sheet.

Variations: Combined fruits are delicious and pretty. Marbleize 2 contrasting-colored fruit purees by swirling equal amounts together on the waxed paper. Or add one of these to the puree:

- a touch of ground cinnamon
- a bit of grated coconut

Satisfying Snacks

We're not opposed to something sweet. Just be sure snacks pack some nutrition too. Cookies and milk don't have to be the standard. How about some of these?

- Egg custard with or without fruit (pages 239–240)
- Banana-Maple Rice Pudding (page 243)
- Cantaloupe-Tapioca Pudding (page 242)
- Stuffed Cucumber Logs with Raisin Ants (page 227)
- Toasted Waffles with Peanut Butter, Jelly, and Fresh Fruit (page 229)
- Bagels or English muffins with Strawberry-Apple Butter (page 282), cottage cheese, cream cheese
- Riding-the-Range Trail Mix (page 234)
- Granola (page 206)

Puddings, Gelatins, and Other SpoonableTreats

Elementary Egg Custard

The basic egg custard is an excellent way to introduce baby to egg yolks. For a milk-free custard, replace the cow's milk with soy or nut milk.

1 egg yolk, beaten
½ cup milk
½ teaspoon vanilla extract (optional)

Preheat oven to 350 degrees. Blend all ingredients together. Divide mixture between 2 4-ounce custard cups. Set custard cups in a pan in preheated oven. Create a water bath by pouring hot water around cups; the water level should reach halfway up their sides. Bake custard for 30 minutes or until done. (A toothpick inserted in the center should come out clean.)

Makes 2 4-ounce custards.

Variation: Add 2 teaspoons of fresh pureed fruit or vegetables to the custard mixture. Divide between 3 4-ounce custard cups and proceed with recipe.

Spoon and Finger Food
for Bigger Babies

Egg Custard with Poached Pear and Raspberry

A more grown-up version of Elementary Egg Custard. This is one treat that baby will have a hard time keeping the rest of the family from eating, so we've increased the quantity to give everyone a taste.

2 Bartlett pears, cored, peeled, and quartered just before cooking
4 egg yolks
2 cups milk
$1/2$ teaspoon vanilla extract
$1/4$ pint raspberries

Preheat oven to 350 degrees. Place pear quarters in a steamer basket set in a pot containing a small amount of lightly boiling water. Steam until tender, about 8 to 12 minutes, replenishing water during steaming if necessary. Check for doneness with a toothpick. Set aside 5 pear quarters; puree the remaining 3 in a food processor fitted with the steel blade or in a food mill. In a small bowl, make the custard mixture by thoroughly beating together the egg yolks, milk, pear puree, and vanilla.

Place a pear slice in the bottom of 5 to 6 ovenproof custard cups. Fill cups $3/4$ full with custard mixture and pop a raspberry in each.

Place a large shallow pan in the preheated oven and carefully arrange all the filled custard cups in it. (The cups should not touch each other or the sides of the pan.) Pour hot water into the pan, filling until the water level reaches $1/2$ to $3/4$ of the way up the sides of the custard cups. Bake custards until a toothpick inserted in the center comes out clean, about 40 to 60 minutes.

Chill custards and serve with a sauce made by pureeing the remaining raspberries. Stir in any leftover pear puree if you like.

Makes 5- to 6 $1/2$-cup servings.

Apple Wiggle

Before Jell-O, every mommy made her own gelatin desserts. Here's our tasty low-sugar version for baby. For more grown-up palates and festive occasions, chill the mixture in a small square pan. Cut into cubes when firm, layer with yogurt or ice cream in parfait glasses, and garnish with whipped cream and a slice of fresh fruit. For baby, simply place a few squares on his high chair tray for a slippery but fun finger food. The following technique can also be used to make a nonsweet wiggle with any of the broths in the soup chapter (pages 214–221). Pieces of fresh fruit or vegetables cooked or raw (except pineapple) can be added to the gelatin mixture too. Add approximately 1 cup when gelatin is almost set.

Spoon and Finger Food
for Bigger Babies

2 cups apple juice
1½ teaspoons gelatin (1 envelope equals 2 teaspoons)
½ cup My First Applesauce (page 116)

Pour ½ cup of the apple juice into a small mixing bowl. Sprinkle gelatin over juice and let sit for 10 minutes to soften. Place bowl in a steamer over boiling water, stirring constantly until gelatin dissolves and mixture turns clear. Remove from heat. Add remaining apple juice and puree, stir well, and pour into small bowls or cups. Refrigerate for at least 2½ hours or until set.

Makes 4 ½-cup servings.

Fruitful Variations: Substitute one of the following for the apple juice and puree

- 2 cups grape juice and ½ cup Pear Puree (page 122)
- 2 cups Iron-Rich Broth (page 221) and ½ cup Sweet Potato Puree (page 132)

Cantaloupe-Tapioca Pudding

**Spoon and Finger Food
for Bigger Babies**

This is an eggless dessert that even the small fry under 1 can enjoy. Try other fruit purees—singly or in combination—in place of the cantaloupe, such as apple, pear, papaya, peach, apricot, and mango or apple-strawberry or apple-raspberry.

½ cup water
½ cup thawed apple juice concentrate
⅓ cup quick-cooking tapioca
pinch of salt
1½ cups Cantaloupe Puree (page 130)
½ cup vanilla yogurt

Bring water and apple juice concentrate to a boil in a heavy, medium-size saucepan. Gradually add tapioca while stirring. Reduce heat to low and cook, stirring constantly, for 5 minutes. Remove from heat, cool slightly, add salt, and fold in cantaloupe puree and vanilla yogurt. Pour pudding into custard cups. Allow to set for 4 to 5 hours in refrigerator before serving.

Makes 3 cups.

Banana-Maple Rice Pudding

An updated version of the creamy, custardy rice pudding that Grandma used to make. When preparing rice to serve with the stir-fry recipe (page 172), be sure to cook extra so that there is enough leftover rice to make this satisfying and nutritious dessert.

Table Food for Toddlers and Grown-ups Too

1 cup cooked white rice
2 cups milk
2 medium-size ripe bananas, peeled and cut into $1/2$-inch-thick slices
$1/3$ cup maple syrup
1 teaspoon vanilla extract
3 eggs, well beaten
$1/2$ cup raisins
pinch of freshly grated nutmeg
$1/8$ teaspoon ground cinnamon
pinch of salt
1 tablespoon unsalted butter, cut into small pieces

Preheat oven to 325 degrees. Combine all ingredients except butter in a large bowl. Stir gently and pour mixture into a 2- to 3-quart round glass or ceramic baking dish. Dot top with butter and bake for 55 to 60 minutes or until custard sets. Remove rice pudding from oven and allow to cool before serving. It's good hot or cold.

Makes 6 to 8 grown-up servings.

Variations:

- Instead of bananas and maple syrup add 2 medium pears, peeled, quartered, cored, steamed, and diced, and $1/3$ cup sugar. Float sliced almonds on top just before baking.
- Substitute $1/2$ cup wild rice and $1/2$ cup cooked brown rice or white rice for 1 cup white rice.

Chocolate Pudding

Table Food for Toddlers
and Grown-ups Too

Our friend Laura shared this recipe with us claiming it's the only way she can get her kids, George and Emily, to drink their milk. For a special occasion, we thicken the pudding with an additional 2 tablespoons of cornstarch; put the pudding into a graham cracker crumb crust; and decorate with whipped cream to make Teddi and Renée's Grandmom Lil's favorite party dessert, chocolate cream pie.

2 cups milk
$\frac{1}{2}$ cup sugar
3 tablespoons cocoa
2 tablespoons cornstarch
1 teaspoon vanilla

Combine ingredients in a saucepan and cook over low heat stirring constantly with a wooden spoon, about 4 to 5 minutes, until the mixture begins to boil and thicken slightly. Immediately remove from heat and pour pudding into 4 individual serving dishes. Eat warm or cool in the refrigerator before serving. Garnish each serving with sliced bananas and whipped cream, if desired.

Makes four $\frac{1}{2}$ cup servings.

Avocado Cream

Avocados may seem startling for dessert, but they are technically fruits, and their creamy richness makes for a delightful dessert.

1 cup frozen vanilla yogurt or ice cream
$1/4$ cup heavy cream
2 ripe avocados
juice of $1/2$ lime
$1/4$ cup confectioners' sugar
2 large unhulled strawberries for garnish

Chill food processor bowl in freezer for 10 minutes. Soften frozen yogurt or ice cream at room temperature. Whip cream until it holds a soft shape and set aside. With steel blade in place, scoop avocado flesh into the chilled bowl of your food processor. Add lime juice, sugar, and frozen yogurt or ice cream and process until smooth—about 20 to 30 seconds. Fold in the whipped cream. Spoon avocado cream into a plastic container and cover tightly. Place in freezer compartment to harden, approximately 1 to $1^1/_2$ hours. About 15 minutes prior to serving, scoop avocado cream into 4 serving dishes and allow to soften slightly. Garnish each serving with half an unhulled strawberry and serve.

Makes 4 grown-up servings (but loved by our kids too!).

Table Food for Toddlers
and Grown-ups Too

Basic Sorbet

■ ■ ■ ■ ■ ■ ■ ■ ■ ■ ■ ■ ■ ■ ■ ■ ■ ■ ■ ■

Table Food for Toddlers
and Grown-ups Too

This recipe will produce simple, refreshing sorbets from many different fruits. We've used raspberries here, but go with what's in season and most luscious. Try strawberries, blueberries, apples, and kiwifruit or fruitful combinations such as banana-strawberry, apple-blueberry, and banana-orange. Leftover fruit purees are perfect for this recipe.

4 cups raspberries (fresh or frozen without syrup)
1 teaspoon freshly squeezed lemon juice
¼ cup sugar

Put all ingredients in your food processor. Using the steel blade, process for 1 to 2 minutes or until smooth, scraping down the bowl once during processing. Strain mixture through a fine-meshed sieve to remove seeds. Spread mixture evenly in a shallow pan and freeze until almost firm. (Avoid using an aluminum pan as it can cause some fruit to discolor.) Scoop out and return to food processor. Process for 45 seconds to 1 minute or until mixture is light and fluffy. (Be careful not to overprocess.)

Store sorbet in an airtight container and freeze for 2 more hours or until firm. (If mixture becomes very hard, for easy scooping, let it sit in the refrigerator for 15 to 20 minutes before serving.)

Makes 1 pint.

Serving Suggestion: Put 1 cup of sorbet in your food processor with ½ cup vanilla (or plain) yogurt. Process until smooth and serve immediately as is or over freshly sliced banana.

Baked Goods

Renée's (Wheat-Free) Applesauce Cookies

Our younger daughter, Renée, was having trouble with wheat early in her life, so we developed this cookie especially for her. Her big sister, Teddi, loved them just as much, especially when we substituted pear "sauce" for applesauce. Omit the nuts if your child is allergic to them.

Spoon and Finger Food for Bigger Babies

³/₄ cup light brown sugar
³/₄ cup vegetable oil
1 cup My First Applesauce (page 116)
¹/₂ cup finely chopped nuts
¹/₂ teaspoon salt
1 teaspoon vanilla extract
1 cup oat bran
2 cups soy flour

Preheat oven to 350 degrees. Combine brown sugar and oil in a large bowl. Stir until all lumps have dissolved. Add remaining ingredients one at a time, mixing well after each addition.

Place level tablespoons of dough 2 inches apart on a greased cookie sheet and flatten slightly with a fork. Bake for 15 to 17 minutes or until golden brown and crisp. Cool before wrapping or storing in an airtight container; the cookies will keep for about a month.

Makes about 4 dozen cookies.

Variations:

- Add ¹/₂ cup chopped pitted dates
- Substitute ¹/₂ cup wheat germ for ¹/₂ cup oat bran

Oatmeal Raisin Cookies

**Table Food for Toddlers
and Grown-ups Too**

The cookie jar staple. Always be sure there's "one for each hand."

½ cup unsalted butter
⅔ cup tightly packed light brown sugar
1 egg, lightly beaten
1 teaspoon vanilla extract
1 cup unbleached all-purpose flour
½ teaspoon baking soda
½ teaspoon salt
¼ teaspoon ground cinnamon
1 cup old-fashioned rolled oats
1 cup raisins

Preheat oven to 350 degrees. Cream butter and sugar together in a large bowl until light and fluffy. Add egg and beat very well. Add vanilla and mix in. Sift together flour, baking soda, salt, and cinnamon in a small bowl. Fold into butter-sugar mixture. Add oats and raisins and mix only until ingredients are incorporated.

Drop dough by level tablespoons onto lightly greased cookie sheets. Bake for 10 to 12 minutes or until cookies are golden brown. Cool cookies on pan for 2 minutes, then transfer with a spatula to a wire rack to finish cooling.

Makes 3½ dozen.

Gingerbread Dinosaurs

Special anytime. For birthday parties, paint each child's name in icing (recipe follows) on a cookie and prop up at his place at the table.

$1/4$ cup unsalted butter
$1/2$ cup light brown sugar, lightly packed
$1/2$ cup molasses
$3^1/2$ cups unbleached all-purpose flour
1 teaspoon baking soda
$1/8$ teaspoon freshly grated nutmeg
$1/8$ teaspoon ground cloves
$1/2$ teaspoon ground cinnamon
1 teaspoon ground ginger
$1/2$ teaspoon salt
$1/4$ cup water

Table Food for Toddlers
and Grown-ups Too

Preheat oven to 350 degrees. Cream butter and sugar together in a large bowl. Add molasses and continue beating until well mixed. Sift together flour, baking soda, nutmeg, cloves, cinnamon, ginger, and salt in a separate bowl. Add the sifted ingredients and the water alternately, a third at a time, to the butter and sugar mixture, beginning and ending with the dry ingredients and blending well after each addition.

Roll out dough on a lightly floured surface and cut dinosaurs (or any other shape, like gingerbread men) with a floured cutter. (Dip edges of cutter in flour every 1 or 2 cuts.) Gently place cookies on a greased baking sheet and add raisin or currant eyes if desired. (Knead scraps briefly and roll and form more cookies.)

Bake cookies for 7 to 9 minutes, depending on their thickness. Check for doneness by pressing on a cookie. If the dough springs back, it is done. Remove from oven and transfer cookies to a cake rack to cool.

Makes 14 to 16 5-inch cookies, depending on your cutter size and the thickness of the rolled dough.

ICING
¼ cup confectioners' sugar
a few drops of water
2 drops of pure vegetable color (optional)

Mix ingredients in a small bowl to form a smooth, glossy glaze (add a drop or 2 of additional water if necessary). Using a small knife or toothpick, paint mouths, ears, feet, scales, fins, hair, horns, etc., on your creatures.

Crusty Teethers

Spoon and Finger Food for Bigger Babies

When sore, teething gums make your normally sweet baby cranky, here's something soothing and delicious she can work them over with at the dinner table or in the stroller.

¼ recipe Pizza Crust dough (page 159)

Let the risen pizza dough rest, covered, in the refrigerator for 8 hours before preparing this recipe. When ready to bake, preheat oven to 375 degrees. Roll dough into a ball, cut into quarters, and roll each quarter lengthwise into a stick shape. Place sticks on an ungreased cookie sheet lightly dusted with cornmeal, cover, and let rest for 10 minutes. Then bake for 30 minutes or until well browned with a crisp crust.

Makes 4 teething sticks.

Blueberry-Applesauce Oatmeal Muffins

This is a good way to use up the egg white after you've fed your infant the yolk. It's also a good recipe for adults who are watching their cholesterol, since these muffins are not only yolkless but use vegetable oil for shortening.

1½ cups old-fashioned oats
1¼ cups unbleached all-purpose flour
1 teaspoon baking powder
¾ teaspoon baking soda
1 cup My First Applesauce (page 116)
½ cup milk
½ cup firmly packed light brown sugar
3 tablespoons vegetable oil
1 egg white
1 pint blueberries, picked over and washed

TOPPING
¼ cup old-fashioned oats
1 tablespoon brown sugar
⅛ teaspoon ground cinnamon
1 tablespoon unsalted butter

Preheat oven to 400 degrees and line a 12-cup muffin pan with paper or foil baking cups. Combine oats, flour, baking powder, and baking soda in a large bowl and mix well. Add applesauce, milk, brown sugar, oil, and egg white. Mix only until dry ingredients are just moistened. Fill the muffin cups until just about full. Push 5 or 6 blueberries into each muffin. In a small bowl, combine the topping ingredients and sprinkle evenly over each muffin. Bake for 20 to 24 minutes or until the muffins are a rich golden brown. They are wonderful served warm. The muffins will keep a few days; reheat before serving.

Makes 1 dozen muffins.

Table Food for Toddlers and Grown-ups Too

BLUEBERRIES

Introduce blueberries at 12 months. Be careful not to feed babies whole fresh blueberries; they can cause choking.

Nutritional Profile: vitamins A and C; potassium.

Select plump, gray-blue berries. Blueberries keep well, at least a week, when refrigerated. Do not rinse until ready to eat, since wet blueberries will turn moldy.

OATS

Oats contain B vitamins for energy and the soluble fiber, beta glucan, which lowers high blood cholesterol and may reduce the risk of heart disease.

Banana-Bran Muffins

Table Food for Toddlers and Grown-ups Too

1 cup unbleached all-purpose flour
$\frac{1}{2}$ cup wheat bran
$\frac{1}{2}$ teaspoon salt
1 teaspoon baking soda
$\frac{1}{2}$ cup (1 stick) sweet butter, melted
$\frac{1}{3}$ cup light brown sugar
$1\frac{1}{4}$ cups pureed ripe banana (about 4 medium-large bananas)
2 eggs

Preheat oven to 375 degrees and lightly grease (or line with paper cups) a 12-cup muffin pan. Place flour, bran, salt, and baking soda in a small bowl and mix well with a fork. In a larger bowl, combine melted butter, brown sugar, banana puree, and eggs. Add dry ingredients and mix only until blended. Fill muffin tins $\frac{2}{3}$ full and bake for 15 to 20 minutes or until a toothpick inserted in center comes out clean. Allow muffins to cool in pan for 5 to 10 minutes before removing. Serve warm. The muffins will keep a few days; reheat before serving.

Makes 1 dozen muffins.

Banana Cake

2¹/₂ cups flour
1 teaspoon baking soda
¹/₄ teaspoon salt
¹/₂ cup butter (1 stick)
³/₄ cup sugar
2 eggs
¹/₄ cup sour cream
3 large, ripe bananas, mashed with a fork

Table Food for Toddlers
and Grown-ups Too

Preheat oven to 375 degrees. Combine in a small bowl flour, baking soda, and salt. Set aside. Cream sugar and butter by hand or with a mixer. Add eggs (one at a time) to sugar mixture. Mix or blend well after each addition. Add vanilla and blend. Then add flour mixture in thirds, blending well after each addition. Add mashed bananas. Mix only until ingredients are well blended. Overmixing will toughen the cake.

Choose and butter (or use liners for muffins) one of the following:

1 12-inch by 4-inch loaf pan. Bake for 50 to 55 minutes

1 12-cup muffin pan. Bake 18 to 24 minutes

Bake until golden brown and toothpick inserted in center comes out clean.

Makes 1 loaf, 8 to 12 slices, or a dozen muffins.

Variations:

- Add ¹/₂ cup chocolate chips to batter
- Add ¹/₂ cup chopped nuts to batter

Cheddar Chip Corn Muffins

Table Food for Toddlers and Grown-ups Too

If your toddler likes spicy food, add 2 teaspoons of chili powder and 1 tablespoon of minced jalapeño pepper for a southwestern taste.

1³/₄ cups yellow cornmeal
3 teaspoons baking powder
¹/₂ teaspoon baking soda
¹/₂ teaspoon salt
¹/₂ cup melted butter (1 stick)
1 cup buttermilk
2 eggs, lightly beaten
1 cup cream-style canned corn
1 cup diced Cheddar cheese

Preheat oven to 400 degrees and lightly grease a 12-cup muffin pan with butter or margarine or line with paper cups. In a small bowl, sift together cornmeal, baking powder, baking soda, and salt. In a larger bowl, combine melted butter, buttermilk, eggs, corn, and diced Cheddar. Mix well. Fold in dry ingredients and mix only until ingredients are blended. Fill muffin cups two-thirds full and bake for 16 to 18 minutes or until edges are lightly browned and toothpick inserted in center comes out clean. Allow muffins to cool in baking pan for 5 to 10 minutes before removing. Serve right away with honey and butter.

Makes 1 dozen muffins.

Carrot Cupcakes

You can influence your child's palate—if you start early enough. When our nephew, Andy, turned 25, he finally admitted that only he (and his teacher) ate these yummy cupcakes his mom sent to kindergarten to celebrate his fifth birthday. The other kids, accustomed to box mixes, couldn't appreciate these homemade goodies.

Table Food for Toddlers
and Grown-ups Too

2 cups unbleached all-purpose flour
2 cups granulated sugar
2 teaspoons baking soda
2 teaspoons cinnamon
1 cup corn oil
3 eggs, lightly beaten
1 teaspoon vanilla extract
1 cup grated carrot (2 large)
1 cup chopped walnuts
½ cup Sultana (golden) raisins
1 8-ounce can, crushed, unsweetened pineapple, drained*

Preheat oven to 350 degrees. In a large bowl, sift flour, sugar, baking soda, and cinnamon. Add the oil, eggs, and vanilla and beat well. Fold in carrot, walnuts, raisins, and pineapple.

Lightly grease (or line with foil cups) a 12-cup muffin pan. Fill cups two-thirds and bake for 20 to 25 minutes or until a toothpick inserted in the center comes out clean. Remove pan from the oven and cool on a cake rack for 10 minutes. Remove cupcakes from the pan and cool completely on a wire rack before dusting with confectioner's sugar or frosting with Pineapple Cream Cheese Topping (page 281). The cupcakes will keep several days, refrigerated.

Makes 1 dozen cupcakes.

*Reserve a few spoonfuls of the crushed pineapple, if you plan to frost
the cupcake with Pineapple Cream Cheese Topping.

Fruit Crisp with Crunchy Oat Crust

When preparing a batch of fruit puree for your baby, reserve some of the steamed fruit and puree to make this quick and easy dessert for the rest of the family. We have used apples in this recipe, but almost any fruit can be substituted. Variations are suggested below. For a shortcut, use Granola (page 206) with melted butter for topping.

¾ cup My First Applesauce (page 116)
5 baking apples, such as Golden Delicious, Granny Smith, or Rome, cored,
    quartered, sliced, steamed *firm,* and skin removed
½ cup Crunchy Oat Crust (recipe follows)

Preheat oven to 350 degrees. Spread applesauce on the bottom of a 5 × 8-inch ovenproof baking dish. Arrange slices of steamed apple in an even layer over the sauce. Sprinkle with oat topping and bake for 15 to 20 minutes or until surface begins to brown. Fruit crisp is best served warm and is especially delicious with a scoop of ice cream or a dollop of yogurt.

Makes 4 grown-up servings.

Variations: After apples, try these fruits:

- peaches
- plums
- pears
- apricots
- nectarines
- bananas
- papayas
- mangoes

Then, for more fun, add to the above fruit base a handful of any of the following:

- plumped raisins
- blueberries
- raspberries
- strawberries
- chocolate chips
- grapes (halved and seeded)

CRUNCHY OAT CRUST

$1/4$ cup unsalted butter, melted
$1^1/2$ cups old-fashioned oats
$1/2$ cup wheat germ
$1/4$ cup dark brown sugar
$1/2$ teaspoon ground cinnamon

Place all ingredients in a large sauté pan and mix well. Then cook slowly over low heat, stirring constantly, for 6 to 8 minutes or until mixture is golden brown. Turn out crisp topping on an ungreased cookie sheet to cool. Store cooled topping in an airtight container in your refrigerator for up to 1 month.

Makes approximately 2 cups.

Variations: For a more interesting topping, add a spoonful or 2 of any of the following to the above ingredients:

- ground nuts (pecans, walnuts, hazelnuts)
- plumped raisins
- shredded unsweetened coconut

Baked Pear Dumplings

**Table Food for Toddlers
and Grown-ups Too**

Apples are good this way too. To save time, you can use prepared pie crust from the supermarket.

½ cup sliced almonds
2 tablespoons unsalted butter
¼ teaspoon ground cinnamon
pinch of dried thyme
pinch of ground cloves
1 tablespoon firmly packed light brown sugar
1 tablespoon unbleached all-purpose flour
1 egg white
8 small *or* 4 large Bartlett pears
1 lemon, quartered
1 recipe Easy as Pie Crust (page 263)

In a food processor fitted with the steel blade, or a blender, chop almonds, butter, seasonings, brown sugar, and flour until mixture is very fine. Add egg white and process briefly until mixture forms a paste. This will yield approximately 8 tablespoons of filling or enough to stuff 8 small or 4 large pears.

Preheat oven to 375 degrees and peel pears, leaving stem intact and removing cores by scooping them out with a melon baller or paring knife from the large end. Place pears in a large bowl as they are trimmed and cored, squeezing a little lemon juice over each as you go to keep the fruit from discoloring. When all the pears are peeled and cored, stuff each with 1 or 2 tablespoons of the almond paste.

Roll out pie dough into a large rectangle and cut into pieces—approximately 5 × 7-inch pieces for the smaller pears and 7 × 9-inch pieces for the larger ones. Center one of these pastry rectangles over the top of each pear. Fold the pastry down around the pear, tucking ends underneath its bottom. Continue until all pears are wrapped, placing each as it is covered upright on a baking sheet. Bake pears for 55 to 60 minutes or until fruit is tender when pierced with a toothpick and crust is golden brown. Serve pears warm, with vanilla ice cream if desired.

Makes 8 small or 4 large pear dumplings.

Sweet Potato-Apple Pie

A delicious slant on that southern favorite, sweet potato pie. The sweetener—molasses—gives the added boost of iron to this delicious dessert.

Table Food for Toddlers
and Grown-ups Too

¹/₂ recipe Easy as Pie Crust (page 263)
1¹/₂ cups Sweet Potato Puree (page 132)
1 cup My First Applesauce (page 116)
¹/₄ cup blackstrap molasses
¹/₄ teaspoon salt
¹/₄ teaspoon ground cinnamon
2 eggs, well beaten
¹/₂ cup milk

Preheat oven to 400 degrees. Line a 9-inch pie plate with crust and chill. Combine sweet potato, applesauce, molasses, salt, cinnamon, eggs, and milk in a medium bowl and mix well. Pour mixture into the pie shell and bake for 40 to 45 minutes or until a knife inserted in center comes out clean. Allow pie to cool before serving.

Makes 1 9-inch pie.

Blueberry-Peach Kuchen

Table Food for Toddlers
and Grown-ups Too

Vary kuchen with the season. Try other fruit toppings, such as rasp-berries, grapes, plums, cherries, or apricots. Serve with vanilla ice cream, whipped cream, or yogurt if desired.

1 cup unbleached all-purpose flour
2 tablespoons sugar
1 teaspoon baking powder
¼ teaspoon salt
3 tablespoons unsalted butter
1 egg
¼ cup milk
½ teaspoon vanilla extract
½ cup blueberries, rinsed and picked over
1½ cups washed and sliced peaches

GLAZE
3 tablespoons unsalted butter
2 tablespoons sugar
or
⅓ cup warmed and strained all-fruit preserves

Preheat oven to 350 degrees. In a large bowl, sift together flour, sugar, baking powder, and salt. With fingers or fork, blend butter into dry ingredients and set aside. In a small bowl, beat together the egg, milk, and vanilla. Add to the dry ingredients and mix with a fork until smooth. (The batter will be quite stiff.)

Spread batter evenly in a *well-greased* 9-inch springform pan. Arrange fruit on top, alternating rings of blueberries and sliced peaches. Prepare glaze by heating butter and sugar in a small saucepan over low heat until sugar is dissolved. Gently brush or dribble glaze over fruit topping.

Bake küchen for 25 to 35 minutes, until a cake tester or tooth-pick comes out clean. Let cake cool in the pan on a wire rack for 15 minutes, then carefully remove from the pan and return to rack to finish cooling.

Makes 1 9-inch cake.

Marble Cake

This cake batter is very dense. But not to worry, the finished product is light and luscious. It can also be baked in a bundt or ring pan. Enjoy the finished cake as is or toast slices and top with vanilla ice cream and Chocolate Sauce (page 282).

2 cups unbleached all-purpose flour
$1/2$ teaspoon baking soda
$1/2$ teaspoon baking powder
$1/4$ teaspoon salt
$1/2$ cup unsalted butter
$3/4$ cup sugar
2 eggs, separated
1 teaspoon vanilla extract
1 cup sour cream
2 ounces semisweet chocolate, melted and cooled

Preheat oven to 350 degrees. Grease a 5×9-inch loaf pan. In a small bowl, sift together flour, baking soda, baking powder, and salt. Cream butter in a large bowl using an electric mixer for 3 minutes. Gradually add sugar and beat for 3 to 4 minutes or until fluffy. Add egg yolks and vanilla and beat for an additional 3 minutes. Mix in flour mixture and sour cream alternately in 3 stages. Using electric mixer, beat egg whites in a small bowl for 1 minute or until they form firm peaks. Fold whites gently into

Table Food for Toddlers and Grown-ups Too

cake batter and divide in half. Add melted chocolate to one half and spoon batter into pan, alternating yellow and chocolate batters until all is used. Run a knife through batter once in a zigzag pattern, then bake for approximately 1 hour or until a toothpick inserted in the center comes out clean.

Makes 1 loaf.

Kiwifruit Tart

Table Food for Toddlers
and Grown-ups Too

¹/₄ cup sugar
2 tablespoons unbleached all-purpose flour
pinch of salt
1 egg, lightly beaten
³/₄ cup milk
¹/₂ teaspoon vanilla extract
1 8- to 9-inch prebaked pie shell (see Easy as Pie Crust recipe, page 263,
    or use store-bought)
3 to 4 kiwifruits, peeled and sliced into rounds

Combine sugar, flour, and salt in a small bowl and mix well. Add egg and stir until blended. Scald milk in a small heavy-bottomed pan by heating just to the boiling point. (A skin will form on the surface; remove it.) Slowly pour scalded milk into the egg mixture while stirring constantly. Return custard mixture to the pan and cook over a very low heat for approximately 5 minutes or until thickened, stirring constantly. Cook for an additional 5 minutes, stirring occasionally. Remove from heat. Pour into a bowl and allow to cool completely. When cool, mix in vanilla.

To assemble tart: Place the baked pie shell on a serving plate. Spread custard evenly over the bottom of the shell. Arrange sliced kiwifruit on top, layering it in circles from the outside to the center. Chill tart for 1¹/₂ hours before serving.

Makes 1 8- to 9-inch pie.

Variations: Other fruits can be substituted for or added to the kiwifruit, but remember that they need to hold their shape and not turn brown. (A list of fruits that brown when cut is found on page 122). Try kiwifruit and:

- raspberries
- blueberries
- strawberries
- tangerine sections

Easy as Pie Crust

You can make this pastry dough in a flash in your food processor! If your recipe calls for just one crust, such as Sweet Potato–Apple Pie (page 259), freeze the other half for another day. Or prebake (directions follow) and use for the Kiwifruit Tart recipe (page 262). (Prebaked shells can be frozen too, for up to a month.)

2 cups unbleached all-purpose flour
1/8 teaspoon salt
1/4 cup unsalted butter, cut into small pieces
1/4 cup cold vegetable shortening
3 to 4 tablespoons ice water

In a large bowl, combine flour and salt and mix well. Add butter and shortening and blend with a pastry cutter or fork until mixture has the consistency of rolled oats. Add water and mix until a ball is formed. Halve dough and pat and shape into 2 flat rounds (to give you a head start on rolling out later), wrap in plastic wrap, and chill at least 1 hour before using.

Food Processor Method: Put all ingredients (except water) in food processor fitted with the steel blade. Pulse processor on and off a few times to cut butter and shortening into flour. With machine running, dribble water in, scraping down sides of bowl once or twice, until dough starts to form a ball. Proceed with recipe.

Makes enough dough for a 10-inch 2-crust pie.

PREBAKED PIE SHELL

½ recipe Easy as Pie Crust dough, chilled

Preheat oven to 375 degrees. On a lightly floured surface, roll out dough into a circle 1 inch larger than your pie pan or tart ring. Lift dough with your rolling pin and carefully lay into pan, pressing gently against the sides and bottom. Even out and trim off excess overhanging dough with a knife or scissors and make a decorative edge by pressing with the tines of a fork or scalloping with thumb and fingers. Thoroughly prick bottom of pie with a fork. Line shell with wax paper and fill with raw dried beans or rice to act as a weight and prevent dough from losing its shape as it bakes.

Bake shell for 20 minutes or until it just begins to brown. (Look at the sides.) Remove from oven and gently lift wax paper and beans out of the shell. (Reserve beans for future pie shells.) Return to oven and continue baking until golden brown, about 10 more minutes. (Cover edges with strips of aluminum foil if they begin to brown too much.) Allow crust to cool completely before filling.

Makes 1 8- to 9-inch prebaked pie shell.

Serving Suggestion: For an extra treat, brush the inside of the cooled baked pie shell with melted chocolate. Harden briefly in the refrigerator before filling with pastry cream and fruit.

Mom's Mighty High Apple Pie

Golden Delicious apples might be baby's first apple, but certainly not his last. For this recipe try a combination of apple varieties, including Granny Smith and Winesap to create your own special pie. Don't be afraid to throw in a pear or even a handful of berries to make this a delicious mixed fruit pie.

Topping:

1 cup flour
$1/4$ cup dark brown sugar
$1/4$ cup sugar
1 teaspoon cinnamon
$1/2$ stick butter

Filling:

7 medium to large apples
1 teaspoon lemon juice
3 tablespoons flour
$1/2$ cup sugar
$1/2$ teaspoon cinnamon

Crust:

See page 263 or use a ready-made crust available in your grocer's freezer case or refrigerator. We like the Oronoque brand (found in the freezer section), which is made with pure vegetable shortening and contains no preservatives.

Preheat oven to 450 degrees. Combine topping ingredients in a bowl and blend with fingers until the ingredients resemble oatmeal-sized pieces. Set aside. Peel, core, and cut up apples in thin slices (about 16 slices per apple). Put apple slices in a large bowl and sprinkle with lemon juice. Add flour, sugar, and cinnamon and toss apple slices until well coated. Place your unbaked pie shell on a cookie sheet and fill with apples. Pile them high. They

---

Table Food for Toddlers
and Grown-ups Too

will reduce in the baking. Now, using your hands, strew and pat the crumble topping evenly over the apples. Place in preheated oven and bake for 15 minutes, then reduce heat to 350 degrees and continue baking 45 minutes longer.

Makes 1 9-inch pie.

Shakes, Smoothies, and Thirst Quenchers

Just Apple Juice

1 apple, peeled, seeded, and chopped, *or* 1/2 cup any chopped, prepared fruit
3/4 cup water or fruit juice (unsweetened apple juice works well if fruit is tart)

Combine ingredients in a blender and liquefy until smooth. Strain and serve immediately.

Makes 1 cup.

For Bigger Babies (over 10 months):

- strawberry-grapefruit
- raspberry-banana*
- pineapple-banana*
- carrot-celery
- apple-carrot
- tomato-celery
- orange-beet

*Thin banana combinations with a bit of juice or water if needed.

Fresh Fruit and Vegetable Juice

Your blender can turn most any fruit or vegetable into delicious juice. Always select fresh, ripe fruit or vegetables that are in season and use them as soon as possible. (Fruits and vegetables tend to lose moisture as they sit in the refrigerator.) If you like cold juice, add some crushed ice to the mixture during the blending process.

In our kitchen we use the Champion brand juicer. It is very well built and versatile. Not only does it extract juice, but it makes wonderful no-sugar-added instant fruit and vegetable sorbets. We just pass frozen, cleaned, cut-up fruit—or vegetables—through the Champion once for a delicious, healthy, all-natural treat. Our girls come flying when they hear the Champion start up.

Grape Juice Cooler with Fizz Ice Cubes

Table Food for Toddlers
and Grown-ups Too

In this recipe frozen fruit serves as the ice cubes and adds some excitement to the glass. Any fruit except fruits that brown (see list, page 122) can be used so long as there is variety and color. Fruits should be big so there's no chance baby can swallow them accidentally. To freeze fruit: arrange cleaned sliced fruit on a cookie sheet lined with waxed paper and place in the freezer. After 2 hours—or when fruit is frozen—peel off paper and store in freezer bags until needed.

1 6-ounce can frozen unsweetened grape juice concentrate
1 pint sparkling water, chilled
1 orange, sliced and frozen
1 lemon, sliced and frozen
1 kiwifruit, peeled, sliced, and frozen

Dilute frozen grape juice concentrate according to package directions. Add frozen fruit to each glass. Fill $^2/_3$ with grape juice. Top remaining $^1/_3$ with cold sparkling water. Serve immediately.

Makes 6 grown-up servings.

Iced Tea

Table Food for Toddlers
and Grown-ups Too

A sugarless, caffeine-free iced tea that's refreshing and appropriate for toddlers and big kids alike. Read the fine print on the tea package to be sure that it's totally caffeine-free and sugarless. Some berry and fruit teas touted as herb teas use regular tea in the blend and are not really caffeine-free. To sweeten the brew, you can add a little frozen apple juice concentrate.

3 caffeine-free blackberry tea bags
3 caffeine-free strawberry tea bags
2 quarts boiling water
1 orange, sliced for garnish
a handful of perfect strawberries

Place tea bags in a big heatproof pitcher and pour boiling water over them. Let steep for 5 minutes or longer. (Tea should be strong.) To serve, remove bags and pour tea into ice-filled tall glasses, garnishing with a whole strawberry or an orange slice.

Makes 8 glasses.

Peanut Butter Bananarama Shake

For an allergen-free shake, omit the peanut butter and use soy milk in place of cow's milk—unless, of course, your child is sensitive to soy products.

Table Food for Toddlers
and Grown-ups Too

1 very ripe banana, peeled and sliced
2 tablespoons smooth peanut butter
1 cup (or more) milk
2 ice cubes
1 teaspoon honey (optional)

Place banana, peanut butter, milk, ice cubes, and honey in a blender. Blend until smooth. Thin with additional milk if needed. Let foam and bubbles settle and serve immediately. (The banana will turn the shake brown if held for any length of time.)

Makes enough for 1 grown-up and 1 child or 2 toddlers.

Nut Milk

We developed this recipe as a way to systematically and safely intro-duce nuts, a common allergen and common cause of choking in young children. If your child is milk-sensitive or lactose-intolerant, but nut milk causes no problem, you can use it in place of cow's milk in the custard recipes (pages 239–240). Nut milks blended with fruit purees also make great shakes! And nut-size balls formed from the paste made by adding a little water or juice to nut powder can be served to tod-dlers as a safe form of nut finger- or spoon-food. The nut paste can also be used on sandwiches, crackers, and fruit slices.

$^1/_2$ cup raw or roasted *unsalted* nuts (peanuts, cashews, almonds, hazelnuts, or sesame seeds)
$1^1/_2$ cups cold water, approximately

Pulverize nuts in a blender or food processor fitted with the steel blade until *finely* powdered. Slowly add water until a smooth, creamy consistency is reached. Nut milk will hold, refrigerated, for up to 4 days. Shake well before using.

Makes 1 pint.

Table Food for Toddlers and Grown-ups Too

NUTS

Introduce nuts 1 variety at a time, at 12 months, for allergy screening. To prevent choking, serve only in pow-dered form.

Nutritional Profile: Almost all nuts (with the exception of cashews) are high in vitamin E and are good sources of vitamin B complex. Almonds contain good amounts of calcium. Cashews are high in magne-sium.

The season for nuts is fall and early winter. Nuts become stale and rancid on standing. Buy nuts in the shell that are heavy for their size and don't rat-tle when you shake them. (Peanuts, which are actually legumes, are the exception to this last rule of thumb.)

Nuts purchased in cans or vacuum-packed jars can be stored for a year or longer on a cool, dry shelf until they are opened. Jars should be placed away from direct sunlight. After open-ing, store cans and jars of shelled nuts, tightly covered, up to one week on the shelf, up to 6 months in the refrigera-tor, or 12 months in the freezer.

Lemon-Lime Smoothie

Dress up these smoothies by frosting the rims of the serving glasses. Dip the glass rims in a plate of lime juice or water and then in confec-tioners' sugar. Grown-ups might want to add a shot or 2 of tequila to the mix. Using commercial frozen yogurt in place of regular yogurt turns this smoothie into a spoonable treat.

1 6-ounce can frozen unsweetened lemonade concentrate or partially thawed
   juice of 2 limes
1 tablespoon confectioners' sugar
2 cups lemon yogurt, well stirred, or frozen lemon yogurt
Fresh mint sprigs and lemon and lime slices for garnish (optional)

In a blender or shake maker, combine lemonade, lime juice, and sugar. Blend for only a few seconds. Add yogurt and blend for 10 seconds longer. Immediately pour into glasses and serve garnished with a fresh mint sprig and slices of lemon or lime if desired.

Makes 4 grown-up servings.

Watermelon Dream

You can use any ripe, sweet melon in this recipe: cantaloupe, honeydew, casaba, etc. Seed watermelon over a bowl to catch the juice and use it in the recipe.

2 cups seeded and roughly chopped watermelon, with juice
$1/2$ cup cold milk
2 cups vanilla yogurt or frozen vanilla yogurt

Place watermelon, juice, and milk in a blender jar or shake maker and blend for 10 seconds. Add the yogurt and blend for 10 seconds longer.

Makes 4 grown-up servings.

Table Food for Toddlers
and Grown-ups Too

WATERMELON

Introduce watermelon at 12 months.

Nutritional Profile: vitamins A and C; potassium. Watermelon's high water content fights dehydration.

Watermelons are related to cucumbers. To check a whole one for ripeness, rap with your knuckles; it should sound hollow. If buying cut melon, look for evenly distributed seeds set in moist flesh (without streaks) and a freshly cut, unwithered rind.

Peaches 'n' Cream Smoothie

Table Food for Toddlers and Grown-ups Too

Peeling the peach is optional in this recipe. Leaving the skin on adds more nutrients, texture, and color. For added punch, grown-ups can spike their portions with peach brandy.

1 ripe peach, peeled, pitted, and sliced
½ cup cold milk
1 scoop peach or vanilla ice cream
2 cups peach yogurt, well stirred

Place peaches, milk, and ice cream in a blender jar or shake maker. Blend for 15 seconds. Add yogurt and blend for 10 seconds longer. Serve immediately.

Makes 4 grown-up servings.

Dressings and Toppings for Dipping, Dunking, and Spreading

My First Salad Dressing

If even our mild vinaigrette, that queen of dressings, makes your toddler pucker, this quick Russian is sure to please the very young and the young at heart.

Table Food for Toddlers and Grown-ups Too

$1/2$ cup mayonnaise
$1/3$ cup ketchup

Whisk mayonnaise and ketchup together in a small bowl. Toss a spoonful or 2 of the dressing with mixed salad greens or serve on the side as dipping sauce for cucumber rounds. Store any extra dressing in the refrigerator.

Makes 1 scant cup.

Variations: Once your child likes it plain, try these additions, or just save them for the grown-ups:
- hard-cooked egg, finely chopped
- 1 tablespoon chopped dill pickle or hot dog relish
- 1 tablespoon chopped stuffed olives
- 1 teaspoon finely grated fresh onion, minced scallion, or snipped chives

A Vinaigrette for All Seasons

Table Food for Toddlers
and Grown-ups Too

This dressing, simple and delicious, is wonderful on tossed salad greens, cold asparagus, artichokes, green beans, and sliced tomatoes. It's also good on cold pasta salads.

1/4 cup finely minced shallots
1/4 teaspoon salt
1/4 teaspoon freshly ground pepper
1/4 cup Dijon mustard
1 cup virgin olive oil
1/4 cup vegetable oil
1/4 cup cider vinegar, approximately
2 teaspoons chopped fresh parsley
1 scant teaspoon chopped fresh tarragon *or* 1/4 teaspoon dried

Combine shallots, salt, pepper, and mustard in a small bowl. Gradually whisk in olive and vegetable oils, thinning as necessary with cider vinegar. Add parsley and tarragon and mix well. Cover dressing and place in refrigerator for at least 2 hours before serving, to develop flavor. Whisk just before serving. (Leftover dressing will keep in your refrigerator in a sealed container for 3 days.)

Makes 1³/₄ cups.

Variations: For extra zip add:

- 3 strips lemon zest
- 1 large garlic clove, peeled and crushed

Tahini Dressing

A great spread, dipping sauce, and topping as well as salad dressing. If you can't find tahini in the supermarket, try a health food store.

Table Food for Toddlers and Grown-ups Too

½ cup tahini (sesame seed paste)
½ cup freshly squeezed lemon juice (about 2 large lemons)
2 garlic cloves, peeled and minced
2 tablespoons minced fresh parsley
2 tablespoons virgin olive oil
freshly ground white pepper to taste (start with a healthy pinch)

Place all ingredients in a blender or food processor. Blend until smooth. Thin dressing with a few drops of water if needed.

Makes 1 cup.

Chickpea Dip (Hummus)

Good with vegetable sticks, pita bread, and pretzel dippers.

Table Food for Toddlers and Grown-ups Too

2 cups Chickpea Puree (page 200)
⅓ cup tahini (sesame seed paste)
1 garlic clove, minced
juice of 1 lemon
1 tablespoon virgin olive oil

Blend chickpea puree, tahini, garlic, and lemon juice for 30 seconds in food processor fitted with the steel blade. Scrape down sides of bowl. With the processor running, gradually dribble in olive oil, processing for 30 seconds more. Store dip for a week in the refrigerator in a covered container. Serve chilled.

Makes 2⅓ cups.

Yogurt Topping for the Youngest

*Spoon and Finger Food
for Bigger Babies*

*Perfect for under-1 dipping and dunking with any steamed vegetable,
fruit, pasta, cracker, or biscuit.*

1/2 cup My First Applesauce (page 116)
1 cup plain yogurt
1/2 cup sour cream
2 tablespoons frozen unsweetened apple juice concentrate, thawed

Place all ingredients in a blender jar. Blend on high for 30 seconds. Chill for 1 hour.

Makes 2 cups.

YOGURT

Yogurt is a great source of calcium, a good source of protein, and supplies vitamins B$_2$ (riboflavin) and B$_{12}$ that aid in growth and development. Studies indicate that there may be a link between daily yogurt consumption and a stronger immune system. Feed your child yogurt that contains live and active cultures. (Heat kills yogurt's beneficial bacteria.) Look for the LAC seal on the container.

Yogurt Topping Grows Up

When baby gets bigger, try this sweet topping.

1 cup fresh blueberries, strawberries, or raspberries
1 cup fruit yogurt of the same flavor
1/2 cup sour cream
2 teaspoons honey

Put all ingredients in blender jar. Blend on high for 30 seconds. Chill for 1 hour. Serve with freshly cut fruit.

Makes approximately 2 1/2 cups.

Berries are not only pretty and tasty, but blueberries, blackberries, and strawberries contain antioxidants (cancer-fighting chemicals).

Eggplant Dip (Baba Ganouj)

Sometimes referred to as "poor man's caviar," this savory gem is great with crudités or steamed veggie dippers, biscuits, crackers, pita wedges, and even as a dressing on cold pasta and vegetables. For one-stop cooking, bake 2 eggplants: puree one plain for baby and prepare the second as follows.

1 large eggplant, roasted*, peeled, seeded, and cut into small chunks
$1/2$ small garlic clove, minced
$1/2$ teaspoon salt
$1/4$ teaspoon freshly ground black pepper
1 tablespoon freshly squeezed lemon juice
1 tablespoon tahini (sesame seed paste)
2 tablespoons virgin olive oil
Finely chopped fresh parsley for garnish (optional)

Place prepared eggplant pieces, garlic, salt, and pepper in a food processor fitted with the steel blade and process for 30 seconds. Add remaining ingredients except parsley and pulse until well mixed but some texture remains. Chill dip for at least 2 hours to let seasonings blend before serving. Serve in a small crock, garnishing top with chopped parsley if desired.

Makes $1^1/2$ cups.

Makes 1 large roasted eggplant or 12 to 14 1-ounce or heaped tablespoon baby servings.

*To roast a large eggplant: Preheat oven to 375 degrees. Pierce eggplant in a few places with a fork and roast on a foil-lined cookie sheet for 50 to 60 minutes or until stem end is tender (easily pierced with a sharp knife tip). When cool enough to handle, cut off stem end and, using a small, sharp paring knife, pull sections of skin off, working from top to bottom. When peeled, cut eggplant lengthwise into quarters, remove seeds, and cut into chunks. Proceed with recipe above or puree for baby in your food processor or strain in a food mill. No additional liquid is required.

Table Food for Toddlers
and Grown-ups Too

EGGPLANT

Introduce eggplant at 12 months.

Nutritional Profile: some vitamin C; potassium.

Select eggplants that are shiny, firm, unbruised, and heavy for their size. Soft, dull, or blemished ones tend to be bitter. The large, dark purple eggplants are most common, but 2 other varieties—the small, white egg-shaped type and the long, thin lighter purple ones—make delicious eating too and tend to be less bitter. Eggplants are available all year but are best in July and August. Store in a plastic bag in your refrigerator for up to 5 days, being careful not to bruise the skin, which causes brown spots to develop.

Tofu Dip

A very healthful and delicious dip, appropriate for lactose-intolerant babies.

1 cup soybeans, cooked (see Soybean Puree, page 200)
1/2 cup tofu
3 tablespoons tomato paste
a few black Greek olives, pitted
2 tablespoons chopped fresh parsley
1 garlic clove, minced
1 teaspoon light sesame oil

Place all ingredients in a food processor fitted with the steel blade or a blender and puree until smooth. Chill well. Serve with whole-wheat crackers or steamed vegetable pieces.

Makes 1 1/2 cups.

Horseradish Sauce

Horseradish Sauce is the perfect partner for the One-Pot Beef Dinner (page 180). It will also dress up any Mommy Made or store-bought roasted beef. Depending on the potency of the horseradish, a few dabs will go a long way.

1 cup sour cream
1 heaped tablespoon prepared red or white horseradish
1/4 teaspoon Worcestershire sauce
1/8 teaspoon salt
pinch of cayenne pepper
2 tablespoons thinly sliced scallions

Place all ingredients in a small bowl, mix well, and chill until ready to serve.

Makes 1 cup.

Summer Pesto

Served over noodles, this pesto is a favorite of both our girls and our Mommy Made customers alike. To store, top finished pesto with additional olive oil and place in an airtight container. It will keep for up to 3 months in your freezer.

Table Food for Toddlers
and Grown-ups Too

1 large bunch of fresh basil leaves (2 cups tightly packed)
$\frac{1}{2}$ cup hazelnuts, walnuts, or blanched almonds
1 large garlic clove, minced
$\frac{1}{2}$ cup virgin olive oil
$\frac{1}{2}$ cup freshly grated Parmesan cheese
$\frac{1}{2}$ teaspoon salt
$\frac{1}{2}$ teaspoon freshly ground black pepper

Coarsely chop basil, nuts, and garlic in a food processor fitted with the steel blade or blender—about 30 seconds. With processor or blender running, slowly add olive oil, scraping down the sides of work bowl or blender jar once during processing. When smooth, transfer mixture to a small bowl. Add Parmesan cheese, salt, and pepper and mix well. Store in covered container in refrigerator for 1 to 2 hours to allow flavors to develop. Pesto freezes perfectly, so it makes sense to make a lot and freeze it when basil's at its peak.

Makes $1\frac{1}{4}$ cups—enough for 1 pound of cooked pasta.

Winter Pesto

Table Food for Toddlers
and Grown-ups Too

When the winter snows cover your herb garden, here's a pesto made with spinach instead of summer's basil. Pesto is perfect on pasta. Create pesto Niçoise with any leftovers by adding flaked tuna, tomato wedges, green beans, olives, etc., to the pasta. Or, for a fast variation, top pasta with pesto and steamed carrots, zucchini, yellow squash, and/or broccoli.

1 cup tightly packed, washed and stemmed spinach leaves
1 tablespoon dried basil
$1/4$ cup hazelnuts, walnuts, or blanched almonds
1 medium garlic clove, minced
$1/2$ teaspoon salt
$1/4$ teaspoon freshly ground black pepper
$1/3$ cup virgin olive oil
$1/3$ cup freshly grated Parmesan cheese

Place spinach, basil, nuts, garlic, salt, and pepper in blender jar or food processor fitted with the steel blade. Process briefly until coarsely chopped. Then, with machine running, add oil in a steady stream and continue processing until smooth. Add Parmesan cheese and process very briefly until just blended. To serve, cook 1 pound pasta according to package directions. Place pesto in a large bowl with 2 to 3 tablespoons hot cooking water from the pasta and stir. Add hot, drained pasta and toss well. Serve immediately with extra cheese and more freshly ground black pepper if desired.

Makes about 1 cup—enough for 1 pound of cooked pasta.

Pineapple Cream Cheese Topping

This semisweet topping not only makes a great frosting for Carrot Cupcakes (page 255) but is terrific as a dip for steamed vegetables or cut-up fresh fruit, as a topping for scrambled eggs or oatmeal, or even as a salad dressing.

1 8-ounce package cream cheese
3 to 4 tablespoons frozen, unsweetened pineapple juice concentrate
¼ teaspoon honey
a few spoonfuls of unsweetened crushed canned pineapple, drained

Place cream cheese, pineapple juice, and honey in a food processor or blender. Blend until smooth and creamy. Add crushed pineapple and mix a few seconds longer or just until the fruit is incorporated. Store topping in the refrigerator in a covered container for up to 4 days.

Makes about 1 cup.

Table Food for Toddlers
and Grown-ups Too

PINEAPPLE

Introduce pineapple at 12 months. Although it's sweet, its high acidity tends to irritate baby's delicate mouth.

Nutritional Profile: vitamin C; potassium.

Select large, heavy pineapples with fresh green leaves. A sweet scent and a stalk end that yields slightly when pressed (but no mold) are the best indications of ripeness since some varieties naturally contain more chlorophyll and stay green even when ready to eat. Keep on your kitchen counter until ripe, then store in the refrigerator up to 5 days.

Chocolate Sauce

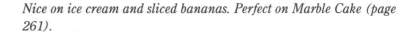

Table Food for Toddlers
and Grown-ups Too

Nice on ice cream and sliced bananas. Perfect on Marble Cake (page 261).

³/₄ cup sugar
¹/₂ cup water
¹/₂ teaspoon freshly squeezed lemon juice
¹/₂ cup cocoa powder, sifted
1 tablespoon unsalted butter

Combine sugar, water, and lemon juice in a small saucepan and cook over medium heat, stirring constantly, until sugar is dissolved. Increase heat to high. Bring syrup to a boil and cook for 1 minute. Remove pan from heat and whisk in cocoa and butter until blended and sauce thickens slightly. Strain into a small bowl and allow to chill before serving. The sauce will keep 2 weeks in the refrigerator.

Makes 1 cup.

Strawberry-Apple Butter

Homemade fruit butters take a bit of doing, but they're worth the effort since kids love them so much. Packed in a jar with a festive bow and label, they make grown-up hostess presents. Use fruit butters as you would jelly. For baby, spread them on toasted whole-wheat bread and bagels, mix with cottage cheese and yogurt, or use as a topping on hot cereals. Fruit butters keep for 2 weeks in the refrigerator and longer in the freezer.

2 cups My First Applesauce (page 116)
1/2 cup strawberry puree
1/4 cup frozen unsweetened apple juice concentrate, thawed
tiny pinch of allspice
pinch of ground cinnamon

Combine all ingredients in a small heavy-bottomed pan. Bring to a simmer over medium heat, stirring constantly. (Puree spits as it bubbles; be careful not to get burned. Don't hold baby on your hip while you stir.) Reduce heat to low and cook for 45 to 50 minutes, stirring frequently. Butter should darken and thicken as it cooks, but take care after 30 minutes that the bottom doesn't scorch. Chill butter well before serving.

Makes 1 cup.

Other Fruit Butters: Substitute 2 1/2 cups of any single-fruit or combination puree for the apple and strawberry. Try:

- pear
- peach
- apricot
- plum
- nectarine
- mango
- papaya
- apricot-nectarine
- mango-papaya
- pear-papaya

STRAWBERRIES

Introduce strawberries at 12 months. Berries in general tend to be allergy-provoking, but especially strawberries.

Nutritional Profile: high in vitamin C and potassium.

Select bright, dark red berries with fresh, unwithered hulls. Smaller berries tend to be more flavorful than the large ones. Store in your refrigerator until ready to serve. Rinse just before using to preserve the most flavor and nutrients.

PART III

Beyond the Basics

Food for Special Situations

UNDER THE WEATHER?

LIQUID DIET

When your doctor orders a liquid diet for vomiting and/or diarrhea, be certain not to use milk as the liquid. This includes milk-based formula and whole cow's milk. Breast milk and soy-based formula are okay, although your doctor may recommend that you water the latter down. In general, use clear liquids. Other appropriate choices are:

- watered-down juices
- caffeine-free Iced Tea (page 268)
- "Just What the Doctor Ordered!" Chicken Soup, without the veggies (page 216)
- Iron-Rich Broth (page 221)
- Very Veggie Broth and Beverage (page 217)
- Grape Juice Cooler, without the fruit (page 268)
- Apple Wiggle (page 241)
- flat room-temperature cola and ginger ale

When your baby feels like eating again, offer small amounts of simple, fat-free foods at first, such as:

- mashed banana
- applesauce or apple shavings (Because of its high pectin content, apple is particularly comforting for upset tummies.)
- rice cereal
- yellow vegetables
- white meat chicken without skin

FOR CONSTIPATION

Prune Puree (page 127) always does the trick.

ESPECIALLY FOR THE LACTOSE-INTOLERANT:

- Egg Noodles with Chunky Fruit (page 193)
- Soybean Puree (page 200)
- Calcium-Rich Broth (page 220)
- Nut Milk (page 270)
- Tofu Dip (page 278)
- Yogurt toppings (page 276)

TEETHING TREATS

Cool and hard are just the ticket to soothe sore, swollen gums. But really hard vegetables such as carrots are out. Your baby's gums are stronger than you might think. She could break off a piece and choke.

- Frozen steamed apple slices head the list. Many parents call to tell us this is a favorite parenting tip from our classes.

- Frozen banana spears are next. As these defrost in your baby's mouth, they turn into easily swallowed mush.

Also good:

- cold peeled cucumber slices
- part–skim milk string cheese sticks
- trimmed celery stalks
- cool chunks of cantaloupe and honeydew melon
- other frozen, steamed fruit slices—pear, peach, apricot, etc.
- Crusty Teethers (page 250)
- bagels
- seedless bread sticks
- the heel of a loaf of French bread

Some children really aren't hungry when they're teething and will howl even louder at the frozen apple slices or banana spears you offer. For a great nonfood teether, moisten a clean washcloth with cold water, wring it out, and let them chew away.

ON THE GO WITH BABY

Even if you're just going around the corner, if you're planning to leave the house for more than an hour it's always a good idea to pack a "feed bag." A feed bag can be a tote, diaper bag, lunch box—anything you put food in!

Foods that travel well:

- ripe bananas
- frozen dollops of purees that defrost on the way (serve with a spoon)
- steamed fruit and vegetable slices

- Cheddar Chip Corn Muffins (page 254) and Banana-Bran Muffins (page 252)
- Carrot Cupcakes (page 255)
- Fruit Leather (page 238)
- Riding-the-Range Trail Mix (page 234)
- Inside-Out Sandwiches (page 224)
- waffle or pita sandwiches (they hold their fillings well)

For slightly longer day trips—picnics in the country, a day at the beach, a visit to Grandma's—we fill a Thermos or 2 with well-chilled purees. If properly chilled to begin with, the foods will remain cool for 2 mealtimes. Just remember to pack a long-handled iced tea spoon for scooping out.

Going further afield for a longer time, where the water and local produce are uncertain? You can even take your homemade baby food. Here's how:

To take along already frozen baby food stashed in your freezer, you'll need a well-insulated picnic hamper and ice packs (as many as possible). The length of time your container will maintain food in a frozen state depends on the quality of the hamper's insulation, the number of ice packs packed with the food, and how solidly frozen the food was to begin with. The average time most hampers hold food in a solid state is about 5 to 6 hours.

If time permits, you can simply prepare your baby food the day before you leave, refrigerate it, and pack as above just before you leave. Then freeze the food when you arrive at your destination. Refrigerated food will remain cold for up to 8 to 12 hours en route.

Always be sure to wrap your food containers in case of breakage, leaks, or other mishaps. If using glass jars, first wrap them in newspaper and then stuff extra newspaper in any loose areas around the ice packs and jars. If you're really ambitious, dry ice is the best coolant, but it is awkward to handle and not readily available. Usually the places that sell dry ice also sell containers to ship it in. If you are serious about this method, buy the shipping container too.

If you're planning to cook on location, here's a checklist of what to take along from home or buy once you arrive. (At the very least you'll need a hotplate for cooking. Hopefully your accommodations will be equipped with a stove or microwave and refrigerator.)

- canvas or vinyl "feed" bag
- medium-size pot with lid
- small metal steamer
- small knife
- vegetable peeler
- baby food grinder
- small plastic containers
- small plastic bowl or dish
- baby spoon(s)
- bibs (disposable)
- small plastic bags
- premoistened baby wipes
- collapsible baby chair

When traveling out of the country, or anywhere with baby for that matter, stick with foods that your baby has already eaten and is accustomed to and use either bottled or boiled water to prepare food. Ironically, there are no regulations for bottled water outside of the United States. So, if you are unsure of the purity of the water supply, purify your own.

To Purify Water: For cooking purposes, start off with more water than you'll need and boil for 20 minutes. Place your small metal steamer in the remaining purified water and proceed to cook dinner. You can also purify your drinking water this way. Simply boil and store in clean, sealed jars. Make ice cubes with any extra water.

RESTAURANT DINING

Just because you have a baby doesn't mean that you can never go out to dinner unless you pay a sitter to hold down the fort. Plenty of parents take their babies and even toddlers along with them—and we don't mean just to fast-food establishments or diners. Here are some tips for making eating out pleasant for all ages:

- Call ahead to check on booster seat and high chair status.
- While you're at it, make a reservation so you won't have to wait to be seated.
- Always take along something for babies and toddlers to eat while waiting for the food to arrive. Finger foods are a good choice.
- Feed the babies right away. Not only does it calm them down, but it also lets you enjoy your food in peace when it is served.
- Clear the table of all things in reach of your toddler—unless you want him to clear the decks for you in record speed.
- Take drinks for your children (especially if you want sugar-free juice) and a plastic training cup or an unbreakable glass to serve them in. Very few restaurants have the latter on hand.
- Take along some toys that your child can easily enjoy in his seat. Books and small cars are good. Particularly useful are those vinyl place mats that have a line drawing and come complete with wipe-off crayons.

A Nutrition Glossary

Vitamins keep the body healthy, prevent deficiency diseases, and act as coenzymes.

Fat-soluble vitamins—A, D, E, and K—are stored in our bodies and do not have to be replenished daily. Consumed in excess, they can be toxic.

Water-soluble vitamins—C and all the B complex vitamins, including thiamine, riboflavin, niacin, folacin, and B_{12}—are not stored in our bodies and should be replenished daily.

Minerals, in small amounts, are needed to maintain the healthy functioning of different parts of the body. They also make up part of the body itself. Some important mineral compounds are calcium, phosphorus, sodium, potassium, and chlorine.

Trace elements, also called *micronutrients,* are required by the body in only tiny amounts. (They can be deadly poisonous when consumed in large quantities.) Trace elements needed for good health are iron, copper, iodine, fluorine, zinc, chromium, copper, cobalt, and manganese.

In the following pages these abbreviations are used:

> g = gram(s)
> mg = milligram(s)
> mcg = microgram(s)
> IU = international unit(s)

FATS (LIPIDS)

WHY WE NEED THEM

Fats serve as an energy reserve system. They are part of the cell membrane structure and important in the transport of fat-soluble vitamins, including A, D, E, and K. Fats also provide essential fatty acids, insulate the body, and cushion its vital parts. (For more information on why fat is essential in baby's diet, see page 59.)

RECOMMENDED (DAILY) DIETARY ALLOWANCE

For children, of the total calories consumed in a day, fats should represent 30 to 40 percent.

BEST SOURCES

Butter	Nuts
Mayonnaise	Sweet cream
Cheese	Cream Cheese
Ham	

CARBOHYDRATES (COMPLEX AND REFINED)

WHY WE NEED THEM

Carbohydrates are used by the body primarily as a source of energy. They also keep baby warm, help the body use protein and fat, and keep the liver healthy. Complex carbohydrates such as starch and cellulose are found in breads and cereals, fruits and vegetables. They supply not only energy but also roughage (fiber), vitamins, and minerals. Refined carbohydrates found in cake, soda, and candy offer little more than high sugar content, contributing factors in tooth decay and obesity. Carbohydrates spare protein from being used for energy, freeing it for more important functions such as tissue growth and repair. Although many adults shun carbohydrates when they're dieting, by themselves carbohydrates are no more fattening than proteins. It's only the butter and sauces we put on the pasta, potatoes, rice, and bread that make them so.

RECOMMENDED (DAILY) DIETARY ALLOWANCE

There is no definitive requirement for carbohydrates; however, adults need from 50 to 100 grams of dietary carbohydrates daily to prevent ketosis, an acid condition of the blood that may occur when fat is used primarily for energy.

CARBOHYDRATES BEST SOURCES

Spaghetti, enriched, cooked (1 cup)	44.0 g
Brown rice, cooked (⁴/₅ cup)	38.2 g
Potato, baked (1 large)	31.7 g
Bagel (1 plain)	30.9 g
Matzo (1 piece)	25.4 g
Beans, white, cooked (¹/₂ cup)	21.2 g
Corn on the cob, cooked (4-inch ear)	21.0 g
Eggo Waffle, frozen (1 waffle)	17.0 g
Whole-wheat bread, toasted (1 slice)	10.9 g

VITAMIN A (RETINOL)

WHY WE NEED IT

This vitamin is needed for growth, normal vision, and smooth skin. It also reduces our susceptibility to colds. Vitamin A is fat-soluble and stored by the body. Too much will make your baby sick. Some foods, such as beef liver, sweet potatoes, and carrots, are very high in vitamin A. Do not serve large portions of these foods or serve them too frequently.

RECOMMENDED (DAILY) DIETARY ALLOWANCES

6 months to 1 year: 1,500 IU
1 to 3 years: 2,000 IU
4 to 6 years: 2,500 IU

VITAMIN A BEST SOURCES	
Beef liver (3 ounces)	45,390 IU
Sweet potato (1 medium)	11,940 IU
Carrots, sliced, cooked (1/2 cup)	8,140 IU
Spinach, cooked (1/2 cup)	7,290 IU
Cantaloupe (1/4 medium)	4,620 IU
Kale, cooked (1/2 cup)	4,565 IU
Broccoli, cooked (1 branch)	4,500 IU
Winter squash, cooked (1/2 cup)	4,305 IU
Mustard greens, cooked (1/2 cup)	4,060 IU
Apricots, fresh (3 medium)	2,890 IU
Watermelon (1 slice)	2,510 IU
Leaf lettuce (1 cup)	1,050 IU
Asparagus, cooked (4 spears)	540 IU
Peas, fresh, cooked (1/2 cup)	430 IU
Green beans, cooked (1/2 cup)	340 IU
Yellow corn (1/2 cup)	330 IU
Parsley (1 tablespoon)	303 IU
Egg, hard-cooked (1 large)	260 IU

VITAMIN C (ASCORBIC ACID)

WHY WE NEED IT

Vitamin C is necessary for healthy blood vessels, bones, teeth, and cartilage. It helps the body overcome infection and heals wounds. Vitamin C is water-soluble and not stored by the body; you need to replenish it each day.

RECOMMENDED (DAILY) DIETARY ALLOWANCES

6 months to 1 year: 35 mg
1 to 3 years: 45 mg
4 to 6 years: 45 mg

VITAMIN C BEST SOURCES	
Orange juice, freshly squeezed (1 cup)	124 mg
Green bell peppers, raw, chopped ($1/2$ cup)	96 mg
Grapefruit juice, freshly squeezed (1 cup)	94 mg
Papaya ($1/2$ medium)	94 mg
Kiwifruit (1 raw)	75 mg
Brussels sprouts (4 sprouts)	73 mg
Broccoli, raw, chopped ($1/2$ cup)	70 mg
Cantaloupe ($1/4$ medium)	56 mg
Turnip greens, cooked ($1/2$ cup)	50 mg
Cauliflower, raw, chopped ($1/2$ cup)	45 mg
Strawberries ($1/2$ cup)	42 mg
Tomato juice (1 cup)	39 mg
Potato (1 medium)	31 mg
Cabbage, raw, chopped ($1/2$ cup)	21 mg
Blackberries ($1/2$ cup)	15 mg
Spinach, raw, chopped ($1/2$ cup)	14 mg
Blueberries ($1/2$ cup)	9 mg
Cherries, sweet ($1/2$ cup)	5 mg
Bean sprouts, mung ($1/4$ cup)	5 mg

VITAMIN B COMPLEX

Originally thought to be a single substance, now known to consist of 11. All are water-soluble and need to be replenished daily.

THIAMINE (B$_1$)

■ WHY WE NEED IT ■

Thiamine keeps nerves in healthy condition, stimulates appetite, and is needed in cell respiration.

■ RECOMMENDED (DAILY) DIETARY ALLOWANCE ■

6 months to 1 year: 0.5 mg

1 to 3 years: 0.7 mg

4 to 6 years: 0.9 mg

■ THIAMINE BEST SOURCES ■	
Soybeans, dried ($^1/_4$ cup)	0.6 mg
Navy beans, dried ($^1/_4$ cup)	0.3 mg
Chickpeas, dried ($^1/_4$ cup)	0.2 mg
Rye flour ($^1/_4$ cup)	0.2 mg
Whole-wheat flour ($^1/_4$ cup)	0.2 mg
Kidney beans, dried ($^1/_4$ cup)	0.2 mg
Beef liver (3 ounces)	0.2 mg
Brown rice, uncooked ($^1/_4$ cup)	0.2 mg
Salmon steak (3 ounces)	0.2 mg
Beef, lean (3 ounces)	0.1 mg
Chicken, white meat (3 ounces)	0.1 mg
Chicken liver (3 ounces)	0.1 mg
Whole milk (1 cup)	0.1 mg
Peanuts, chopped ($^1/_4$ cup)	0.1 mg
Salmon steak (3 ounces)	0.1 mg
Wheat germ, toasted (1 tablespoon)	0.1 mg

RIBOFLAVIN (B$_2$)

WHY WE NEED IT

Riboflavin is needed in oxidation and energy release in all cells and is responsible for tissue repair (prevents sores around mouth) and healthy skin.

RECOMMENDED (DAILY) DIETARY ALLOWANCE

6 months to 1 year: 0.6 mg

1 to 3 years: 0.8 mg

4 to 6 years: 1.0 mg

RIBOFLAVIN BEST SOURCES	
Beef liver (3 ounces)	3.6 mg
Chicken liver (3 ounces)	1.5 mg
Whole milk (1 cup)	0.4 mg
Beef, lean (3 ounces)	0.2 mg
Soybeans, dried (¹/₄ cup)	0.2 mg
Swiss cheese (2 ounces)	0.2 mg
Chicken, white meat (3 ounces)	0.1 mg
Chickpeas, dried (¹/₄ cup)	0.1 mg
Egg, hard-cooked (1)	0.1 mg
Rye flour (¹/₄ cup)	0.1 mg
Kidney beans, dried (¹/₄ cup)	0.1 mg
Navy beans, dried (¹/₄ cup)	0.1 mg
Peanuts, chopped (¹/₄ cup)	0.1 mg
Salmon steak (3 ounces)	0.1 mg

▲ ● ■
NIACIN

■ WHY WE NEED IT ■

Niacin is necessary for cell respiration. It also helps maintain healthy skin, digestion, and the nervous system.

■ RECOMMENDED (DAILY) DIETARY ALLOWANCES ■

6 months to 1 year: 8 mg
1 to 3 years: 9 mg
4 to 6 years: 11 mg

■ NIACIN BEST SOURCES ■	
Beef liver (3 ounces)	14.0 mg
Chicken, white meat (3 ounces)	10.6 mg
Salmon steak (3 ounces)	8.4 mg
Peanuts, chopped ($1/4$ cup)	6.2 mg
Beef, lean (3 ounces)	3.9 mg
Chicken liver (3 ounces)	3.8 mg
Brown rice, uncooked ($1/4$ cup)	2.4 mg
Whole-wheat flour ($1/4$ cup)	1.3 mg
Navy beans, dried ($1/4$ cup)	1.2 mg
Chickpeas, dried ($1/4$ cup)	1.0 mg

VITAMIN B$_6$

WHY WE NEED IT

B$_6$ helps the body use protein to build tissue and use carbohydrates and fat for energy. It also helps maintain healthy skin, digestion, and the nervous system.

RECOMMENDED (DAILY) DIETARY ALLOWANCES

6 months to 1 year: 0.6 mg
1 to 3 years: 0.9 mg
4 to 6 years: 1.3 mg

VITAMIN B$_6$ BEST SOURCES	
Salmon steak (3 ounces)	0.6 mg
Chicken, white meat (3 ounces)	0.5 mg
Beef liver (3 ounces)	0.5 mg
Chicken liver (3 ounces)	0.5 mg
Soybeans, dried ($1/4$ cup)	0.4 mg
Chickpeas, dried ($1/4$ cup)	0.3 mg
Navy beans, dried ($1/4$ cup)	0.3 mg
Brown rice, uncooked ($1/4$ cup)	0.3 mg
Beef, lean (3 ounces)	0.2 mg
Kidney beans, dried ($1/4$ cup)	0.2 mg

VITAMIN B$_{12}$

▦ WHY WE NEED IT ▦

This vitamin aids in the function of all body cells and the formation of red blood cells. Assists in the maintenance of nerve tissues.

▦ RECOMMENDED (DAILY) DIETARY ALLOWANCES ▦

6 months to 1 year: 2 mcg
1 to 3 years: 3 mcg
4 to 6 years: 6 mcg

▦ VITAMIN B$_{12}$ BEST SOURCES ▦

B$_{12}$ is found only in animal foods—liver, meat, fish, shellfish, milk, milk products, eggs, and poultry. Vegetarian diets should include milk or a B$_{12}$ supplement.

Beef liver (3 ounces)	49.0 mcg
Chicken liver (3 ounces)	16.5 mcg
Salmon steak (3 ounces)	3.0 mcg
Beef, lean (3 ounces)	1.4 mcg
Swiss cheese (2 ounces)	1.0 mcg
Whole milk (1 cup)	0.9 mcg
Egg, hard-cooked (1)	0.7 mcg
Chicken, white meat (3 ounces)	0.3 mcg

VITAMIN D (CALCIFEROL)

WHY WE NEED IT

Better known as the "sunshine vitamin," vitamin D is needed by the body in order to assimilate calcium and phosphorus in the formation of bones and teeth. Few foods are naturally abundant in vitamin D, but 15 minutes of sunshine every day will supply the necessary amount. Cow's milk is fortified with vitamin D, as are many prepared foods, especially cold breakfast cereals ($3/4$ cup of Product 19 contains 200 IU of vitamin D). Vitamin D is fat-soluble and therefore stored in our bodies.

RECOMMENDED (DAILY) DIETARY ALLOWANCES

6 months to 1 year: 400 IU
1 to 3 years: 400 IU
4 to 6 years: 400 IU

VITAMIN D BEST SOURCES	
Salmon, Atlantic, canned ($3^1/_2$ ounces)	500 IU
Sardines, canned in oil ($3^1/_2$ ounces)	300 IU
Vitamin D-fortified milk (1 cup)	100 IU
Egg yolks (1 medium)	27 IU

CALCIUM

WHY WE NEED IT

Calcium is best known for its role in the formation of bones and teeth. But this highly versatile mineral is also important to the functioning of our neuromuscular system and in blood clotting.

RECOMMENDED (DAILY) DIETARY ALLOWANCES

6 months to 1 year: 540 mg

1 to 3 years: 800 mg

4 to 6 years: 800 mg

CALCIUM BEST SOURCES	
Swiss cheese (2 ounces)	544 mg
Yogurt, skim milk (1 cup)	452 mg
Provolone cheese (2 ounces)	428 mg
Monterey Jack cheese (2 ounces)	424 mg
Cheddar cheese (2 ounces)	408 mg
Muenster cheese (2 ounces)	406 mg
Colby cheese (2 ounces)	388 mg
Brick cheese (2 ounces)	382 mg
Sardines, Atlantic, canned (3 ounces)	371 mg
Mozzarella cheese (2 ounces)	366 mg
American cheese (2 ounces)	348 mg
Skim milk (1 cup)	302 mg
Salmon, Sockeye, canned (3 ounces)	274 mg
Broccoli, cooked (1 medium branch)	158 mg
Cheese pizza ($^1/_8$ 14-inch pie)	144 mg
Blackstrap molasses (1 tablespoon)	137 mg
Soy flour ($^1/_2$ cup)	132 mg
Collards, cooked ($^1/_2$ cup)	110 mg
Tofu (3 ounces)	109 mg
Kale, cooked ($^1/_2$ cup)	103 mg

IRON

WHY WE NEED IT

Iron is needed for the formation of hemoglobin for red blood cells. A lack of iron causes anemia.

RECOMMENDED (DAILY) DIETARY ALLOWANCES

6 months to 1 year: 15 mg
1 to 3 years: 15 mg
4 to 6 years: 10 mg

IRON BEST SOURCES

Cooking in an old-fashioned iron skillet will add iron to your diet, as will the following foods:

Beef liver (3 ounces)	7.5 mg
Blackstrap molasses (1 tablespoon)	3.2 mg
Roast beef (3 ounces)	3.1 mg
Ground beef, lean (3 ounces)	3.0 mg
Lima beans, dried, cooked ($^1/_2$ cup)	2.9 mg
Soybeans, dried, cooked ($^1/_2$ cup)	2.5 mg
Prunes ($^1/_2$ cup)	2.2 mg
Avocado, raw, California (1 medium)	2.0 mg
Turkey, dark meat (3 ounces)	2.0 mg
Apricots, dried ($^1/_4$ cup)	1.8 mg
Broccoli, raw (1 medium branch)	1.7 mg
Spinach, raw, chopped (1 cup)	1.7 mg
Almonds, slivered ($^1/_4$ cup)	1.6 mg
Peas, fresh, cooked ($^1/_2$ cup)	1.5 mg
Beet greens, cooked ($^1/_2$ cup)	1.4 mg
Raisins ($^1/_4$ cup)	1.3 mg
Kidney beans, dried, cooked ($^1/_4$ cup)	1.1 mg
Turkey, white meat (3 ounces)	1.1 mg
Chicken, white meat (3 ounces)	1.0 mg

OTHER VITAMINS, MINERALS, AND TRACE ELEMENTS

VITAMIN E (ALPHA-TOCOPHEROL)

The human uses of vitamin E are not completely understood. This vitamin aids in the formation of red blood cells, muscle, and other tissues and protects vitamin A and essential fatty acids from oxidation. It is fat-soluble. The best food sources include vegetable oils and products made from vegetable oils such as margarine, salad dressing, and shortening. Whole-grain cereals and breads, liver, dried beans, and leafy vegetables are lesser sources.

VITAMIN K

Vitamin K plays a role in the clotting of blood and is needed for the formation of prothrombin, a substance used in the clotting process. This vitamin is manufactured in the liver and in bigger babies and adults in the intestine. Vitamin K is fat-soluble. Food sources include leafy green vegetables (turnip greens), cauliflower, peas, broccoli, beef liver, and cereals.

MINERAL SALTS

PHOSPHORUS

This mineral salt is needed for building bones and teeth. Sources of phosphorus include meat, poultry, fish, eggs, dried beans, milk, and milk products.

POTASSIUM

Potassium maintains water balance in the body fluids and is important in the transmission of nerve impulses and the release of energy from carbohydrates, proteins, and fats. Food sources of potassium: potatoes, avocados, raisins, flounder, orange juice, squash, and bananas.

CHLORINE

Chlorine regulates the balance of body fluids—acids and bases; activates enzymes in saliva; and is necessary for the formation of hydrochloric acid in the stomach. Food sources include table salt and vegetables.

SODIUM

Sodium maintains water balance in the body fluids. It is found in vegetables and table salt.

MAGNESIUM

Magnesium is necessary for the building of bones. It also helps nerves and muscles work and regulates the use of carbohydrates and the production of energy within the cells. Food sources include legumes, whole-grain cereals, milk and eggs, meat, green vegetables, and nuts (especially almonds and cashews).

TRACE ELEMENTS

CHROMIUM

Chromium is needed for normal glucose metabolism. Food sources include meat, cheese, whole-grain breads and cereals, dried beans, and peanuts.

▒ COBALT ▒

Cobalt is an essential part of vitamin B_{12}. Food sources include canned tuna, peanut butter, asparagus, broad beans, Brussels sprouts, cabbage, corn, mushrooms, and spinach.

▒ COPPER ▒

Copper is needed for the formation of red blood cells and as part of several respiratory enzymes. It is found in beef liver, dried beans, nuts, raisins.

▒ FLUORINE ▒

Fluorine is needed for the formation of strong teeth and the maintenance of strong bones. It is found in most animal foods and fish—eggs, cheese, cod, mackerel, canned salmon and sardines, hot dogs, chicken—as well as kale, potatoes, spinach, brewed tea, and fluoridated water used for cooking and drinking.

▒ IODINE ▒

Necessary for proper functioning of the thyroid gland and for normal reproduction. Food sources include seafood, saltwater fish (especially haddock), whole milk, mozzarella cheese, Cheddar cheese, cottage cheese, and iodized salt.

▒ MANGANESE ▒

Manganese is necessary for bone structure, functioning of the central nervous system, and reproduction. Food sources include nuts, whole grains, vegetables, and fruits.

▒ MOLYBDENUM ▒

Molybdenum is part of the enzyme xanthine oxidase. Food sources include lentils, cereal grains (especially buckwheat), rye flour, tomato sauce, green beans, rib lamb chops, and lean pork.

▨ SELENIUM ▨

Selenium prevents the breakdown of fats and other body chemicals and interacts with vitamin E. Food sources include seafood and fish (especially canned tuna), whole-grain cereals, beef, egg yolk, chicken, cashews, roasted peanuts, milk, molasses, and garlic.

▨ ZINC ▨

Zinc is part of approximately 100 enzymes and insulin. Food sources include meat, liver, seafood, milk, and whole-grain cereals.

This information is drawn from the following sources:

Brody, Jane E. *Jane Brody's Nutrition Book*. New York: W. W. Norton & Company, 1981.

Committee on Nutrition, American Academy of Pediatrics, Forbes, Gilbert B., M.D., ed., and Calvin W. Woodruff, M.D., assoc. ed. *Pediatric Nutrition Handbook,* 2nd edition. Elk Grove, Ill: American Academy of Pediatrics, 1985.

National Dairy Council. *Nutrition Source Book*. Rosemont, Ill: National Dairy Council, 1985.

Pennington, Jean, A.T., Ph.D., R.D., and Helen Nichols Church, B.S. *Food Values of Portions Commonly Used,* 14th edition. New York: Perennial Library, Harper & Row Publishers, 1985.

Editors of *Prevention Magazine. The Prevention Total Health System: Understanding Vitamins and Minerals.* Emmaus, Pa: The Rodale Press Inc., 1984.

"Best Sources" information drawn from: Editors of *Prevention Magazine. The Prevention Total Health System: Understanding Vitamins and Minerals.* Emmaus, Pa: The Rodale Press, Inc., 1984.

RESOURCES

TEMPERATURE CONVERSIONS

Degrees Fahrenheit (°F)	Degrees Celsius (C°)
32 degrees	0 degrees
40 degrees	4 degrees
140 degrees	60 degrees
150 degrees	65 degrees
160 degrees	70 degrees
170 degrees	75 degrees
212 degrees	100 degrees
275 degrees	135 degrees
300 degrees	150 degrees
325 degrees	165 degrees
350 degrees	175 degrees
375 degrees	190 degrees
400 degrees	205 degrees
425 degrees	220 degrees
450 degrees	230 degrees
475 degrees	245 degrees
500 degrees	260 degrees

WEIGHTS AND MEASURES EQUIVALENCIES

Dash	less than $1/8$ teaspoon
3 teaspoons	1 tablespoon ($1/2$ fluid ounce)
2 tablespoons	$1/8$ cup (1 fluid ounce)
4 tablespoons	$1/4$ cup (2 fluid ounces)
$5 1/3$ tablespoons	$1/3$ cup ($2 2/3$ fluid ounces)
8 tablespoons	$1/2$ cup (4 fluid ounces)
$10 2/3$ tablespoons	$2/3$ cup ($5 1/3$ fluid ounces)

12 tablespoons	¾ cup (6 fluid ounces)
14 tablespoons	⅞ cup (7 fluid ounces)
16 tablespoons	1 cup
1 cup	8 fluid ounces (240 milliliters)
2 cups	1 pint (480 milliliters)
2 pints	1 quart (approximately 1 liter)
4 quarts	1 gallon (3.75 liters)
8 quarts	1 peck (8.8 liters)
4 pecks	1 bushel (35 liters)
1 ounce	28.35 grams (rounded to 30)
16 ounces	1 pound (453.59 grams rounded to 450)
1 kilogram	2.2 pounds

HINTS AND TIPS FOR CALCULATIONS

To convert ounces and pounds into grams:
multiply ounces by 28.35
multiply pounds by 453.59

To convert Fahrenheit to Celsius:
subtract 32 from Fahrenheit, multiply by 5, divide by 9

1 gallon = 4 quarts = 8 pints = 16 cups (8 fluid ounces) = 128 fluid
   ounces

1 egg white = 2 fluid ounces (average)
1 orange = 3 to 3½ fluid ounces of juice
1 lemon = 1 to 1¼ ounces of juice

1 measuring cup holds 8 fluid ounces. A coffee cup typically
   holds 6 fluid ounces.

WEBSITES

www.mommymade.com—Our own website with up-to-the-minute information, new recipes, parenting tips, and new products.

www.lalecheleague.org—The world's authority on breast-feeding.

www.kidshealth.com—Topics include immunization, infection, safety of toys, and nutrition, among others

www.foodallergy.com—The Food Allergy Network

www.non-dairy.org—Non Dairy: Something to Moo About Inc.

www.foodsafety.gov—U.S. Government information on food safety

www.eatright.org/news—What's in the news about health

www.quackwatch.com—Information on health fraud and quackery

www.ama-assn.org—American Medical Association

www.fda.gov—Food and Drug Administration

www.nih.gov—National Institutes of Health

www.newmommies.com—A site with upcoming events and products for new parents

www.medela.com—Information about Medela breast pumps and where to rent or buy them (or call 1–800–435–8316)

FOOD INTRODUCTION RECORD

REMEMBER: The first year is your best time to detect food sensitivities or reactions your baby might have to any food. Your baby can be sensitive to any food, but reactions to cow's milk, eggs (whites in particular), corn, peanuts, tree nuts, wheat, chocolate, shellfish, tomatoes, and soybean are the most common. Happily most babies affected by food sensitivities and allergies outgrow them during their first years. (See Chapter Two for more detailed information on food introduction and allergies.)

Steps to follow:

1. Use the Food Introduction Road Map (pages 20–21) as your guide.

2. Start with one new food, for three days straight, no later than the midday meal. (Avoid introducing new foods late in the day. If a new food upsets your baby's system this could make her irritable. Better for you during the day and not all night long if this should occur.)

3. Keep a written record.

FOOD	DATE OF INTRODUCTION	REACTION (IF ANY)

FOOD	DATE OF INTRODUCTION	REACTION (IF ANY)

Cut here

FOOD	DATE OF INTRODUCTION	REACTION (IF ANY)

INDEX